ALSO BY JOHN SANFORD

NOVELS AND OTHER FICTION

The Water Wheel (1933)
The Old Man's Place (1935)
Seventy Times Seven (1939)
The People from Heaven (1943)
A Man Without Shoes (1951, 1982)
The Land That Touches Mine (1953)
Every Island Fled Away (1964)
The $300 Man (1967)
Adirondack Stories (1976)

INTERPRETATIONS OF AMERICAN HISTORY

A More Goodly Country (1975)
View From This Wilderness (1977)
To Feed Their Hopes (1980)
The Winters of That Country (1984)

LETTERS

William Carlos Williams/John Sanford: A Correspondence (1984)

AUTOBIOGRAPHY

The Color of the Air, Scenes from the Life of a American Jew,
    Volume 1 (1985)
The Waters of Darkness, Scenes from the Life of an American Jew,
    Volume 2 (1986)
A Very Good Land to Fall With, Scenes from the Life of an American Jew,
    Volume 3 (Spring 1987)

JOHN
SANFORD

THE
WATERS
OF
DARKNESS

VOLUME 2

SCENES
FROM
THE
LIFE
OF
AN
AMERICAN
JEW

BLACK SPARROW PRESS ■ SANTA BARBARA ■ 1986

For permission to reprint herein certain material from *To Feed Their Hopes,* the author is grateful to the University of Illinois Press.

LIBRARY OF CONGRESS CATALOGING-IN-PUBLICATION DATA
(Revised for vol. 2)

Sanford, John B., 1904–
    The color of the air.

    Vol. 2 has title: The waters of darkness.
    1. Sanford, John B., 1904–   —Biography.
2. Novelists, American—20th century—Biography.
I. Title. II. Title: Scenes from the life of an American Jew. III. Title: The Waters of darkness.
PS3537.A694Z64   1985   813'.52[B]   85-13514
ISBN 0-87685-643-1 (pbk. : v. 1)
ISBN 0-87685-644-X (hard : v. 1)
ISBN 0-87685-645-8 (lim. ed.: v. 1)
ISBN 0-87685-671-7 (pbk. : v. 2)
ISBN 0-87685-672-5 (hard : v. 2)
ISBN 0-87685-673-3 (signed : v. 2)

This book is for my cousin
Mel Friedman
who has also been my friend

Water is a movable and wandering thing.
　　　　　—Blackstone's *Commentaries*

A NOTE ON THE INSERTS

As in the previous volume, *The Color of the Air,* the scenes of this one are interspersed with pieces commenting on the history of the country. Numbered I through XIII, they are meant to give "the color of the air," the political element in which the principal character lives.

J. S.

Contents

The Waters of Darkness:
Scenes from the Life of an American Jew
Volume 2

THE COLOR OF THE AIR, I

NORTH AMERICA—A.D. 1000
A PLACE CALLED HERE

> *We found sweet water in Vinlandiam, or Vinland, which we named it for its grapes, and voluntary wheat grew thick there, as if sown, and fruits that were new to us tinselled the trees. Day lasted longer than day at home, nor did the grass so soon wither, and for that savory smoke came down the wind, the air seemed brewed of spice and herb. A fair land to fall with, agreed we all, and we wintered well upon its shore. We slew some few inferior people before we left. Skraelings, they were. . . .*

If you'd been the first blue-eyed blond to make that landfall, you'd've been Leif, Vicar of Christ to the West, or, dressed in a skin shirt and skin buskins, you'd've been some thrall at the oars and blown your nose in your hair — and, known or nameless, you'd be a pinch of carbon now, a tooth turned to stone. If you'd seen the world as the world was then, you'd be a thousand years dead, but even so, even so. . . !

SCENE 1

ROUND-TRIP TO ENGLAND (September 1927)

Was it you that night, you losing sight of Pier 56, you walking the decks to Bishop Light? were you on hand for The Lizard, Beachy Head, the Goodwin Sands? and did you land at Woolwich? was that truly you at the Norfolk a step or two from the Strand? Were you actually there, you sometimes wonder, were you there as you suppose in the fall of that year, and is it fact that you recall or merely fancy?

The hard evidence is scant — your name on an Oxford pamphlet and the same and Cambridge in a copy of *Lear.* How were such things come by: could you have been in Trumpington Street, could you have walked down the High?

Images flash at the edge of your eye—the tracery of towers, flamboyant quads and cloisters, lacework in stone, are all these imagined, or had you known the Isis, the bell called Tom, the courts, the chapels, the gardens? Do you remember, or only think you do, a day of railways, of fruitless journeys through shipshape landscapes like lifesize maps, do you remember a silence as if no one in England had spoken and no two solids had met? A day of trains across a green and rolling world—and not a sound remains. Whatever it was you sought, you did not find it on the Cherwell, nor was it found by the Cam.

So complete was the failure of your expedition that when you came to write of it, you could hardly bear to report that you'd fared far for fruits that weren't there. You sailed for home the poorer for your wastrel ways, your days of nothing learned and nothing done, and all you let yourself recall of the voyage was a sunset you'd seen on the last day out:

> . . . The lowest arc of the sun was touching the top line of the still water. Reflected perfectly and making an orange figureight, there was another sun round and unbroken in the water. After a while, the sharpness of the eight went away and the sun became red, deep red like a poinsettia. The hips of the eight were the hips of a sitting woman. *And the woman was arrayed in purple and scarlet color, and decked with gold and precious stones and pearls, having a golden cup in her hands full of abominations and filthiness of her fornication.* When the poinsettia went away, the woman, and the clouds that made her voluminous floating sleeves, became darker than dried blood on linen . . . *And every shipmaster, and all the company in ships, and sailors, and as many as trade by sea, stood afar off, and cried when they saw the smoke of her burning, saying, What city is like unto this great city!* Sanford looked around for those who stood afar off. The only person he saw was a barefoot sailor. The man was hosing off the decks. . . .*

SCENE 2

THE APPRENTICE (1927-29)

If your father had thoughts about your vain excursion, he kept them to himself or expressed them elsewhere: he let you off in silence, as though you hadn't

---

*The Water Wheel, 1933.

been away. You weren't quite so kind—you didn't spare yourself. You'd known from the start that, going forth with little purpose, you'd return with little gain, and unable to explain what had driven you, you suffered the question like a foreign body, a splinter you couldn't reach, and you bore it until it encysted and the pain was contained.

But what he did speak of was your clerkship, the twelve months of fetch-and-carry required of all applicants for admission to the Bar: if you were ready, he said, he'd place you with one of his professional colleagues. You were, you told him, and soon your year of servitude began. In that period, you shagged for four law firms in succession, and in every case, it *was* servitude. You filed pleadings in all the courthouses between the East Bronx and Graves-end Bay, and you did so (swift courier!) early and late and in the snow and rain, and you did so too when the days were fine and you longed to laze in the sun and watch the clouds and girls pass by. Only at the weekend were you manumitted—at all other times, you ran with brief and deposition, with lien and lis pendens, writ and summons, letters to mail or deliver by hand. You ran!

§

On one such weekend, you went to Boston. *Do come,* she'd written, *and don't lose your enthusiasm before you get here. Isn't life glorious?* and she'd signed herself *Lou.*

She lived in a two-room flat on a sloping street (Lynde, was it, or was it Pinckney?), and she took you there after meeting your train. She wore gray, you remember, something of gray wool, a suit, it might've been, and it comes back with a ray of yellow that quickly goes away—a locket, you suppose, or a flower on one of the lapels.

There were six thousand sea-miles to be explained, there were thoughts, sensations, moods, intentions old and intentions new, and while you talked, the day grew dim, and at last (*don't lose your enthusiasm*) you were talking in the dark.

You had dinner somewhere, or she prepared it, and then you walked about the Hill, along Beacon and Charles and through Louisburg Square, and once more you were in two small rooms wondering what was glorious and what was not.

Your bed for the night was a couch outside her room, and you lay there looking out at a few black windows and a few square white holes in the sky, and you were thinking *She'd be good for you* when a door opened, and you heard silk slide on silk, and then she was sitting beside you saying, "Fix my wagon, Jule. Fix my wagon."

You put your hands on her nightdress and moved them over her chest—a boy's, it might've been, but for its pair of buttoning buttons. "Fix it, Jule," she said, but everywhere in the room there seemed to dwell another presence. It was as inescapable as an element of the air—it *was* an element—and you drew it in at every breath only to poison your blood with it. He was there, you felt, and you could fix nothing.

"Why?" she said

"He's here with us. He always is."

"He's in New York, playing the piano for another girl."

"I've never asked you about him," you said. "I would've doubted the answer."

"That's a bad way to be."

"If you said he'd had you, I'd've wondered, and I'd've wondered if you said he hadn't."

"Which would've made you wonder more?" she said, and when you didn't reply, she bent over you to say again, "Fix it, Jule."

You said, "I can't fix anything while I'm being watched."

"Then take your hands off my tits," she said, and she went back to her room. The sister that had no breasts, you thought.

§

The letter was meant for delivery at Oxford, but by the time it arrived, you'd come and gone, and you were gone too from where a postal clerk had sent it—*Norfolk Hotel,* he'd written, *Surrey St. Strand.* It overtook you only after another crossing of the ocean, a lavender envelope addressed to *Julian L. Shapiro,* and as you look at it now, at worn edges and blurred ink, at old cancellations, at an old name, even, you think through the paper to words grown fifty years old. *We are not advanced enough to receive either a fellowship or scholarship from the Juilliard M. F.,* she wrote. *We don't much care, we may add: we are to sing for Mrs. Jacob Schiff next month with the intention of being financed by said party.* And she wrote *I'm expecting a certain type of letter,* and she wrote *Have you read between the lines?* and she signed herself *Olia.*

The letter reached you at your father's office, and you must've opened it there, with typewriters hacking at platens, with voices and smoke on the air, and turning the lavender sheet, you must've tried, as she'd wished, to read between the lines, but all you found were lavender blanks. You hadn't seen her since your return from England, and one day when Boston was behind you and lost in a haze, you called on her to say that her letter had been received.

She was standing near a window, you remember, and looking down at the park when you said, "I couldn't read between the lines."

And still looking at cars, trees, people, she said, "There was nothing between the lines."

"You were expecting a certain kind of answer, you wrote. Answer to what?"

"I wish you hadn't gone away, Julian."

"Why?"

"I wrote that I'd be singing for Mrs. Schiff."

"Ah, and did you please her with Heine's lyrics and Schumann's music? Did she cry *bitterlich* when she gazed at *deine Augen*?"

"I sang," she said, "and she found me a backer."

"And now," you said, "it's you who'll go away."

"Yes."

"Then of course you're right," you said. "There could've been nothing between the lines."

You awaited her no more at the door of the Ziegfeld, and when you saw her now, she was always in her brother's company, at a concert, at an art-show, or at the dancing-class where he played Chopin and Berlioz for Isadoras in gauze or crêpe de Chine. You recall Saturday afternoons in one of the salles at the Hall, where you leaned against the piano and watched figurantes flee in fear or shame—watched her, really, though she was too full a girl to dance with grace. Terpsichore on the Nevsky Prospekt, you'd think, and once, when you caught her glance, she seemed to have heard the thought.

In that time, any encounter with her was a sore one, the more so for what did not occur, for what had to be suppressed, but you made no effort to avoid her, nor, you suppose, did she go out of her way for you. The meetings simply came about, and when your ways crossed, you both were civil. *Civil,* you'd say to yourself afterward, and it soon became a hateful word.

Somewhere one day or night (over a table at Child's, was it, Hicks? the Russian Tea Room?), you heard of her backer—a banker, someone said, a patron of the Arts. She was there, and if she looked at you to learn your mind, she could only have seen what you saw of her—a face receding, as if you were both going away, and in a sense, both of you were. Arrangements had been made (by the backer, the banker, the patron of the Arts?) for a course of vocal studies in Italy, and one winter evening, from the North River pier of the Navigazione Generale, she sailed on the *Conte Biancamano.* You were elsewhere.

§

On returning from England, you'd been invited by your Grandma Nevins to share her small flat on West End Avenue. When you moved in, you'd found old friends among the furnishings, some chairs and a couch that you'd known in Harlem, a Kazak rug, a Circassian walnut chiffonier. The couch was in the sitting-room, and it became your bed for the better part of a year. From it, five mornings each week, you turned out numb and stumbling to start your round on subway, bus, and crosstown car. *Ready for the plaintiff!* you'd cry in the City Court, and *I offer an affidavit* in the Supreme. There were long rides in all weathers, long waits in dead air, and then long rides back in the winter dark or the spring and summer evening.

§

The going rate for a law-clerk was four dollars a week, and on Friday afternoons, the office manager would count four new singles into your held-out hand. Why four? you'd wonder. Why not three? five? seven? Indeed, why any pay at all? But if pay was proper, how had four been hit on? Had it been chosen by vote, had it been picked from a hat, or had someone rolled a Little Joe from Kokomo?

On one such Friday afternoon, you left the Tribune Building, your then place of work, and headed for your father's office across City Hall Park. It was a day after a snowy day, and the streets were half awash in gray slush, and there were clouds that made you think of sheets in bluing. At the entrance to the Emigrant Bank, you paused for another look at the colors, and leaving one last breath on the air, you went upstairs.

Several of your father's associates were lounging in his suite, some of them smoking but he not, for the sun was going down and the Sabbath had begun. He greeted you with one of his old ones, saying, "Is it true what I heard about you, kid?"

And you replied with another. "I deny the allegation," you said, "and I defy the alligator."

"Who're you working for, Josh?" Sam Ellerstein said.

"Arthur Hutter."

"Good trial lawyer," Barney Chambers said. "What does he pay you?"

"You know the answer," Jack Freeman said. "Why ask?"

"When I was clerking," your father said, "I made four dollars a week."

"We all made four, Josh," Sam Ellerstein said.

"I'm going to organize the law clerks," you said. "We're getting skinned."

"Remember the waiters you tried to organize," your father said. "You were a vanguard, but you had no army."

Loath to leave, the lawyers jawed on till the sky was almost dark, and then one by one they set out for home.

"Anything on your mind?" your father said.

"Nothing special," you said. "I just might be here because I like to see you."

"I'm flattered, but I'm not fooled. No one with two girls has time for a father."

"One is in Boston, the other in Milan. My flush days are over."

"There'll be others."

"What if I treat them as I treated these?"

"Did you treat them badly?" he said.

§

In the fall of 1926, Nat Weinstein called you at your father's office and asked you to meet him in front of the Sub-Treasury; he was going to France, he said, and he wanted you as a witness to his application for a passport. You walked down Nassau to Wall, where you found him standing near the statue of Washington, staring off, as the bronze was doing, along Broad past the Stock Exchange. Six years earlier, almost to the day, an explosion had taken place only a hundred feet away, but you took no notice of the patches in the pavement or the scars on the face of Morgan's; you were thinking of Paris, not of thirty burst bodies and the bloody strip of hide that once had been a horse. Within a few moments, you'd sworn or attested to Nat's being the male Caucasian (brown eyes, brown hair) described in the questionnaire, and some weeks later he left the country.

During his absence, you heard nothing from or about him, but on his return, he invited you to his home. There for the first time you met his mother, who put you in mind of your Grandma Nevins, and his father, whom he introduced as Max, a quiet sunken-eyed man, consumptive-thin and mild. Mild, you thought when you heard him speak, and whatever his actual size, he comes back to you as small beside his thick-bodied Anna. Nat, he called his son, but her name for him was Natchie.

He proposed a walk, and while he changed his shirt and tie, you peered through glass at shelves of books.

"Brought most of 'em back from Paris," he said. "There's one for you. That Leonardo sketchbook."

You opened the case and took it out, knowing quite well that it'd been bought for himself. *Die Skizzenbucher,* you read, and you said, "Thanks."

(After fifty-five years, you turn the pages, only a dozen or so, and you stare at sepias of old men, rampant chargers, monumental machines, and you feel now as you felt then, that you were an afterthought, that the book had never been meant for you.)

"Look at some of that other stuff," he said. "God, what you can buy over there!"

(What still stirs after fifty-five years? Pater, you think, and *Marius the Epicurean,* and the caricatures of Max Beerbohm, and the Coleridge—what was it?—the *Biographia Literaria,* and a memoir by Pound on Gaudier-Brzeska. You see pen-and-inks by Grosz of overstuffed soldiers and bristling profiteers, you see the photos of Man Ray, the title *Tarr,* and still alive too are names— Persse, Carco, G. S. Street. Who in hell was G. S. Street?)

The Weinsteins lived on 79th Street, only half a block from the Museum of Natural History, and when you were passing it later, you said, "The Museum of Nat's Ural History."

"Nathanael," he said, "with an a-e-l. I hate Nat, and I hate Nate, but the worst is Natchie!"

"When we met on the golf course that day, you told me you were writing a book. I've thought a lot about that."

"I've written six versions of it, and it still isn't right."

"Why does it give you so much trouble?"

"I want it to be lean, and in places it's fat."

"I never heard of fat writing," you said.

"Read Tolstoy. There's plenty of lard in Tolstoy."

"I read *War and Peace* last year. I didn't see any."

"He should've left out every other page."

"He'd've left out half of Russia. Of course, I'm no writer."

"You want to know about Russia, read Turgenev," he said. "And most of the time, he was in France."

"What was he doing in France—a Russian?"

"Chasing a singer named Viardot. He actually moved in with her and her husband."

"Where do you get that kind of dope?"

"*La vie de bohème!*" he said. "To coin a phrase, the life of a writer is an open book."

You'd rounded Columbus Circle by then, and, crossing 57th, you were headed for Fifth. It was a cold evening, you remember, and the air was sharp enough to feel going in, and against the lamplight, your breath hung for a moment before shredding away.

As you neared the Avenue, a woman came from one of the dark doorways and touched Nat's arm as he passed, saying, "Would you like a little pleasure?"

He stopped, and you went on for a few paces before turning to wait for him. You heard him say, "How much?"

"Ten dollars," the woman said, and those were the only words she had a chance to speak.

"Ten dollars!" Nat said. "And what would you charge *without* that chancre? Don't tell me it's only a cold sore! And don't say you cut yourself shaving! It's a syphilitic lesion, and it's mine for ten dollars!"

24

The woman looked at him, expressing nothing you were able to read, and then she went back into the doorway.

He rejoined you, and as the two of you walked away, you said, "That was kind of rough."

"*Bubu de Montparnasse!*" he said.

Not knowing what he meant, you said, "You could've said No. Even No thanks."

"I should've punched her in the face!"

"Kicked," you said. "Like Baudelaire."

And then you and he went down the Avenue, you listening while he spoke of the Pierian spring, the Cumaean sibyl, and La Coupole, and you heard too of the Areopagitic Maloney in *Balso Snell,* of rosy-fingered morns (in italics), of *Alcools* and Apollinaire. But your mind all the while was somewhere else, further and further behind in a dark doorway.

Why had he scolded the woman away? you wondered, what lay beneath his heat and hatred? He couldn't've meant to quit you for a pickup in the street, you thought . . . and suddenly it came to you that the scene had been rehearsed, saved for an occasion, acted out to earn applause.

But always there was that woman in the doorway, and you said, "You didn't have to piss on her. You could've walked away."

§

"How're things going at Arthur Hutter's," your father said.

And you said, "Not so good."

"How so?"

"I don't like the managing-clerk."

"You're not supposed to like him."

"Her," you said. "She gives me all the long-distance assignments. Calendar-calls on West Farms Road, New Lots Avenue, Staten Island."

"That's what those four bucks are for."

"I know," you said. "But when she hands me one of those jobs, she enjoys herself. Especially if it looks like rain."

Your father gazed at you for a moment, and then he said, "I've noticed something about you, kid. You're like my brother Aaron—you don't get along with people."

Before the year was out, you'd change employers three times, always for the reason your father had observed: *You don't get along with people.*

§

Under the date of February 27, 1928, your Uncle Romie wrote to you from the State Asylum at Napanoch, N. Y.:

My dear darling Nephew Julian,

I received your welcomed letter, and I certainly am glad to hear from you, after all these years.

It has been six years since I heard, or saw you, and your letter surly was like being brought back to life.

Please tell your sister Ruth dear to write me a letter, as I haven't seen or heard from her as long as I did you.

Outside of a severe cold, I otherwise feel O.K.

You want to know something about myself, well dear nephew Julian, there is not much to tell you, except that I work in the tailor shop, making buttonholes in coats, pants, shirts, and overalls.

In the summer we have parade dress twice a week, if it doesn't rain. My eyesight is getting much poorer, have to read everything with a magnifying reading glass.

Thanks very much for your picture, and hope you'll send me another one, but a fuller picture, legs, pants, and all of you. Tell Grandma Nevins I thank her for the 3 dollars.

Some time this summer I am going to have 6 pictures taken of myself, and the first visit I receive, I will give 5 of them to you, your sister Ruth, Uncle Dave, Aunt Ray, and Edith, and Grandma Nevins. I will keep one for myself.

It was very sad about your Grandpa Nevins. He was a devoted Father, Husband, and Grandfather. May his soul rest in peace. Don't take this hard Julian dear.

Well Julian dear, I will be 34 years old the 23rd of August, 1928.
(read other side)

I hope some day, you'll be a Judge and will try big cases, and that you'll get your name and picture in all the newspapers, and will get a lot of publicity.

Well my darling Julian if what I am going to ask you send me dosent put a whole in your bankrool, I would like you to send me the following.

1. 1928 diary so that I can keep a record of the things I have in mind.
1. aluminum soap box to hold one cake of soap.
6. sheets of carbon paper you probably have some in your office.
1. Sat. Eve. Post., don't subscribe it for me as it will last a month.
1. Liberty Magazine   "   "   "   "   "   "   "   "   "   "   "

The 2 magazines will last me 2 months, as I can read a little of each every night. The carbon paper I can use for the 2 grocery orders. I can put one carbon paper between the 2, and write my order on one, and then I need them for other work I have in mind.

You certainly look mighty good to me in the picture. I don't see anything wrong with your looks.

26

Have Ruth write, and send me her picture in her letter to me.

Since I have been hear, I had a visit from your Aunt Edith, Grandma Nevins, and also your Uncle Dave was up to see me several times. You can put the carbon paper in one of the magazines and send it all (5 articles) in one small box.

Well Julian this will be all for now, and I hope you will answer soon.

Your loving Uncle
Romie
Jerome P. Nevins #528

§

In the spring, twice again you went to Boston, twice more you walked with Lou the streets of Boston, twice the same unlighted room, the benighted jag of sky, the same soft persuasions in the dark.

After you'd gone, she wrote *I think our misunderstanding lies in our individual interpretations of the overworked and ill-used word love. It is impossible for me to analyze my feeling for you — but most emphatically it is not a possessive or demanding one, and I doubt if it should be called love. I have an affection, sympathy, liking, which cannot easily be shaken — what more would you?*

and she wrote *I was supremely happy every moment with you, Jule, and you are the most delightful refuge for my thoughts,*

and she wrote *I love you.*

§

"Here's a story for you, Scotty," Nat said. "A traveler in Tyana — that's in Asia Minor — was looking for the sage Apollonius when he saw a snake crawl into a man's rectum. He said, 'Pardon me, my good fellow, but a snake just entered your . . . ,' and he finished by pointing. 'Yes, sir, he lives there,' the man replied. The visitor responded by saying, 'Ah, then you must be Apollonius of Tyana. Here's a letter of introduction from my brother George. May I see the snake? Now the rectum. Perfect!' "

It was another of those nights in your clerkship year, and you were walking the streets, or riding the bus up or down the Drive, or crossing the bay on the St. George ferry. You forget which it was, but you were somewhere with Pep Weinstein (Nathanael, Nathan, Natchie), and when he finished the story, he said, "That's from the first few pages of *Balso*."

"It's funny," you said.

"You get the point, of course. The tourist, you understand, always armed with credentials."

"I get the point," you said. "I understand."

"Just as the snake is in the rectum of Apollonius, Balso is in the rectum of the Wooden Horse of Troy. A rectum within a rectum, so to speak."

"That makes it twice as funny."

"Balso finds the horse in the long grass outside the ancient city, and he decides to go in. There are only three openings—the mouth, which is too high to reach, the navel, a cul-de-sac, and the rectum. He uses the last."

"There are four openings," you said.

"What do you mean—four?" he said. "How do you get four?"

"What about the trapdoor of the Greeks?"

"Jesus Christ, you're killing the joke!"

"Nail up the door," you said. "That'll do it."

"I'm a writer, not a carpenter.!"

§

You learned of her whereabouts from her brother George: she was at the Villa d'Este on Lago di Como. You'd never recall what you wrote to her, nor would you ever be certain why you'd written at all. You have only her reply to suggest an intention:

> Received your letter yesterday, Julian. It did come as a surprise, and tho I had a fair idea of what you were attempting to tell me of your mood, I found it impossible to read some parts of it, one part in particular which might have made the meaning a good deal clearer.
>
> Life is dull just now, as it usually is during a holiday. However, am planning a winter of very hard work in Milan, so a forced rest is necessary. It will all be over, though, in a few days, and just as well. I'm not the person to wait for things to happen. Want to work, and if it's to be, get the debut over and done with.
>
> Hope to hear from you again, J.
>
> Olia

What had you said? you wonder. Did you speak of what she herself had spoken of once—the space between the lines? Did you tell her to look for signs of words erased, to read the blurs of thoughts withdrawn? Or were you airy and knowing about the Villa (180 rooms, 135 with bath)? Did you descant on the formal gardens, the Renaissance statuary, the restricted beach, and did you permit yourself a jest about her *stanza di bagno*—was it private, did you venture, or was her *gabinetto* somewhere down the hall?

A winter of very hard work, she'd said, and if the debut was to be. . . .

§

It was not to be.

Soon after hearing from her, you were told (by whom?) that she was on her way home. There'd be no winter in Milan, no practicing the tones of the gamut, no lessons in breathing, phrasing, drama, languages, in the bearing of the body and the head. There'd be no days at La Scala to watch the ways of others, no marking of scores, no choices made for a repertoire — there'd be no cold ateliers and no more notes from J. for Julian. There'd be no debut: it was not to be.

No one had bespoken your presence, but when her ship arrived, you were at the pier, self-invited, and standing near the Customs fence, you watched her watching hands slide through her folded clothes. She knew you were there, but she did not speak, and soon she left with her brother George. You recall that most, her walking away. What was it, the sway of her skirt? a color she wore? a flashing stone? You still can see her walking away.

§

You remember a day in the fall of the year. You were to call for George in the afternoon and walk across the park to the Museum, where a new bequest was on display, the Havemeyer, it might've been, with Degas by the dozen on the walls. When you reached his building and went upstairs, you found a note rammed between the door and the jamb: *Julian,* it said, *Olga is in Mt. Sinai.* You didn't wait for the elevator: you ran six flights down to the sidewalk.

A taxi took you through the 96th Street transverse, and you arrived at the hospital as George and his mother were coming down the steps.

"Those God damn adhesions!" he said. "This time, she's dead."

A hard winter's work, she'd written, *and if it's to be. . . .*

§

Wenn ich in deine Augen seh!

The coffin was open, resting on trestles in the middle of the parlor, and from time to time a woman would rise from a ring of chairs and gaze down at the dead, a girl of twenty-three. From where you sat, outside the ring, all you could see above the rim was a small affray of hair, and you stared at it, the last of her, the last, you thought, that involute of hair. You watched the woman reach out and touch it, redistribute it, thin it here and gather it there, and you wondered, as she drew back to note the effect, whether Azrael was now more pleased.

So schwindet all mein Leid und Weh

In the hallway of the flat, there were muted greetings, and from the chairs came upturned looks and recognitions, but you saw no grief, and save for the encircled coffin, the occasion might've been an evening: in a moment, you thought, the girl might enter, quite alive, and begin to sing her songs. They were called Lieder, she'd told you once, poems in music, poetry sung, and many, she'd said, were concerned with love. The woman was leaning against the coffin again, changing her arrangement, adjusting strands of hair. *Doch wenn ich küsse deinen Mund. . . .*

Your mind seemed to come back to you from somewhere, space, night, nothing, and you saw that the room was crowded now. All the chairs were occupied, and callers stood behind them, ranged along the walls. The woman was hovering about the coffin again, and again she was trifling with that little floss of hair. She moved it with deft touches, hardly more than passes of her hand, and then she pressed it down and out of sight, and at last she seemed to be satisfied. You could see nothing inside the coffin now, nothing, and you could no longer stay in the room.*

You remember, in discontinuous instants, in stills of thought, a ride through a white tile tunnel, a long hill, and, on the western side a cemetery, a slope of stones like broken steps, and at the bottom, you remember, a river twined among its reeds. There the slides of memory end, and you do not see the mother, the brother, the friend or two, the man of the cloth if one was there; what follows is an area of light, a blank brightness, as if you had no more views for your magic lantern.

§

When next you saw the parlor of the flat, the ring of chairs was gone, and there were no mourners seated or standing against the walls. The coffin, though, seemed all but present, and you almost saw that puff of hair, and you knew that, in that room, you'd always be aware of a box on a pair of trestles and of someone reaching in to rectify the dead.

There were other days, other times with brother George, and you recall a Tristan at the Met and a Jupiter at the Hall, and you remember the books he spoke of, the Courbets he said were like Zola on a wall. And through all those days, a dead one moldered on a hillside, just across the river only a million miles away. She was never mentioned now. Her few possessions had been put out of sight — a brooch or two, a pair of earrings, what more

---

*from *To Feed Their Hopes*, 1980.

could she have owned? — and in her room, always spare, even her flavor was gone from the air.

But whenever you stood at the windows, whenever you stared at the park below, bright in the sun or dark, under snow or overrun by rain, she was there behind you still. When you were alone in the flat one day — alone except for her — you came upon her photo, and you stole it. You stole it, as once you'd done with a pretty stone.

§

It was a Saturday afternoon, you remember, and walking uptown with your father, you were passing through Washington Square.

He indicated the Arch, saying, "Stanford White."

"I'd forgotten that," you said. "Or maybe I never knew it."

"Smoke, if you like, kid."

"On Saturday?"

"You never promised your father you wouldn't."

You lit a cigarette, and as you tossed the match away, you said, "I wonder what my word would've been worth."

"People always wonder what they'd do *if*."

"How old were you when you promised grandpa?"

"Oh, about fourteen," he said.

"Did you know then that you'd keep the promise?"

"I know that I meant to," he said. "But I'm only fifty, and I may still break down."

"Not you."

Crossing Madison Square, he nodded at the Garden, saying "Stanford White."

"Odd thing," you said. "Getting shot in a building he designed."

There was no more talk for a while, not until you were going past the Waldorf, and there he said, "Bad luck for that girl you knew."

"How did you hear about it?"

"Clients. People from the old days in Harlem. They say she had promise."

"Yes," you said.

And you were halfway from there to the Library when he said, "I'm sorry, kid."

And again you said, "Yes."

§

Your Grandma Nevins had gone to Cedarhurst to visit her daughter Ida, and you were in possession of her flat. From one of its rear windows, it overlooked the Drive, and you might've been there when the impulse came, taking in a chink of river, earth, and sky, or you might've been in the other room, sitting, standing, staring out at the airshaft gloom. You can't say what you were doing or give the time of day, you can't place yourself in this chair or that corner or recall the sight, the sound, the shift of light that spun your mind back years to a night in Easton. You saw the snow of that night, the lamps of Third Street, the red glow in curtained windows, and you remembered a theme you'd written, *A Personal Experience.* And now you had another, you thought (thought where? in which room, in what chair?), and you began to hunt for pen and paper.

It all began there in one of those rooms, the one that gave on a brick wall or the one that held a gore of water, Jersey, sky.

§

I'm writing a book, your friend had declared, and it seemed for a while that you were doing the same. He'd never shown you the actual work, the white or blue or yellow pages of typed or scrivened words; you'd not yet seen the butcher paper, the unfolded envelopes, the underside of throwaways; you had no written proof of Saint Puce, the flea that lived in the armpit of Jesus. But you'd heard enough to accept the book's existence, not merely in the mind of Nat, Nathanael, Natchie, but also on foolscap lines, on a sheet of cardboard from a laundered shirt. You believed that what he'd had in mind had *become*; the book you'd heard so much about, *The Dream Life,* was real. If so, you thought, what you'd put on paper was also real—you too were writing a book!

Alas, you were not, as soon you found when you fished your stream, cast the riffles and pools of memory; you brought in weeds, twigs, trash, but nothing that seemed alive. You'd wanted to write of the dead girl, to say what you hadn't said to her, but the words lay as still as she did on the side of a hill in Jersey. You held the loose leaves before you, turned them over, shook them even, hoping for a sign, an emanation, but all that stirred, and not for long, was weed, black and tangled trash. You thought of a grief that had issued undefiled—*Fondly do we hope, fervently do we pray, that this mighty scourge of war may speedily pass away*—and you knew that yours was only ink.

§

Your father called you one afternoon while you were clerking for a lawyer named David Porter Siegel, and he asked you to join him for supper at the Hotel Astor Grill, and that evening, when you entered from the 44th Street side, you found him sitting alone against one of the dark wood-paneled walls. He motioned you toward a facing chair, and you spoke of nothing consequential until smoke was entwining with coffee steam.

"You'll be glad to hear," he said, "that Josie and I have come to the parting of the ways."

The painted woman, you thought, but you said nothing.

"From the start, I was living with a stranger while my blood was somewhere else. All along, I hoped you'd relent. I hoped, as you grew older, that you'd understand. You never did, though—and here it is, nine years, and you've never set foot in your father's house."

"I guess I'm what you called me—a tough nut." You watched your cigarette burn on the edge of an ashtray: a rope of blue smoke grew as high as your face before it began to fray. "I shouldn't've listened to the Perlmans, Pop. I should've left grandma's and gone to live with you."

"People said I was wrong to let you stay there, but I knew what I was dealing with."

"Aunt Rae always called her *the painted woman.* I must've heard that fifty times. *How was the painted woman, Julian?*"

"The Perlmans tried to make her out as fast," your father said, and he waved at the smoke as if it were a cloud of time. "But they really *wanted* me to marry her."

"How can that be?" you said. "They never missed a chance to run her down."

"That was to stir up your Grandpa Nevins," he said. "It would've spoiled their plans if I'd thrown Josie over."

"What plans?"

"You surprise me. I thought you were smarter."

"What plans?"

"I represented your grandpa from 1903, when I married your mother, to 1920, when I married Josie. For seventeen years, I stood between the Perlmans and grandpa's money. Harry always wanted the use of it, and I always made him put up security for its return—bonds, a mortgage, anything that would protect grandpa."

"I still don't see any plans," you said.

"Harry didn't like to repay," your father said, "and as long as I was grandpa's lawyer, he knew that he'd have to. He got me out of his way with slander and scandal: *the painted woman,* the fast and frivolous divorcée to whom I gave your mother's diamonds. Your grandpa was poisoned by that kind of talk."

"Why didn't you tell me this before?" you said.

"You were poisoned too."

"The Perlmans are bastards."

"Not bastards," he said. "People."

"People who like money that much are bastards."

"Don't be so quick to draw the line. You might be on the wrong side of it some time."

"Never."

"I was telling you about grandpa," he said. "One day, right after Josie and I were married, he sent someone down to my office for his papers, his folders, his corporate books and seals—and Phil Shapiro was no longer his lawyer. Unfortunately, he wound up with *Harry's* lawyer."

"I can see the wolves licking their chops," you said. "Poor grandpa."

"So that's the sad story. I married a woman who happened to be nothing like the one they invented. So far from being flirty and free in her ways, she's a woman to admire. Your grandpa thought otherwise, which didn't trouble me, but you thought so too, and that did. It spoiled everything for Josie and me. She's always known that I'd sooner be parted from her than you, and now the time has come. I'm moving out."

You said, "I'd've been glad to hear that once, but not any more."

"You're late," he said. "By nine years."

§

At your father's request, you went to Washington Heights in the morning, and with the key that he'd given you, you entered his flat for the first and only time. By arrangement, no one else was there, and you stood for a moment in a long hallway and breathed its unfamiliar air. For all you knew, you'd gone to the wrong place, opened the wrong door, let yourself into a privacy that you had no right to share. Quite clearly still you remember a parlor, a corner room with two exposures, and clearly too you can see a suite in dark and damasked velour, blue portières, silken lampshades with spangled fringes. The rest of the flat was a train of cars—a pair of bedchambers, a bath, a kitchen, a pantry, a diningroom. Between the two last, there was one more opening off the hall, an archway hung with bamboo segments strung like beads. They were always in collision, always xylophonic, and through the strands you saw the room you'd never used, the promised bath of tile. Between you and the space they screened, there were only strings of reeds that played for a sigh, a breeze made by a passerby. You didn't try to part them, though; you knew they wouldn't give.

You followed your father's instructions: you packed his belongings and took them away.

§

In the spring of 1929, you were living with your father and sister at the Peter Stuyvesant, a hotel on Central Park West, and while you were at breakfast one morning, a waiter handed him a packet of mail. He glanced at several envelopes, putting them all aside, but when he reached a penny postcard, he read both sides with care before tossing it across to you.

It was addressed to *Julian L. Shapiro, Counselor at Law,* and turning it over, you read the reverse:

COURT OF APPEALS
Albany, N. Y.

Dear Sir:

I have this day received and filed the affidavits of your admission to practice as an Attorney at Law in the courts of this State.

Yours,
William J. Armstrong

May 1, 1929   Clerk

"Congratulations, kid," your father said.

You felt him shake your hand, but for some reason your mind was set on something else. You were thinking of a man named 528 at a place called Napanoch. You were thinking of an aluminum soap box, a diary, carbon paper, and a pair of magazines. Had you sent them? you were wondering (5 articles!), but you couldn't remember.

THE COLOR OF THE AIR, II

HERNANDO DE SOTO — 1542

ADELANTADO OF FLORIDA

He was with Pizarro in Peru. Where else could a captain of horse, a spic *condottiere,* have put together as his share of the pickings two hundred thousand cruzados in gold, enough to buy him the groin of Doña Ysabel de Bobadilla, with coin to spare for an usher, an equerry, and a chamberlain, and pages and footmen and other servants requisite for the menage of a brand-new Marques — where but in Peru?

His portion for ending a civilization, two hundred thousand likenesses of the crusader's cross — and he lavished them on the wines and whores of Estremadura. When, therefore, Cabeza de Vaca, that had sailed with Narvaez, returned with tales of a place where gold (let God judge him if he lied!) sprang from the earth, where it flashed in the waters and depended from the trees, who will wonder that Ysabel's minor lips were forgot, along with the major-domo?

Once only the Marques sent tidings to the Court. *Very noble gentlemen,* he wrote, and he told of a new land that was nothing if not a magazine of plenty, a depot that would subsist an army without its knowing a want, and he spoke of a town that was called Ocale, so large and so extolled that he scarcely dared repeat what the air was rife with—the multitudes of turkeys kept in pens, the herds of deer tended as kine were tended in Spain, the rumor of pearls. . . .

What more there was straggled in with the survivors. The figs as big as a fist; the anane, whereof the pulp was like a curd; the mamei, that recalled the peach; the guayaba, in form a sort of filbert; the humpbacked cows and the conies; the bagre, a third of which was head, and the barbel, and the pereo, and the peelfish, with a snout a cubit long; in short, the gold that grew, that swam, that flew and ran—no man had sought it, alas, no man born in Spain.

The treasure that had drawn them was the kind that would weigh in the purse and chime in the palm, it would shine when shone on and sometimes glow in the dark, it would buy the heart's desire and take the place of fire in a woman of stone.

Three years had they wandered, only to be stopped in the end by a flow of water so great that it tore loose the earth and bore it away, and it was there, by that spate, that the Marques had sickened and died, and his men, those that were left, wrapped his body in a blanket weighted not with gold but sand and sank it in the stream.

SCENE 3

A SUMMER THAT BEGAN IN MAY (1929)

One day early in the month, your father sent you down to West End to rent a cottage for the coming season.

"What kind of cottage?" you said. "How many rooms?"
"Well," he said, "there'll be us three—you, me, and Ruthie—and we'll need a housekeeper."
"Four bedrooms, then,"
"Make it five. I've asked your Grandma Nevins to be our guest."

On the following morning, you boarded the steamer *Monmouth* at the Jersey Central pier, and as you rode downriver on her open upper deck, you thought of what your father had said when he saw your expression of surprise.

"She was always good to me, Julian."

"I know," you said, "but grandpa wasn't. He hated you. He tried to take your clients away."

"Only after the Perlmans crazed him. Before that, remember, he gave us a home for six years."

In your lap lay the booklet you'd brought along, an old issue of *Poetry*, the one that contained "At Melville's Tomb" and Crane's explication of its imbricated metaphor. You'd read both often, and that day you'd meant to compare once more his prose and the verse he'd been asked to unfold. All you could do, though, was stare at the bay-green hue of the little magazine.

"What did she say when you invited her?"

"I don't recall that she said anything."

"Then what makes you think she'll accept?"

"You ought to know your grandma by now," he said. "Whenever she's happy, she cries."

Somehow you must've taken in the islands of the upper harbor, the tugs, the scows, the car-ferries, but they seemed hardly more substantial than recalls from other trips, and it was so too with the tramps riding high at anchor and the ships lying to at Quarantine. Unopened, the magazine was in sight but hardly seen, a gull, it might've been, a spar- or bell-buoy, a hull-down crate, and Crane's illuminations went unread that day. You simply sat in a camp-chair watching brush-strokes of sunlight shuttle on the bay.

Through the soles of your shoes, you felt the twin-screw throb of the *Monmouth*, and it shook you as it did the housing and the halyards and the rail. She was swift, you might've noted at another time, good for twenty-some knots even against the tide in the Narrows, but speed that day was thought of not at all. Your mind was fixed on your father, on the good that he remembered and the ill that he forgot, the aspersions of your grandpa, the backbite, the shrill and constant word-of-mouth. The silver son-in-law did not hate the old man, you thought, and how much finer therefore was silver than gold!

At Atlantic Highlands, there were trains on trestles running out from the shore, one of them the Long Branch local. You had no need to look at the engine—it could only be a 4-4 American, tall-stacked and gaunt—and the cars would be the same soot-gray you'd seen in the past. Within moments, you were reading station-signs long familiar—Low Moor, Sea Bright, Water Witch—and you were reaching shingled houses, the Shrewsbury bridge, unmoved chunks of rip-rap on the beach, and it pleased you that nothing appeared to have changed. These minor things had been overlooked by the crowd in its quest for the majestic—the gorge, the falls, the tall timber. They were all where and as you'd left them, as though they belonged to you.

By midafternoon, you'd put down a deposit on a cottage a mile or so inland of West End village. It was one room short of the number required, but at the rear of the grounds, in the loft of a carriage-house, you found a fifth room—yours, you decided, once you'd heard birds differing in the eaves. The two stalls on the lower floor were still redolent of hay and harness, and in the corners skiffs of straw still lay. You'd like that steep-roofed room, you thought—you could hardly wait to sleep there in the rain.

No hedge or fence marked the limit of the property, which ravelled into a field of milkweed and thistle. You strode through the undergrowth, picking up foxtails that clung to your cuffs like crickets, and some way in from the road, you reached a reed-ringed pond where redwinged blackbirds flew and flashed. You'd seen the place years earlier, and to your eye nothing seemed to have changed: what was not the same was so similar that the very birds might've been those of the times before.

A path led away from the pond through roughs and fairways toward a long pillar-porched hotel, now being readied for the coming season. A crew of workmen were trimming lawns and whitewashing stones while a line of rockers kept watch like an array of paying guests. Soon such guests would be there, and the air would hum with summer talk, and children would play in the sun, and girls in white, yellow, light blue, green would wait in the shade, one of them for you.

"It's on Cedar Avenue," you said. "A ten-minute walk from where Aunt Sarah lives."

"Good," your father said.

§

The pleasures of sin for a season, you thought.

She was waiting for you at the far end of the portico, near the ballroom door. Between you, along the hotel wall, ran a row of wicker chairs and rockers, and there sat elders gazing at the summer night and through it at a host of ghostly summers of the past. There must've been talk, music, laughter, the resonance of footsteps on the porch, but sight diminished sound (the white dress, the black sash, the red rose), and you went seemingly amidst a silence toward the pleasures of the season. In the autumn of that year, there'd be a silence more profound, and mighty men would drown in their deliquescent chink, sink and scream but make no sound, as in a dream of falling. But that time was still in the making, this was the season of sin, and its pleasures wore crêpe de Chine, a velvet sash, and a red red velvet rose.*

§

She was a beauty, you think as she comes to mind, and you're surprised to find that she comes in colors, always the same as those of that dress; in recall, she has no other, as if she'd posed for a picture and were costumed once for all. You see her in unconnected slides, images like a strewn deck of cards. You see her walking toward you and away, you see her on the sand, in the surf, and standing still, waiting, as on that long verandah, you see her in black, red, white, and now and again you see her without that dress at night, and then she herself is in color, red and black and white. She was a beauty.

§

It was a good summer.

Your father had provided you with a book of commutation tickets good for fifty trips to and from New York, but it was the rare day when you made the round. Instead, you drove him to the station in the morning and met his train in the afternoon. In between, you sunned on the sand, watched children dig down to water, stared out at ships towed by their own smoke, lay beside a spread of long black hair.

"Why didn't you speak to me last year?" she said.
"I didn't know you last year."
"You could've known me. I was there."
"I was in Boston last year," you said.

You had the use of your father's Marmon, and sometimes you'd call for her at the hotel, and then the two of you would take your grandma for an evening ride into the dark and quiet country, past truck-farms and stands of pine and through the rills that cut across the roads. *Wie schmeckt!* your grandma would say as some fragrance blew in from a bank of shrubbery, a damp fall

---

*To Feed Their Hopes, 1980.

of leaves. *Wie schmeckt!* she'd say to the lamplit night. And you'd think ahead to your carriage-house room, to its remnant smells of feed and leather, to salt on long black hair, and then it'd be your turn to say *Wie schmeckt!* and she'd say, "I hope you're not in Boston now."

On the engine-room deck of the Jersey Central steamers, there were card-games going and card-games coming back, and one day while watching the play, you saw a man you knew gazing out at water passing at twenty knots.

You walked over to him and said, "I'm Phil Shapiro's son. How are you, Mr. Rossi?"

He continued to stare at the opaque bay.

"Are you all right?" you said.

"I had a bad day at the Market," he said.

"Oh, I'm sorry," you said, and you turned to go away.

"I only made four thousand," he said to the swales in the stream. "God damn it, I should've made twenty!"

In the fall, he shot himself, but it was a good summer.

She was so striking, so bright, that she was lost in her glare, like the sun, and you failed to see that she was freeing you from Boston. One night, as you were coming from the carriage-house, she said, "Does all this mean anything to you?"

You were in the driveway, and you listened to gravel grind underfoot, to the call of a distant bird, to your voice saying, "There was a girl I knew. She died last year."

"The one in Boston?" she said.

You shook your head. "The one who came next."

"You have a bad habit, Julian," she said. "You live backwards. Why don't you get your ass behind you, where it belongs?"

And later, when you were walking on Cedar Avenue in the nightshade of the chestnut trees, you said, "I haven't had my ass behind me since I was ten."

"What happened when you were ten? Another girl?"

"In a way. I lost my mother."

"I shouldn't've said that."

But you spoke over her, saying, "It was like losing an eye. I could still see, but only half as well."

As you went toward her hotel, you wondered whether, if you asked, she'd've gone back to the carriage-house, and after you'd left her on the verandah, you wondered why you'd let the summer end where it began, before a row of empty rockers.

A good summer.

SCENE 4

AND ENDED IN OCTOBER (Fall 1929)

It was over, that summer, when the sycamores turned, and their brown and grasping leaves fell and filled the roads. The shingled homes were shuttered then, and their porches, bare of chairs, gave on lawns and hedges going dry. Fast-flown clouds made fleeting shade, and sudden showers passed, leaving webs of mist that grayed the trees, and the season, like its pleasures, went, and there were no more drives in the dark, no nightbird cries, no rustlings above your bed below the eaves.

In the city, sin had a different flavor. It was wine that did not travel, and in that different place, even the girl, bright all summer, changed. How soon it faded, her sunburn with its shoulder-straps of white!

SCENE 5

THE PEOPLE vs. ADOLPHUS ROCK (February 1930)

On your admission to the Bar, you'd been given a room in your father's suite of offices, and from its single window, across a quarter-mile reach of roofing-tar, you could see the Hudson River and a wedge of Jersey. When alone, as you were that morning, you'd sometimes stare at the far and near, at other windows, at clouds, at smoke and steam against the sky and traffic in the stream. And sometimes you'd turn to the view within, to a desk that bore only a telephone and its lynched receiver, to a bookcase filled with first editions, to pictures of flowers, soldiers, ruins, to the frosted glass of the door and its legend in reverse: *namtrO & oripahS*. namtrO was somewhere else that day.

Your father entered with a folded legal document in a pale blue cover. He placed it before you on your desk, where it lay slowly expanding, as if inviting search. *Proceedings of the Grand Jury of Bronx County*, you read, *in the matter of Adolphus Rock and another.*

"Who's Adolphus Rock?" you said.
"Your first client," your father said.

41

"I don't know any Adolphus Rock."

"Go up to the County Jail. They'll introduce you."

"How did I get to be his lawyer?"

"You've been appointed by the Court."

You reached for the paper and shook it open to the gravamina: *Count One— Conspiracy to commit Robbery; Count Two—Carrying a deadly weapon after a Felony Conviction.* Looking up at your father, you said, "You arranged this, didn't you?"

"I spoke to Tom Cherry, the Court clerk," he said. "I told him you had to start somewhere."

"I was perfectly happy."

He glanced at your books and decorations, saying, "I don't wonder. There's nothing to remind you of your profession. What's Winslow Homer got to do with the law?"

The People of the State of New York vs Adolphus Rock, you thought, and you said, "You know what's going to happen to Adolphus Rock, don't you?"

"He's going to be convicted."

"A better lawyer might get him off."

"He can't afford a better lawyer."

In the detention section of the Bronx County Courthouse, you were shown into a room with four walls of woven wire. It contained a marred table of golden oak and a few marred chairs to match. The smell of piss and disinfectant drained in from the cells, and sound drained in from everywhere, the sound of voices, footsteps, running water, small sound, all of it strained down to an undertone, as if a town were hurrying by. Far off, a steel door rang, and you saw two figures coming toward you along a hallway, one in blue behind the other's gray, and soon, across the rilled and flaking table-top, you were facing Adolphus Rock.

"I'm your lawyer," you said.

His stare unfurled into a smile, and turning to the guard outside the crisscross wire, he said, "He's my lawyer."

The guard said, "You'll be a free man in no time," and then he and the prisoner laughed.

Lettered in gilt on a glass prism was the name of the Prosecutor—*Sylvester Ryan*—and struck by the sun, it seemed to float in light. Beyond, on the desk-top, lay a short-barreled pistol and a length of rubber hose taped shut at the ends.

"I just saw Rock," you said. "He claims to be innocent."

"Did you believe him?" Ryan said.

"I'm only supposed to make a jury believe him." You watched Ryan reach out and make a slight adjustment in the position of the pistol. "No, I didn't."

"But you're going to try the case anyhow."

"I was appointed by Judge Barrett," you said. "What else can I do?"

"Plead him to possession of the gun. We'll drop the conspiracy count."

"He says No."

"He'll be saying no when he comes back down the river several years from now."

"I told him that, and he still said No."

Ryan picked up the hose, held it suspended for a moment, and let it fall: it fell like a solid. "Rock and an accomplice are arrested in an alley on a snowy night," he said. "There's a loaded S. & W. .38 in his pocket, and his accomplice is carrying a sap filled with lead shot—this one. When the patrolman asks them what they're doing there, a foot deep in the snow, they say they wandered in and fell asleep. They were sleeping, they said."

"It isn't much of a story."

"The jury won't even leave the box," Ryan said. "Well, it's Rock's funeral." He watched you rise and start for the door. "You haven't asked me about the accomplice. You don't even know his name."

"It's Vincent," you said. "Rock told me."

"Did he tell you Vincent pleaded guilty last week?"

"No, he didn't tell me that."

"They're both Barbasians," Ryan said, and you said *Barbasians* under your breath as you closed the door.

At the trial, which lasted through a morning and part of an afternoon, Adolphus Rock sat alone several chairs removed from you and your law partner, and never did he address either of you or turn his head to the courtroom world. He faced the Bench and the jury-box because his seat was so placed, but he did not appear to see them or to be aware of voices, scraping shoes, the racket of paper, or sounds from the street below. His expression was the absence of expression, as if he were all surface and that in repose—all skin and cocoa-colored, you thought, and the word *Barbasian* came to mind. What was a Barbasian? you wondered, and you glanced at the Prosecutor, as if he might reply.

Ryan had just called a witness to the stand, the patrolman who had made the arrest, and you heard a name and a shield-number given and the slurred recitation of a bailiff's oath. "Officer Foley," Ryan was saying, "were you on duty on the night of December 12th last?"

"Yes, sir, I was," Foley said.

"What was your beat?"

"Southern Boulevard between Hunts Point and Intervale Avenues."

"Will you describe the condition of the weather that night?"

"It was cold," Foley said. "It was snowing, like it done the day before."

"Were any pedestrians abroad?"

"Yes, sir. A movie-house was letting out, and people was going home."

"Do you recall any of them in particular?" Ryan said.

"Two. A man and a woman."

"What brought them to your notice?"

"I was standing in a doorway on Simpson near Aldus, and these people was walking towards me, and all of a sudden, when they come to an alleyway, they begun to run."

"What did you do, if anything?"

"I stopped them, and they said there was somebody in there."

"Meaning in the alleyway?"

"The alleyway, yes."

Ryan drifted to a table, where, inert and incompatible, two tagged objects were displayed—a pistol and a foot-long piece of hose. He had never seen these things before, it seemed, and he was spelled by their presence. It was the hose that worked the greater witchery, and he took it up and trifled with it, tested it for weight, rigidity, balance, and finally, still possessed of it, he returned to the witness Foley, saying, "Somebody in the alley, you said."

"Yes, sir."

"Did you take any action?"

"I drew my gun and proceeded to the alleyway."

"And was it true, as you'd been told, that somebody was there?"

"Yes, sir."

"Who?" Ryan said.

Foley indicated Rock, saying, "That man was there."

The hose slipped from Ryan's grasp, and, falling, it made dust dance up from the cracks in the floor. Ryan retrieved it and said, "I'm sorry. Please repeat your answer."

"That man there—Adolphus Rock."

You glanced at Rock, ten feet distant but all space away: out where he was, you thought, there were no resonations.

"Was the man alone?"

"No. There was a man name of Vincent."

"Were they armed, these two men?"

"Rock had a pistol, and Vincent had that club."

"This club?" Ryan said, and he struck the ledge of the witness-box with the hose.

"That's the one," Foley said.

"Do you see the man Vincent in the courtroom?"

"No, sir."

"Do you know where he is?"

"Yes, sir."

Holding up a hand to Ryan, the Judge summoned you with the other, and when you stood before the Bench, he said, "For God's sake, counselor, can't you even make it *look* good!"

"I'm doing my best," you said.

"You're doing nothing! Where the hell did you study law?"

"Fordham, Your Honor."

"Fordham!" he said. "What did you do—cut all your classes in Criminal Law?"

"Nobody cuts classes on Joe Crater, Judge. He gave me a B."

"He'd've had to be drunk to give you a B. You don't know beans from bullshit. If you did, you'd see where the D. A. is heading. One more question, and he'll have it in the record that Vincent pleaded guilty. Do you know what that does to Rock—having a guilty accomplice?"

"I wish I could do better, Judge."

"Do something!" he said. "Or the jury won't be out long enough to squat!"

A recess was called, and you returned to the counsel table and your dumb show of lawbooks.

"What was he telling you?" your partner said.

"Herb, my boy, he told me I was losing."

"He saved me the trouble. That God damned club! Ryan is killing us with it. Why don't you make him put it down?"

"I don't know yet," you said. "Maybe I'm hoping he'll kill himself."

"Every time he hits something, he's hitting the jury."

"Maybe the jury will think he's taking advantage of my ignorance. I'm the underdog, they'll figure."

"You think people care for the underdog?" Herb said. "Jules, they piss on the underdog. They're pissing on Rock."

"Ryan calls him a Barbasian. What's a Barbasian?"

"A snotty way of saying Barbadian. Somebody from Barbados."

"The Judge warned me to keep Ryan off the subject of Vincent."

"He did?" Herb said. "Why?"

"It'd hurt Rock if the jury knew his accomplice had pleaded guilty and gone to prison."

"And the Judge doesn't want to hurt Rock—he wants to hurt the State of New York! Is that what we're supposed to believe?"

"A Judge has to be impartial," you said. "He can't be for either side."

Herb looked at you, slowly shaking his head. "Jules, you're in for a hard life," he said. "Where's this Vincent?"

"Downtown in The Tombs. After Rock is convicted, they'll both go up the river."

"Send for him."

"Send for Vincent! What for?"

"Something's fishy," Herb said. "They should've been tried together."

When the trial was resumed, you rose to say, "If the Court please, I ask that a subpoena be issued for the man Vincent. . . ."

Early in the afternoon, when the State had presented its case, Vincent was brought into the courtroom and seated alongside Rock. His skin was lighter-colored, with less Negro and more Indian, almost buff, you thought, like suede. He too sat staring straight ahead, he too betrayed nothing occurring within.

"What do I do with this guy?" you whispered to Herb.
"Put him up there," he said. "Maybe something will happen."

On the stand, he stated that his first name was Hillaby, and that he'd been so called by his mother after Mt. Hillaby, the high point of Barbados. He was thirty years old, he told you, and he'd come away from the island some ten years earlier, after having worked there cutting cane at times and at others in a distillery; unmarried, he'd never before been arrested anywhere.

You returned to the table, ostensibly for some notes. "Why the hell did he confess?" you said to Herb.
"Don't ask me. Ask him."
"Here goes."

You turned back toward Vincent, stopping on the way to pick up the shot-filled hose lying before Ryan.

Carrying it to the witness-box, you showed it to Vincent. "Hillaby," you said, "have you ever seen this hose before?"
"Damn right," he said.
The dangerous word *where* rose through your mind, and you heard yourself say, "Where?"
"I seen it the night I was arrested with Dolphus Rock."
"Where, I said, not when."
"In the station-house."
"You mean you didn't have it with you in the alley?"
"I never had nothing in the alley."
"Then where did the hose come from?"
"The cops brung it in the room."
"What room?"
"The one where they was keeping me."
"Keeping you and Rock?"
"Just me."
"What did the cops do with the hose?"
"What did they do?" Vincent said, and he half came up from his chair. "I tell you what they done. They beat the shit out of me."
After a full beat of silence in the courtroom, you said, "Like this?" and you slammed the hose against the witness-box.
"Like that," Vincent said.

46

"And like this?" you said, and now you struck the jury-box.

"Like that," Vincent said.

Finally you hit the Bench, saying, "Beat the shit out of you, you say?"

"The living shit," Vincent said.

"And is that why you confessed?"

"Beat the shit out of me," he said. "The living shit."

"Stand up and take off your jacket and shirt."

Vincent did as told, stripping himself to the waist. On his chest and belly, there were many dark brown ridges, like earth pushed up by burrowing animals.

"Turn around," you said.

Vincent's back was jackstrawed with everywhichway welts, all bloody once and some raw and suppurating still.

"And you say the cops did that to make you confess?"

Vincent put both hands on the rim of the Bench and spoke directly to the Judge. "Beat the holy shit out of me," he said.

There were summations, charges to the jury, motions to the Court, but the trial actually ended with Vincent's testimony. The jury was out for only five minutes—as the Judge had said, hardly long enough to squat.

"How do you find?" the bailiff said.

And the foreman said, "Not guilty."

The Judge spun his swivel-chair once around and said, "I dismiss you idiots without the thanks of the Court." Then he thrust a finger at Adolphus Rock, saying, "You! Get to hell out of Bronx County. If you ever come back, you'll be arrested on sight!"

Rock rose and with all elegance dusted himself off. "I won't come back, Judge," he said, "because I won't have to. I'm not going to leave."

Turning, he passed you, still without expression, and strolled from the courtroom.

When you reached your father's office late in the day, the usual after-hours smoker was in progress. Most of his associates were there—Billy Goldman, Jack Freeman, Barney Chambers, your Uncle Arthur—and at your entrance, they stopped their talk to take stock of you.

"Well, kid," your father said. "Would a better lawyer have gotten him off?"

"He didn't need a better lawyer," you said. "This one got him off."

After a still moment, there were whoops and hollers, handshakes, praise, and then the story was called for and told in detail. Of what was said by Billy, Barney, Jack, your Uncle Arthur, all is now gone; only what your father said remains:

"Why didn't you move for a new trial for Vincent?"

SCENE 6

FROM THE NIEMEN RIVER AND THE RIVER MOY (1930)

After her West End summer with your father, your Grandma Nevins had moved to Cedarhurst to reside with her daughter Ida, and to keep her company, Ellen Lang had been brought there too. The door between their rooms was always open, and always they were to be found in one or another, sitting close together as if still in the Harlem kitchen, still conniving under the cover of some household task. They were tiring now, the younger as well as the elder, and on the calls you made so seldom, you noted that they moved more slowly and spoke less often, though they seemed to see further when they stared at the walls. You'd sit with them, try your grandma's crystallized ginger and bear the Sligo scorn of Ellen as the fat boy had done before, and if for you the past was still near, for them it had far receded, stranding empty shells, worn stones, drying foam. The Jew and the Mick, you thought, the two ways, the two Testaments. Turn the heart, the first one ends, lest the Lord smite the earth with a curse. What a marvel, that no curse falls here!

SCENE 7

A ONE-ROOM FLAT ON BANK STREET (Early 1930)

It was in a red-brick walkup, and it held a mattress, two straight-back chairs, and a small kitchen table—ten dollars worth of furniture, all of it secondhand. There were no rugs, pictures, or lamps, and through an uncurtained window, the place confronted other red bricks and other staring windows across the way.

Opening the door for you, Pep West said, "Montparnasse, Scotty. Come on in."

You were there at his request to read galley proof with him. After years of writing and revision, *Balso Snell* had gone to press a few weeks earlier, and lying on the table now was a sheaf of printed sheets. Nearby, in a binder of green canvas, was the manuscript, and turning back the cover, you let some pages run, many of them dense with interlineations scrawled in a spasmodic hand.

"So it was all true," you said. "You *were* writing a book."

I'm writing a book, he'd said, and you'd been awed as by word of some wonder, but here the wonder was, a Sixth Day reenacted especially for you. Here was what he'd given rise to, this order, this ruling of misrule, and you knew then that what your mother had begun for you in that little Harlem library—*a building made of books!*—had grown to be the world.

"How do we go about this?" you said.
"You read, Scotty," he said. "So far, I've only heard my own voice."

And taking the galleys, you read him his inscription (*to A. S.*), his epigraph (*After all, my dear fellow*), and the opening line of his text (*While walking in the tall grass*), and then with Balso Snell, the poet, you entered the anus of the Wooden Horse, where on meeting the guide, you were treated to the story of the traveler in Tyana, known to you from before. *Ah, then you must be Appolonius of Tyana,* you read, and you failed to catch the double-p and the single-l, and there they are yet. Other errors, though, were found, and using a proofreader's chart, you made marks in the margins for alignment, transposition, and spacing, and wrote *stet* for *let it stand.* You spoke Balso's apostrophe to beautiful names for Jewish girls—Hernia, Paresis, Paranoia— and when you glanced across the table, Nathan, Nate, Natchie Weinstein was looking down. And now you came to names that meant nothing to you— Notker Balbus, Ekkenard le Vieux, Hucbald le Chauve—but you read them as if familiar with medieval monks and abbots, with a Swiss saint a thousand years dead. And on the reading went, through Maloney the Areopagite, the Crime Journal of John Raskolnikov Gilson, and the teacher Miss McGeeney, and there were deletions, inserts, new paragraphs, and changes back from *stet,* and killed cigarettes filled the ashtray, and the room grew blue and gray, and still to come were Beagle Darwin and Saniette.

There were two dozen galleys, coming in all to some twenty thousand words—the lean book of the West ideal. There were no long straights of narrative or description, no roads without a bend, but though its course twisted like its locale, the journey through it was swift. By the time the reading ended, snow had begun to fall, and between the window and the facing wall, it settled slowly, like sediment in a jar. For a while, neither of you spoke, and presently his silence informed you that you were not expected to speak: you'd been brought there to read, it said, and having read, you were free to talk of other things or go. Your opinion didn't matter, he seemed to be saying.

But what if he'd sought it? you wonder. What would you have told him if he'd asked you what you thought. Would you have praised his wit, his literary inventions, and the scope of his lore, would you have endorsed his trope (*carrying fear as an ant carries a caterpillar thirty times its size*), and would you have remarked on the fact that only the author was actually in the horse—I mean, you'd say, there are many voices, Beagle's, Balso's, Gilson's, but all of them are his?

Would that have made him say, "What the hell are you talking about, Scotty?"

And would you have said, "They're all *you* in there, Pep, every one of them."

And would he have closed the discussion with, "You don't understand"?

But nothing was said. There were three more sessions in that room and at that table—for revised galleys, for page proof, and for revised pages. Four times running you read him his book, and never did he ask (nor did you tell him) what you thought.

SCENE 8

AUTUMN DAYS (Late 1929)

The restaurant, known simply as Hargus, was named for Harry and Gus, its proprietors. It was in a block-long alley near Wall and Nassau, and often in the fall of that year, you'd lunch there with your friend, Olga's brother George. He was employed by a stock and bond house called J. A. Sisto & Co., and he'd call you, or you'd call him, and amid the noontime crowds, you'd walk downtown from your father's office and join him at the Morgan corner, blind to the scars of the explosion and deaf to the one that even then was on the way.

Hargus was narrow and deep, rather like a burrow in the building that rose above it, and it held an oyster-bar and two long lines of tables, one at either hand. At the midday hour, it would be thronged throughout its length, always with similars in sack suits or cotton jacket—brokers in wrongful regimentals and traders off the floor of the Exchange. Ever on the air was the compound flavor of the cuisine. It seemed to have become the element itself, like the blended breath of a forest—and for all you knew of the world you were in, you might well have been wandering the woods. All about you here, numbers were growing smaller, and glowing names were turning dim. There were cries you did not hear from those you did not know, and soon there'd be falls from heights that made bloody piles of clothing on the street — the Street!

At every table, there was a turmoil of talk and gesture, but you were unaware of the excitement roundabout you, of silver flatting on china, of seat-backs creaking, of the sound of passing feet. For you, your table alone was occupied, and there the bronze tone of Brahms was discussed, the despair of a poet deplored. Only later did you perceive that George's mind was at other tables, that he spoke as he did to be kind to your ignorance. He was thinking of those fading names and shrinking numbers, he foreknew those headlong flights from upper floors.

No forces were at work for you, though. No charges were laid on you from without, no duties assumed from within. You pry into the silt, the drift-down of the years, and you try to recreate the place, the table, and you across from George, but there's no one in your chair. You're somewhere else, with a hand outstretched for your father to fill. You're not there.

SCENE 9

OF PHIL, THE SILVER SON-IN-LAW (March 1930)

Soon after the turn of the year, your father rented a furnished apartment at 99th Street and Riverside Drive. It was on the ground-floor, and across a strip of park, it faced the Hudson and a wavering line of Jersey hills. From the windows, you could watch the color-change at sunset, when a dye, all shades of blue to black, spread upward over the sky. A sign would come on then at the foot of the Palisades, and its upside-down equivalent would electrify the stream. A mile away from you, a flow-past of letters and numerals would begin — IT IS NOW, the lights would say, 7:54, but it would be so for only a moment, for time would be passing too.

On one such evening, the doorbell rang, and when you answered it a long flat parcel was handed in by the building superintendent. It was addressed to *Philip Shapiro — Apt. 1B.*

"Who sent this? I wonder," you said.

Your father glanced at the parcel, saying, "A cousin of your mother's— Jack Smolens."

"Ida Smolowitz' son?" your sister said. "I didn't know you knew him."

"I know more Nevinses than you do," your father said.

"Grandma used to take me down to Cousin Ida's," you said. "Her husband had a delicatessen-store under the Delancey Street bridge. They were poor, and they were always crying, I remember."

"But not because they were poor," your father said.

Ruth fingered the package, saying, "I wonder what's in it."

"I don't have to wonder. It's part of a bolt of cloth. Enough for a suit of clothes."

"Tell me," you said. "How do you know that?"

"Jack has been doing this for years. He deals in woolens, and whenever he has something fine, it turns up at the office or at my tailor's."

You thought of the gold son-in-law, and you said, "Does he do the same for Uncle Harry?"

"I don't think so."

"Why does he favor you?"

"Your cousin Ida had two sons," your father said. "Jack for one, and a younger boy called Danny. Danny was a drummer—that is, a traveling salesman—and his territory was out in Ohio and Indiana. I don't recall the line he sold, but he thought he could sell more by using a car instead of the trains. That's what killed him, I'm sorry to say. When his people cry, they cry because of him."

"How did it happen?" Ruth said.

"He was driving from one town to another on a rainy night, and at a B. & O. grade crossing, his car was hit by a flyer."

"What a terrible thing!" Ruth said.

"Was anything done about it?" you said.

"The father and mother came to the office and told me the story. I thought there was a possibility that the railroad was at fault, but I wasn't admitted to the Ohio Bar, so what I did was get a referral from the Lawyers' Association. It put me in touch with a negligence man in Chillicothe, a town in the county where the death occurred, and from then on, he handled the case."

"How did it come out?" you said.

"In the complaint, it was alleged that the railroad had been guilty of negligence: there was no watchman at the crossing, there was no sign saying LOOK OUT FOR THE CARS, and there was no automatic signal. In the railroad's answer, it was claimed that Danny had been guilty of contributory negligence, in that he failed to heed the engine whistle, which was blown as required. There was some real doubt, but rather than risk a jury's verdict, the railroad settled the case for $10,000. The Ohio lawyer took a third plus expenses and sent $6,000 to the father and mother."

"Small pay for a son," you said.

"It might've been smaller if there'd been a trial. It might've been nothing."

You turned to your sister, who was opening the parcel at the diningroom table. "And merely for referring the matter to an Ohio lawyer," you said, "Jack Smolens keeps on sending you the finest woolens he can find?"

"I've tried to stop him," your father said, "but it does no good."

"Look at this!" Ruth said. "It's gorgeous!"

A few nights later, while out for a walk on Broadway, you met Jack Smolens as he came up from the 91st Street subway kiosk. He lived close by, and you kept him company as far as his door.

About to part, you said, "I was there the other night when your gift arrived."

"I hope Mr. Shapiro liked the goods," Jack said. "I saved it for him special."

"Oh, he liked it, all right. But what I don't understand is why you sent it."

"Why shouldn't I? He's a good man, Mr. Shapiro."

"Is he the only good man you know?"

"There's lots of good men."

"Do you send four yards of worsted to them all?"

He laughed. "I would have to be made of money."

"Why do you single out my father?"

He studied you for a moment, and then he said, "I can see from your face that he didn't tell you, but I should've known he wouldn't. He's not that kind of a man."

"What kind of man?"

"You heard about the case of my brother Danny, I guess—how he got killed by a train?"

"That much my father told me."

"And you heard about the settlement, $6,000 for my father and mother?"

"Yes."

"And about the lawyer out there in Ohio—$4,000, his share come to?"

"Yes. My father told me about that."

"But did he tell about the lawyer divvying up with him fifty-fifty? Did he tell you he got $2,000 from that settlement?"

You stared at him. "My father split a fee!" you said. "Is that what you're saying?"

"That's what I'm saying, Julian."

"Well, you're a God-damned liar!"

"Wait. It isn't all. The day he got the check, he come around and endorsed it over to my father and mother."

You shook your head, saying, "I'm sorry I got sore."

"He wouldn't take such money," Jack said. "Blood-money, he called it."

You smiled away up the street at nothing you can now remember and perhaps at nothing at all.

"So that's why I send him the suiting," Jack said.

"He didn't tell me," you said.

"He's not that kind of a man."

At home, you found your father smoking a final cigar. "I just met Jack Smolens on Broadway," you said.

"Did you?"

"He told me the *whole* story—about how you gave up your share of the fee."

He waved at the conflict of smoke going on about him. "Anybody else would've done the same," he said.

"I'm not so sure of Uncle Harry," you said. "And I'm not so sure of me."

SCENE 10

THE LAUREL IN THE PINES (Early 1930)

Your room was at the rear of the apartment. The steep slope of 99th Street cut its view in half, and you could see outside only through the upper part of the window. Passersby were reduced to legs and feet, and now and then you'd wonder about faces you never saw, about their color, expression, and age. The sill was a yard lower than the sidewalk and rarely free of dust, and sometimes snow came in and sometimes spattered rain. All the same, you rather liked the dim little room, its narrow couch, its table, chair, and chest of drawers, its single decoration—a Manet reproduction called *Mlle. Victorine as an Espada.*

Your sister occupied what once had been a music-room. It was at a front corner of the apartment and bright always with light from three windows, two of which looked out at trees, water, and the Jersey sky. In that part of the year, though, she was far less aglow than her surroundings. She spent much time in her room, closed off from you and your father, and on her infrequent appearances, she sat quietly, tapping a foot on the floor. You remember thinking of it as disembodied, like the feet you saw from your room.

Such behavior made your father take you aside one day, saying, "Julian, have you been watching Ruth lately?"

"Yes," you said.

"What's troubling her?"

"A guy."

"That's what I suspected. Do you know him?"

"Very well," you said. "And you do too."

"I don't care who he is. I just want to know whether it's going to come to anything."

"I'm afraid not. She likes him more than he likes her."

"Did she tell you that?"

"He did," you said. "I felt I had to do something, so I went to him and put the question."

"What question?" your father said.

"The only one there is — What do you have in mind?"

"You were taking a lot on yourself, weren't you?"

"Somebody had to do it," you said.

"Maybe, but it didn't have to be you."

"She's as thin as an umbrella."

"Did you tell her what you'd done?"

"Yes."

"And how did she take it?"

"She said I'd ruined everything."

"It just might be true," your father said. "You should've kept your two cents out."

"I didn't expect her approval, but I did expect yours."

"For what? Butting into the business of a girl who's twenty-two years old? If she can't manage it, how can you?"

"A brother ought to look after a sister," you said. "Especially when she schleps around like an invalid."

"She does look bad — I'll spot you that."

Before long, looking bad became feeling bad, and with a cough as one of her symptoms, the family physician arranged for an x-ray of her chest: it revealed a small blur in one of her lungs. A period of rest was prescribed, preferably away from the city, and your father chose Lakewood for her and a stay at the Laurel in the Pines.

"And you're going with her," he said. "After all, you're the dutiful brother."

The hotel was a great outspread of tawny brick with a long glassed-in verandah, and there your sister passed her days sitting in sheaves of sunlight gathered by the trees. Each morning, after you'd installed her in a suitable place, you went for a walk among the laurels and the pines. In the steady cold, a thin snow lay long, candle-wicked everywhere with tufts of grass and weed. The resort was no longer in fashion, and you saw boarded houses, shops in disrepair, streets that seemed dejected. In its palmier days, your mother had been there often — *Money has a tendency to melt in this neighborhood,* she'd written in 1912 — and though you remembered the name of her hotel, you couldn't bring yourself to look for it, as if, when you found it, you might look for her too.

The loveliest women are stopping here, she'd written, but they'd gone away, those lovely women, and as you knew so well, she was with them.

Your sister had little to say, but her shoe-tip no longer tapped without her knowing, and she sat quite still, looking out at barren branches piped with snow. There was a time, though, that she spoke so that you remembered.

"He told me how you put it," she said, "—that I wasn't thriving on his neglect. How could you be so foolish, Julian? A man hates to hear he's being depended on."

"You've dealt with men," you said. "You're an authority."

"Maybe not, but I know that one."

"There's a girl he's been gone on for a long time. Is that one of the things you know?"

She looked at you for a moment and turned away again to the trees, the sun, the snow.

"She gave him the gate about a year ago," you said, "and he's still hoping to get her back. He even sent me around to plead his case, but she stopped me as soon as I started. Tell your client his motion is denied, she said."

"I care for him, and he cares for her," your sister said, "and the one she cares for probably cares for someone else. Why can't people get what they want?"

"I'm going to read," you said, and you opened a book you'd brought along from New York. "Maybe Stendhal has the answer."

While talking with your sister, you hadn't noticed a dozen or more guests gathering about a radio set a little distance off along the verandah. They'd seated themselves in a half-circle facing the screened speaker, and they were waiting quietly for some broadcast to begin.

In the Scott-Moncrieff translation, you were reading of a small town in the Franche-Comté, of Verrières

. . . sheltered on the north by a high mountain, a spur of the Jura
. . . a torrent which comes tearing down from the mountain passes
through Verrières before emptying its waters in the Doubs. . . .

when suddenly sound, tidal in power overwhelmed and drowned the verandah. Quickly, though, it was subdued to the lazy slur of vaudeville blackface. This, you found, interfered with the printed page, and, rising, you crossed over to the radio and switched off the set. Then you returned to your seat and took up your reading again, this time of

. . . the sawmills that have made the little town rich.

There was a moment of silent suppression before you heard the guests explode. *Hey!* someone said, and someone else said *What a God damned nerve!*

56

and still another said *Who the hell does he think he is!* and a fourth switched
on the set again, and out came the same syrup-talk of before.

"What happened?" you said to your sister.
She laughed, saying, "Don't you know what you did?"
"I turned the thing off."
"You turned off Amos and Andy, Julian."
"Who are Amos and Andy?"
"The most popular show on the air."
"Well, they were bothering me," you said.

THE COLOR OF THE AIR, III

THE SCARLET LETTER — 16--
AD LIBS BY A FICTITIOUS CHARACTER

> *Child, what art thou?*
> *Oh, I am your little Pearl!*

As Mr. Hawthorne says, the first thing I saw was the scarlet *A* on
the breast of my mother's gown. It was a nearby brightness in a
gray-green world, and it drew me as any other would've done, a
red flower, a red bird or berry, or fire as it played. It was there at
the start, and it stayed, as much a part of Hester as her eyes. But
Mr. Hawthorne seems to have been unaware of the second thing
I saw, a strange lack since it was a second *A*, this one black.

I was three months old at the time and in my mother's arms on
the pillory, pilloried too, the fruit of her sin and therefore no less
vile than she. All Boston had come to view us, and faces paved the
market place, paned the windows, grew on trees. There was an
absence of color in the crowd — the uniform garb was black — but a
certain conical hat seemed somehow blacker than the rest, and so
too a certain cape that fell in folds and flared, and I stared at the
shape my father thus made: a sable *A* on a sable field.

I seemed to know him at sight, though I've never known how.
He stood among the crowd, concealed by it, as he thought, like a
shadow lost in the shadow night, but there was my begetter, the
black letter *A*. Dimmesdale! Mr. Hawthorne says I touched him once
(it was at the Governor's, he claims, and I was going on three), but
if so, I must've done it to test whether one who looked so dead was
still alive. His eyes were deep in his head, bits of sky in a well, and

his hair lay senseless, nonconductive, and his skin was dry, like slough. If, as said, I touched him once, let it be known that once was all, but quite enough.

My mother must've touched him too, and not his hand, as I did, nor merely with her cheek; it must've been some other member that she reached, sunless, sallow. Mr. Hawthorne describes the result of that collision—I, a wild and flighty elf named Pearl, an airy child, the friend of weeds, sticks, rags, and the *ferae* found in the forest. He dwells long, Mr. Hawthorne, on the wrong they worked on me, but mum's the word on why. How could she have borne him bare, how endured that prying candle, that tallow finger in her private hair? and where, in what field did she lie, what pine-bough bed, to what rocks was her fall revealed? and did she cry aloud when his small flame singed her, did she pray when he came or wait till he went? Ah, the reverend Arthur! Pale psalmer, scratcher of itches, charmer of skirts, snake in the pubic grass—what did she find in his leached-out phiz, what soul sat behind those rank clothes, what imbued his sour stuffing?

To my mind, she sinned only in sinning with him. It was her affair that she chose to be ridden, and I didn't care where the rider took her, on the run or standing still or during a swim in a stream— but to receive such a one and make him my father! to couple with that quick-spent dip, that one-cent wick! my God, to be lit but once and then so dimly! And thereafter, for seven years, she wore the badge where the world could see it, while he sequestered his in his room. It was not enough that he carved it with a whip, it didn't matter that it bled and festered and appeared to glow in the dark: he let my mother alone be stoned by eyes.

Mr. Hawthorne says that she took me overseas when he died and, after a span of years, returned without me, and rumor ran that writings reached her from time to time, some wearing seals of an unknown bearing, and that monies made her late days easy and paid for the slate over her bones and Arthur's. But with no blood of my own, is it likely that blood would wed me? With no name but Pearl, would I be apt to flash his ring and bring to bed some belted earl, would I become My Lady, would I be called My Lady Pearl? Or would I, so to say, lie below nobility and sell what Hester had given away?

SCENE 11

THE LITTLE MAGAZINE *TAMBOUR** (Spring and Summer 1929)

They're bound in buckram now, your snotty screed to the editor and a pair of tin-pot sketches that you can hardly bear to read. "You, Drum Major," you wrote, and with fury you assailed his slogan: *Every form of artistic expression is tolerable,* he'd proclaimed, and you aimed to make him take it back. Whatever you may have meant, though, was lost in rant, in termagant language—or were you saying nothing in an arcane way?

And when you composed "An Old Lady," what, you wonder, did you have in mind? She was your father's mother, that lady, and indeed she was old, but were you outraged by her age or merely outrageous? Were you offended by her twisted fingers and swollen feet? Did her wig distress you, her smell of saffron? Did it gall you that she'd never call you Julian, that you were always Yonkel Layv? Did her carved and high-backed chair, did her footstool and cushions remind you of a throne? And is that why you tried to demean her—because she was a queen?

And what of that other spate of spleen—"Terpsichore on the Nevsky Prospekt"? For a dance-class in one of the salles of Carnegie Hall, your friend George played the piano on Saturday afternoons, and now and then you'd join him there and sit through an hour or two of heavy flight, of gauze and Greece. The piano was often out of tune, a string or two sounding as if damped by paper, and there was a taint of sweat in the air, and dust was raised by black-soled feet. All true, but why did you go, or having gone, why did you not go away?

*Beginning in March 1929, eight issues of *Tambour* were published in Paris by editor Harold J. Salemson. The three pieces of early writing mentioned here appeared in Nos. 3, 4, and 6.

SCENE 12

THE PEOPLE vs. JESÚS CORTEZ (April 1930)

There were two judges in the Bronx County Court. The senior was John Barrett, before whom, on his own appointment, you'd defended Adolphus Rock. After you'd won an acquittal, he'd made it known that he'd never again assign you a case: you'd tried too hard, he said. The junior judge, Harry Stackell, had just been elected, and in a small way, you'd contributed to his campaign by handing out flyers and tacking VOTE FOR posters to telephone poles. Not long after being installed, he sent you a True Bill found by the Grand Jury against one Jesús Cortez.

The crime imputed to him was burglary — specifically, pants burglary, an offense wherein the breaking and entering is committed by a part of the body only, an arm, say, or by the introduction of an instrument, such as a stick or a hook, provided such breaking and entering is done for the purpose of theft. According to the indictment, Cortez was accused of having, in the night-time, climbed a fire-escape leading to residential quarters with the intention of stealing a wallet from a pair of trousers lying across a chair near a bedroom window. To the necessary element of darkness was added that of the necessary trespass, in that when seized, Cortez actually had his hand in the complainant's pocket.

Dropping the indictment on your father's desk, you said, "What am I going to do with this?"

"Another hard one?" he said.

"They nail this Puerto Rican on a fire-escape two flights up from the street in the dead of night, and in his fist is the tenant's poke. How do I explain that? How do I make him look innocent?"

"Maybe he isn't," your father said. "Not everybody is, you know."

"This guy's guilty. As a juryman, that's how I'd have to vote."

"Don't try to be everything in a courtroom. Just be what you are — a lawyer."

"Poor Jesús Cortez, " you said. "I wonder who gets the easy cases."

"There are no easy cases."

At the Courthouse, you were shown as before into the conference room, and soon, through the weave of wire, you watched the approach of your client, Jesús Cortez.

After seating himself, he studied you from across the table, and then he said, "*Como se llama usted?*"

60

You shook your head, saying, "I speak very little Spanish."

"What name is you have?"

"Julian Shapiro," you said, and you pointed at yourself. "I'm a lawyer. *Abogado.*"

"Zapiro. Is eSpanish name, no?"

"Jewish."

He leaned toward you a little, as if you'd become harder to see. "You *un judío?*" he said.

"Don't you like Jews? Do you want another lawyer?"

He shrugged, saying, *"Es mejor, un cristiano?"*

Showing him the indictment, you said, "It says in this paper that you tried to steal money — *robar dinero* — from a house near Crotona Park."

"Yo soy inocente," he said.

At the trial several days later, a plausible case against the accused was spelled out by a set of four witnesses. The first of these was the complainant, a minor official of the county, who testified that he was the lessee of the flat where the alleged burglary had taken place. The household, he said, consisted of himself, his wife, and a sister-in-law; the last occupied an alcove in the parlor, where she slept on a davenport, and the others the only bedroom, located at the opposite end of the hall. On the date of the break-in, the complainant related, his wife was absent from the city, and he and his sister-in-law were alone in the flat. Shortly after midnight, he was awakened by a sound — a scraping sound, as he described it — and by the light from a street-lamp below, he saw an arm reaching into the room from the fire-escape, whereupon he rose, and moving quietly, he managed to shut the window on the intruder's hand, pinning it between the sash and the frame. At the same time, he called out to his sister-in-law to telephone for the police. Taking the stand as the second witness, the sister-in-law testified that the outcry had roused her and that she'd done as bidden; by the time the police arrived, however, the accused had freed himself and gotten away. The third witness, a patrolman, deposed that he had seen the accused running — fleeing, he called it — and that on taking him to the station-house, he was confronted by the complainant and identified. The final witness was the precinct sergeant, who swore to seeing a fresh laceration on the wrist of the accused, an injury consistent with having been caused by . . . and there you objected, and the objection was sustained.

While the evidence was being given, Cortez showed no anger, no aloofness, no disagreement. He seemed, rather, to be entertained, as if he were part of the audience, but he did not grasp that *he* was the entertainment and that its end might be tragic. He watched the proceedings brightly and listened with care.

You too watched and listened, but throughout the course of the morning, you found little to challenge, little ground for hope. The presentation had been straightforward and relentless: there'd been no errors of law that you knew enough to seize on, and possessed of a solid case, the district attorney let it speak for itself to the jury. Your cross-examination was futile from first to last, evoking only a repetition of what appeared to be the truth, but for some opaque reason, you reserved the right of recall. After the noon recess, with nothing in view but keeping the defense alive, you summoned the sister-in-law back to the stand.

What could you adduce from her? you wondered, what fact, what opinion, what attitude would make the jury doubt her word? and unable to find a line of questioning, you let yourself be led by your mind—and it led you to the burgled flat.

"Miss McQuade," you said, "tell me more about the floor-plan. Describe the layout, please, in greater detail."

"Well," she said, "I guess it's what you'd call four rooms—parlor, dining-room, kitchen, and bedroom, and of course a bathroom. They're all in a row, and they open off a hall."

"With the parlor at one end," you said, "and the bedroom at the other? I'm trying to picture the place."

"Four rooms ain't much to picture."

"How far would you say the parlor is from the bedroom?"

"I guess about twenty-five feet, door to door."

"When your brother-in-law called out to you, how long did it take you to reach the telephone?"

"I didn't have to reach," she said. "It's on a table next to the bed?"

"And by the time the police arrived, the accused had fled?"

"And broke the window doing it. There was glass all over the floor."

The Judge intervened. "Counselor," he said, "we've been over most of this before. You're not bringing out anything new, and you're wasting the time of the Court."

On a table next to the *bed*! you thought. The telephone, she'd said, was on a table next to the *bed*—but there *was* no bed in the parlor alcove; there was only a davenport.

"Miss McQuade," you said, "I'd like to go back to an answer you gave a moment ago. You said the telephone was on a table next to the bed."

"That's right. That's where it is."

"On a table next to the bed—in the alcove?"

"Who said in the alcove? The table with the telephone on it is in the . . . ," and there the woman stopped.

"In the what, Miss McQuade?" you said, but she was looking at the Prosecutor, and he was looking at the Judge. "Isn't this what you were about to say—that the telephone is in the bedroom?"

"No," the woman said.

"Then where is it? Tell us."

"It's . . . ," she said, but she could find no predicate, and she stopped again.

"Maybe I can help," you said.

"I don't need your help! The telephone was next to the davenport!"

"Oh," you said. "Then there are two telephones."

"One! Can't you get that through your head?"

"Why are you so worked up, Miss McQuade? Is it because the telephone is next to the bed—in the bedroom—*and you were in the bed*?"

"That's not right!"

"You weren't sleeping on the davenport that night. With your sister out of town, you were sleeping with your brother-in-law."

"That's a lie!"

Again breaking into the proceedings, the Judge rose from the Bench and beckoned to you and the District Attorney. When you joined him in his chambers, he said, "Julian, what the hell are you trying to do?"

"If Your Honor please, I'm trying to show that the woman's testimony is unreliable."

"Why unreliable—because she was copulating with her brother-in-law?"

"They weren't copulating, Judge—they were fucking."

"Whatever they were up to, how does it affect your client? They caught him in the act of lifting a wallet."

"And he caught them in an act of adultery."

"And you're out to smear that all over the record just to save a lousy pants-burglar."

"He claims he's innocent. *Yo soy inocente,* he says."

"They're all innocent, God damn it!" the Judge said, and he turned to his Court Clerk. "See if you can find out from the bailiff how the jury is leaning."

When the man returned, he said, "Looks bad for the spic, Judge. They had a show of hands while they was waiting."

"Julian," the Judge said, "I strongly advise you to plead your client."

"To what, sir?"

"I'll quash the burglary if he admits an attempt."

"What would that cost him?"

"Three-to-five at Sing Sing. He could be out in two."

Addressing the Court Clerk, you said, "How did they split?"

"Eight guilty, the bailiff told me, two undecided, and two in the toilet."

"If you let them bring in a verdict, Julian," the Judge said, "I'll give Cortez five-to-ten, out in four. Keep on, and you'll cost him an extra two years."

You had Cortez brought to the chambers from the courtroom, and through an interpreter, you explained the fix he was in. He kept saying *Yo soy inocente,* and for their *inmoralidad,* he scorned the *focking* woman and her *cuñado.* In the end, being helpless, he let himself be swayed. When the jury returned to the box, it was informed of the defendant's plea and dismissed. As the courtroom began to clear, you gathered a few papers and were about to rise from the counsel table when you saw the Foreman of the jury standing before you.

"Why'd you plead that guy?" he said. "You was going good."

"Thanks," you said, "but I heard otherwise."

"Then you heard wrong, counselor."

You stood up, staring. "You mean to say . . . ?"

"Oh, he was guilty, all right," the Foreman said. "But, shit, he didn't get away with nothing, and them two no-goods did. The wife is away, and there's the husband jazzing her sister. That being the case, we don't let 'em swear nobody up the river."

"But you took a vote, and the vote was bad."

"Who says bad? It was ten to two for acquittal, and when we got done pissing, it would've been unaminous."

"God damn the law!" you said.

Later in the day, in your father's office, you said, "Cortez got jobbed."

"I fail to see it," your father said.

"That poker-game friend of yours, that Harry Stackell, he took me in with that lie about the jury."

"Look at it this way, Julian. Your client was guilty of burglary, certainly of attempted burglary. Or do you take issue with that too?"

"Guilty or not is for the jury to say. If it weren't for the lie, the jury would've given Cortez his walking papers. A judge sits up there making believe his only interest is the truth. I got a sample of the truth today, and so did Cortez— three-to-five on the rocks. I feel sick, pop."

"Well, I'm not going to defend Harry," your father said. "Lying to you was wrong."

"You go to his home, you play cards with him, you've known him since your butcher-boy days. How could he do such a lowdown thing?"

"Didn't you ever do a lowdown thing, Julian?"

SCENE 13

SHAW'S FARMHOUSE ON LONG LAKE (May 1930)

His first name was one you'd never encoutered before—Ai, two single-lettered syllables each pronounced long. It was Biblical, he told you, and in Hebrew it meant *a heap of stones.* When you looked it up in a Concordance, you were referred to Joshua, where you read of *Ai, which is beside Bethaven, on the east side of Bethel.* A city in Canaan once, it had been pulled down in battle and left to be overgrown, and in time it was lost except to old men's minds. You wondered how Shaw could bear a reminder of his history from birth to death whenever he heard his name: Ai, you thought, a city that was, and is no more.

When you came to know him, he was fifty-and-some, six feet of lean meat. No longer was he a farmer, having tired of tilling stones and growing thistles — *Lord,* he said, *if only a crop would grow like weeds!* When the region began to attract summer sojourners, he'd taken to providing them with rooms and board, and he'd worked up a seasonal trade that carried him through the year. His place lay a dozen miles beyond the Raquette Lake railhead over a one-way logging road. Your first sight of it was across the causeway that divided his pond, and it showed itself to you against a ruck of trees and the dim and distant ridge of Kempshall Mountain. Three or four brooks came down the slopes to feed the pond, and through your windows you could hear the constant pour of water over a spillway, and at night it would put you to sleep.

You were there to shuck the city, the Law, the People vs Jesús Cortez (vs Jesus!) while you wrote your way past the opening pages of what you hoped would become a book.* On paper were a few thousand words, all of them concerned with a character called John B. Sanford, your own approximation of you. The disguise you wore concealed no more than your name: the rest was open to view.

The Hudson River was a quarter of a mile from his window,

you'd written, and when he turned to face the room, he saw what you did — a table, a typewriter, a bookcase, a name in reverse through the door, and he saw the pictures you'd hung on the walls, the Homers, the da Vinci prints, Forain's seated soldier, and he toured with you the shelves, ticking off a pocket Marlowe, a Mermaid Massinger, *A Winter's Tale,* and *Much Ado.* As Shapiro, you'd written of Sanford's girls, and one was

A vapor, a wraith,

and there she was on ruled yellow paper, a girl whose breasts were merely red-ringed nipples. On the glass half of the door was *drofnaS B. nhoJ,* but John was only Julian ass-end-to.

---

*A first novel, published in 1933 as *The Water Wheel.*

There were trout in both parts of Shaw's pond, and with one of the rods that were kept for guests, you tried for them from the banks and the causeway. You were a poor hand at fly-casting, your only catches coming when you still-fished with bait. A sport only in the sense that trapping was hunting, it was little to your liking, and it grew even less so one day when you were joined by the Long Lake parson. You'd heard him deliver a sermon a few days before, and while paying scant attention to his homely text, you could not escape his voice, which had a physical property beyond that of sound; buoyant and blown up round, it seemed to emerge from his mouth as a cartoon balloon, and it hung long on the air before it lost its fill and fell. His name was Peabody.

You were watching your bob, and the little ball was beginning to jig on its axis when the man took a folded sheet of paper from his pocket and held it out to you. It was a warrant for his arrest in a bastardy proceeding brought by the County of Warren. The charge was the fathering of a child on a servant at the parsonage, a girl named Marjorie Brown.

"Mr. Shaw tells me you're a lawyer," he said. "He'd like you to represent me."

"How about you?" you said.

"I would too."

The hearing was held that night at Inlet, a good forty miles away, and what you recall most clearly is the two-hour ride through the navy-blue woods. Still damp from a day-old rain, the dirt road was sand-smooth, and from either hand came the fresh exhalation of trees, earth, and fallen leaves. When the car stopped for someone to ease himself, a pair of eyes stared back at the staring lamps, and for a moment you heard only the still motor ticking and a dwindling spill at the roadside, and then the eyes turned away and went out.

On the witness-stand, the girl told a story that put you in mind of a tenement hallway, of soiled walls, rank cuisines, and happenings under the stairs — and yet what she spoke of had happened here, in the clear and tonic air. At a salary of five dollars a month, she'd been taken on as a hired girl, she said, but when Mrs. Peabody became an invalid after her second confinement, her duties were heavier than ever and almost endless. Often, as she made her way home in the dark, she'd cry with fatigue and despair. One night, though, the parson had saved her the walk by driving her there in his car.

"Miss Brown, what happened in the car?

Fellows got fresh when they had you alone somewhere, she said, but not

Mr. Peabody. He was kind, and when he asked her to, she went with him to the back seat.

"What happened in the car that night?"

You rose, conceding what the witness had implied, and on she spoke, telling of other kindnesses and other nights, one of these in the indoor darkness of the parsonage hall.

"What happened in the hall, Miss Brown?"
"The same thing. We did it twice."

After a few months, she said, when her pregnancy began to show, she was forced to stop working at the parsonage. Then the baby was born, but the County officials made her bring legal action before they would give her any help.

Knowing it would be useless to cross-examine her, you called your only witness, the parson, and when he'd taken the stand, you asked him a single question.

"Mr. Peabody, you've heard what Miss Brown had to say. Is her story true?"
"Yes. It's absolutely true. I'm guilty."

You turned him over to the Prosecutor, a man named Plumley, who rushed at him, calling off questions all the while.

"But why? Why did you do it, Peabody? How could you forget your church, your position, your wife?"

You still remember the parson's answer.

"Mr. Plumley, my wife is sick."

After that, there was only the drive back to Long Lake in the dark, but the fragrance of the woods seemed not to be there now, and all you were aware of was a story that made you think of the uric smell of tenements, the shop-worn look of the halls.*

§

You'd been writing for the better part of a morning when, in a vacant moment, you heard music coming up the stairwell to your room. In the parlor below, there was an old and weathered upright, and though never quite in

---

The dialogue given above is from a story called "Once in a Sedan and Twice Standing Up," published in *Contact*, October 1932.

tune, it was being played now. You listened to the music, trying to name the composer and, if possible, the score. It was a game you played often — identification by sound — and while you rarely won, that day you caught a few bars in the Spanish idiom that brought to mind a composition you'd heard at the Hall. You went downstairs and stopped in the parlor doorway. The pianist was a gray-haired man with a face that was less than gray-hair age. Seeing you, he stopped playing.

"Lalo?" you said. Lalo, you guessed. You knew nothing of Lalo's but the *Symphonie Espagnole,* and that you'd heard but once. What phrase, what gust of notes, had stirred your memory? "Lalo," you said.

"A piano transcription of the violin part," the man said. "Did you ever hear Menuhin play it?"

You remember your glow of recognition.

He was a friend of Ai Shaw's, the man said. He came from Glens Falls, and, as district game-warden, he was on a tour of sportsmen's resorts in the western Adirondacks. His name, one you'd never heard before, was Beakbane, and he favored you (for your lucky stab at Lalo?) by inviting you to go fishing with him that afternoon. You used one of the guest rods, but Beakbane had his own, a split-bamboo beauty; a dozen feet long, it tapered to a tip that was match-stick thin, and when whipped, the top agate would almost touch the reel.

On leaving the farmhouse with him, you made for the pond, but Beakbane said, "I'd sooner fish in an aquarium." He indicated one of the brooks running down off Kempshall Mountain. "That's where the sport is."

About half a mile up a slightly sloping pasture, he found a spot along the run that suited him, a few bends lying in high grass, and there he began to lay Silver Doctors and Gray Hackles down on surfaces hardly larger than the brim of a hat. It was a skill you didn't possess, and after a spell of casting into the banks, you broke off to watch Beakbane. He didn't catch trout, you thought; he lured them with a fly and made them catch themselves.

You left the farm a few days later and never saw Shaw again. You did see Beakbane, though.

SCENE 14

FATHER AND SON (Late Spring 1930)

He said, "Come into my office, Julian. I want to talk to you," and when you followed, he gestured for you to close the door.

"I know what you're going to say," you said.

"Do you?"

" 'Julian, isn't it about time you got down to practicing your profession?' Right or wrong?"

"Well, I've thought that, but I'd never say it."

"My trouble is, I've got two professions."

"One in the hand and the other in the bush," he said. "But it happens that I want to talk about me, not you."

Discussing himself had never been his custom. He had restricted areas, you'd found, places where no other presence was welcome, not even yours—and you his only son.

"Your Grandpa Nevins used to say you didn't know the value of a dollar. You were a kid then, but you're twenty-six now, and I'm afraid you still don't know it."

"My mind is on other things," you said.

"Yes, things like Tolstoy."

Removing the band from a cigar, he was about to strike a match when it occurred to him to glance at the time, and then he put the cigar away. Too late to finish before sundown, you thought, and you recalled the promise he'd made to his father—when had that been, at fourteen?—and the care he'd taken to keep it, as though his father would know in the grave. What if the promise were broken? you wondered. No one had heard it but a man now twenty years dead—how could he be hurt? with what dust of memory would he grieve? It came to you then that your father was ruled by his *own* memory and that as long as he lived his word would be good.

"I want to talk about me and money," he said.

The value of a dollar, you thought, and you remembered another expression of your grandpa's: found money. It's like found money, he'd say of this, that, and what not—but to you, *all* money was found. You found it in your pocket, you found it in your hand, and there it was on a table, a counter, and coming through the mail. It was magic stuff—you waved, and it materialized. It fell in a fall of green-gold leaves.

"It's been scarce in these parts since the Crash," your father said, "and I look for it to be even more so. Many of my clients got hurt, and those that skinned through are scared of what's ahead. Things don't look very good, Julian."

Did you hear the words or merely store their sound for hearing now? What stood in the way of meaning then—a girl (and which girl?), the climb to Kempshall summit (3,300 ft.), the phrase *Ripeness is all,* the *Tristan* you'd stood through at the Met?

He said, "The practice has fallen off to where I have to retrench. As you know, or maybe as you don't, I support two households—our own and Aunt Jo's. Things being what they are, that has to stop. She and I have been talking it over and we've decided to join forces again." He paused there briefly, almost without punctuation. "Provided you agree."

"What have I to say about it?"

"If you stay away because she's there . . . she won't be there."

"I stayed away once. It was the biggest mistake I ever made."

"You'll welcome her, then? You'll show her respect?"

"I will."

"A wise son maketh a glad father."

"How about a dumb one, pop?"

SCENE 15

THE HOUSE ON NORWOOD, IN WEST END (Summer of 1930)

The lesion in your sister's lung had healed, leaving a lime-salt scar, but to make the cure more certain, your father decided on another summer at the shore. As you knew, he could ill afford it. There were no crowds in his office now, only the occasional buyer or seller, the hopeless broker, the desperate mortgagor, and from the six typewriters came scattered firing instead of fusillades. There were days when you could hear the clock on the waiting room wall, the belch in the water-cooler, the spring in the seat of a swivel-chair. A nice quiet law practice, your father had called it once, and the quiet had come again.

He sent you to Jersey notwithstanding, and at the rental he had authorized, you signed a lease for the season on a house in West End. You have pictures of it yet. It was steep-roofed and sided with shingles, and there were unattainable little balconies, filigreed brackets, porch-posts of turned wood, and lawns appear that you'd forgotten, and shrubbery you never knew was there, and trees bearing fruit too dim for you to name.

You'd made the trip down in the morning, and had you wished, you could've returned on the same day, but as always, you found it hard to leave, and when evening came, you walked back to the cottage through black shadows on the blued ground: everywhere else was strange country, you felt, and only here was home. It was a notion you couldn't easily account for. Though you hadn't been born there, it seemed to be your native land, and you were loyal to its foot-wide torrents, the shade trees that made its forests, its mountains shoulder-high. What did you see in its frame castles? you wondered, how did its sand differ from other sand? why did the surf bow and scrape as to no other shore? Home, you thought—did that explain it? had times there been good because of your mother? did it make you think she was alive?

Without illumination as yet, the house was darker than the night outside, and you inched your way in on touch and memory. A couch became your bed and a rug your blanket, and you lay a long while listening to leaves brushing leaves, to a periodic bird-call, to tires on a gravel road, and there were sounds within as well, small feet racing on an attic floor, a dripping sink, sudden frictions within a wall. You breathed deep a familiar mix of privet, salted sand, and winter just gone from wood and wicker, and somehow you were made to feel that you were among your own peculiar possessions in a setting known as home.

§

At the West End station a few days later, you waited for her train. In the quiet afternoon you could hear it a few miles off toward Red Bank, the raucous whistle, the pulmonary engine, and soon dust began to dance at your feet, and a great black presence came at you spraying steam. A Pacific, you thought, a 2-3-1, and then you saw *the painted woman* a car-length away. Even at a distance, you could tell that she had changed—her figure was a little fuller, her hair a little grayed—but even so she seemed to glitter, as though she still wore sequins here and there.

"Aunt Jo," you said, and you kissed her, "I'm only ten years late, but I'm glad you're here."

It was a good summer. The house was always filled with your friends and your sister's friends, and there were swimming parties and fishing parties and rides into the country after dancing at The Farms, and there was a girl named Bernice and a girl named Florence (or was it Frances?), but there was only a wave in passing from the girl of the year before. Still, it was a good summer.

SCENE 16

THE EVILS OF CAPITALISM (Fall 1930)

The law offices of J. Sidney Bernstein were on Broadway near Columbus Circle, and at his request, you presented yourself there one autumn afternoon. His greeting was in keeping with the season, thinly warm, and when neither of you offered a handshake, he nodded you toward a chair. During the moment he took over some arrangement of papers, you watched light glide on his scalp between sparse strands of hair; these tended to slide, and he held them in place whenever he moved his head. You heard the tear of perforated paper and saw a check being launched across the desk.

Signed by him as executor of the Abraham Nevins Estate, it had been drawn to your order. "Two thousand dollars!" you said.

"The earnings of your trust fund last year," he said.

"But the fund is only ten thousand dollars. How could it earn 20% interest in a year?"

"I didn't call it interest, did I? The two thousand was a premium for lending the money."

"Do you mean somebody borrowed ten and only got eight?"

"You ask a lot of questions," he said, and he indicated the check. "That's yours. Are you fastidious about how it was made?"

Fastidious, you thought. You'd never looked up the meaning of the word, taking it to imply a delicacy of taste, but as just now used, it seemed to convey that you were falsely right-minded, that though your tone was high, you yourself might well be low. Therefore, you thought, how do you answer?

"Yes," you said. "I am."

The sound he made was meant as a laugh, but it came forth mirthless, and what you heard was more like a cough. "You'll spend it all the same," he said. "And you'd've spent the principal too if Mr. Nevins hadn't put it out of your reach."

72

"If *you* hadn't, you mean," you said, and you flicked the check. "But wherever this came from, what I spend is none of your damn business, Mr. Bernstein." Between you lay a black metal strongbox marked NEVINS ESTATE, and you put your hand palm-down on it, saying, "Don't ever make any mistakes with this, counselor."

When you left his office, it was too late in the day to return to your own. Instead, you walked northward along Broadway, crossing side-streets through slices of the going-down sun. In the Circle, Columbus was still bright atop his column, but below him all was gray and lavender evening. You followed the park wall for a way, watching trees founder in the shade. Passing the Century Theatre, you remembered having been taken there by Olga (Olia, you thought, how long since you'd called up the name?) for a midnight rehearsal of *Dantons Tod,* and you'd sat hand in hand in the dark (dead Desmoulins, you thought, and dead Danton), and now she was dead too.

Words rose in your mind—*I'm writing a book,* Pep West had said—and you thought of the check in your pocket, and you thought *Now you can write one too,* but you did not think of your Grandpa Nevins, from whom the money had come, or of your father, to whom it ought to go.

SCENE 17

A DISSENTER'S DISCIPLE (Fall of 1930)

He was a first cousin named Melvin Friedman, the youngest of your Aunt Sarah's children, and to the dismay of the family, he chose you as a pattern for his life. He was four years your junior, a spread in age that hardly made for constant association, but on your occasional encounters, you could see the effects wrought on him by your rebellion. His tastes had strayed far and forever from his elders' occupation, the construction of blocks of flats: he frequented the art-shows now, he was a reader of Keats, of Congreve and Synge, and twice a week he sat in the hard cheap seats at the Hall. You saw too some of your views and ways, the cut of your clothes and the make of your shoes, and he even dug up a copy of the fedora you wore, a velour in olive green. A tall, lean, and unusually handsome young man, he carried himself well, stiffly, almost, as if in parade dress, and being quiet and observant, he spoke only when it was time to speak, and then in a low and resonant voice. Flattered by his little emulations, you might've liked him more if you hadn't sensed in him the makings of a rival, though you could not have said where the competition lay.

During your year at the Fifth Avenue Hotel, you saw rather more of him than usual, and one evening the two of you went to see a foreign film at a playhouse up the street. He got no further than the vestibule: there he was stopped, as one stricken with a spell, by a pretty usherette dressed in a black velvet bolero and tight black pants to match. You saw nothing else of him that night, nor did you hear from him again until, some days later, he called to request the key to your room and a few hours of privacy. The request was renewed from time to time, and once, late in clearing out, you met the girl in the corridor—*Olivia Perrin,* he said, meet *my cousin Julian.*

The spell did not wear off, and though you were seldom in their company, you knew that the relationship had continued; his people, however, were unaware of its existence. After three years of it, he informed you that the girl was ill, and that together with her mother and sister, she was leaving for a winter's sojourn in the Alpes Maritimes; they were sailing that night on the *Statendam,* he said, and he'd be pleased if you joined them on the pier. Herb Ortman, your friend and law partner, went with you on the ferry to Hoboken and the docks of the Holland-America Line; unable to find your party among the departure throng, you boarded the ship and asked the purser for the location of Mrs. Perrin's staterooms. You were directed to a pair of adjoining cabins on B-deck. On the door of the first, a card read *Mrs. C. Perrin and daughter Anne;* on the second, the card said *Mrs. M. Friedman.*

Herb stared at you, saying, "My God, he married the *schicksa!*"
And you said, "Now there's hell to pay."

SCENE 18

THE TIME NOW IS . . . (November 1930)

It was a gray Sunday morning, and you were walking with your father on the Drive. In the narrow little park, bare trees like nervous systems branched against the sky. Through them, you could see the river and, at the base of the Palisades, the electric-sign that would begin to run at dusk. In the shadow of the cliff, it would flow from nowhere, glow for a moment, and disappear, lasting only long enough to let you know that you were flowing too, that you were going as well as the sign and its reflection in the stream. THE TIME

74

NOW IS . . . , they'd say, and you'd feel as if you were being bled.

"I got some money from the Estate the other day," you said.

"Don't spend it all in one place," your father said. "When my mother gave me a nickel, that's what she'd tell me: don't spend it all in one place."

"This was no nickel. It was two thousand dollars."

He glanced at you with the down-drawn features of surprise. "How come so much?" he said.

"The way Bernstein explained it, it was a premium for a loan. But I still don't understand why a man would borrow eight and pay back ten."

"The extra two is called vigorish. What the word means, I never knew, but when you're pressed for money, you'll pay vigorish to get it."

"Sounds like another way to say usury."

"Which is exactly what it is."

"So this two thousand was really wrung out of some hard-up son-of-a-bitch."

"That's about the size of it, kid."

You went for some way in silence toward the granite charlotte russe of Grant's Tomb, and then you were crossing the plaza leading to the portal.

"I want to go to Europe again," you said.

Your father paused at the entrance, as if to consider going in, and he must've remembered the guide's palaver, the sunken sarcophagi (red porphyry, folks), the flag rooms, the alto-reliefs, and turning away, he headed for the grounds of the Claremont Inn.

You were passing the old mansion when he said, "I'm glad you told me. I was about to ask what you were going to do with all that vigorish."

THE COLOR OF THE AIR, IV

GENERAL EDWARD BRADDOCK—1755

WHAT WILL THE DUKE SAY?

The General, having been inform'd that you exprest some desire to make the Campaigne, has order'd me to acquaint you that he will be very glad of your Company. . . .

—Capt. Orme to Col. Washington

The Monongahela fell to low water at that time of year—July, it was—and Braddock's two-mile train took it on foot, getting wet in the crossing only as high as the knees. There were thirteen hundred men, give or take a dozen, about half of them Lobsters and half in Colonial fringe, and when their van of six Light Horse ran into Pontiac's Ottawas and a hundred-odd French under Beaujeu, their rear was still at the ford. There was no ambush: the British fired first.

An early volley laid Beaujeu dead, and some of his Indians took French leave. Those that stayed, though, had scalps to show for it, for the British had been found in column, the right way for a walk in the woods but the wrong way to fight there. The road that six hundred axes had made for them was only twelve feet wide, and in that aisle four hundred and fifty men died in two hours.

"Is it possible?" Braddock said through blood from his lung, where a bullet had struck it rich. "Is it possible?" he said from the arms of Orme. "Who would have thought it?" he said to no man named— to Orme, it may have been, or to himself, or to someone soon forgot, or even to the red and buckskin rout that fled over his feet and sash. Orme cried out for bearers, offering, when none would stop, sixty guineas per head—five years' pay! "We shall know better another time," Braddock said, but the time, if it came, was in another world.

He was buried in that twelve-foot road, and for fear the Indians would scalp his corpse, the broken army was marched over it, and it was lost for seventy years. When found, finally, it was bones wearing the insignia of a Major-General. The high-ranked relics were taken a little way off, and four hemlocks were planted to mark the grave.

The battlefield, the long gash in the woods, has been marked by other things: by coke-smoke, more ash than air, by black ballast, by a forest of ties under track, by oil-slicks flowing like spiral rainbows, by dead dogs in the mud of Turtle Creek, by the carcass of a car.

"What will the Duke say?" General Braddock said.

SCENE 19

S. S. ST. LOUIS (December 1930)

She flew the burgee of the Hamburg-Amerika Line, and she comes back to mind as an ill-shaped little ship, rather like an overweight dog. You'd always admired form—in motor-cars, in locomotives, even in a suit of clothes—and you still can't understand why, once you'd seen her picture, you'd permitted yourself voyage in a packet so ungainly. But voyage you did, and all you can recall of the departure is that your father wasn't there. You'd had no quarrel about your going, no discussion, even, and from your manner while together, no one would've known the density of the air. It was as dimensional, though, as mist, but since nothing was said or done, when you left for the pier, you might only have been taking a walk. Others may have come to see you off, but your father wasn't there.

As you went down-bay that day or night, did you suppose you were on a second excursion, or did you know it was a second flight? Were you the lightsome pilgrim watching land go under, watching gulls, smoke, clouds against the sky, or were you watching yourself in mere motion, as mindless as a star? Did you think of your Uncle Dave, always driven from home, of Uncle Romie, drawn always back, did you wonder where you were going, never knowing why you'd left?

§

When you woke in the morning, you thought for a moment that the ship hadn't sailed after all; you could see a steeple through the porthole, you could hear the sound of donkey-engines, voices, water pouring into water, and the bulkhead beside you shook no longer. You rose and looked out at wharves, red brick buildings, and a hill that wore a golden dome—Boston. Dressing against the cold, you mounted to the topmost deck, and from there, between two lifeboats, you stared across the city as if to find one certain window on Lynde, Garden, Pinckney, Vernon. You stared through the wind, through steam and dusted sunlight at the hill—she was somewhere within sight of it, you thought, and you wondered whether, awakened, she was staring at it too.

§

There were some two hunded passengers aboard, but you remember only one of them by name—Arthur Johnson. You met him when the ship was only a few hours out of Boston; on one of your rounds of the deck, he joined you and introduced himself.

"May I tell you why I fell in with you?" he said.
And you said, "Of course."
"I overheard you speaking to someone in the saloon last evening."
"What did I say?"
"*Cela ne fait rien.* It was how you said it. You used the one-one construction."
"I'm afraid I don't know what you mean."

"Most people would say, for instance: 'As one goes through life, *he* comes to believe,' et cetera."

The one-one usage, as he called it, had been a stilted way of speaking, even for highflown you, but once praised, it was hard to disclaim. "People ought to speak with care," you said. "Not with their flies open."

§

He was a man of about fifty, you supposed, not very far from your father's age, but there all likeness ended. He bore himself as though he alone wore satin breeches in a world of worsted knaves. Others, who did not share his fellowship, must've found his presence hard to bear; you, though, were rather set up by his recognition of the purity of your speech. That your one-one arrangement had been affectation detracted only slightly from your satisfaction. On the crossing to Cherbourg, you spent a great deal of time in Johnson's company. Indeed, for all that survives of the other two hundred, the ship might've been a private charter for the pair of you only. At his invitation, you changed your seating in the *Speisesaal*, taking both lunch and dinner with him daily, and you walked together, talking of law and literature, and drank Canadian at the bar before parting for the night. In sight always were some two hundred faces, forms, and get-ups for the *voyageur*, but they were scarcely seen and did not mar the view.

At Cherbourg, as you were going down the gangplank, a passenger bound for a further port called to you from the deck, saying, "He like young boys, *nein?*"

And looking back at many, any of whom might've spoken, you said to all, "You bastard son-of-a-bitch!"

§

By the time you cleared Customs, a wind off the channel had turned a cold day colder. The only train for Paris would reach there late at night, and when Johnson proposed a lay-over till morning at one of the harbor hotels, you thought *He like young boys*, but all the same you agreed. On entering the room he'd registered for, you found that it contained a double bed (*young boys, nein?*), and you kept well to your side of it after the thirty-watt light was out. You lay awake for a time, listening to tires on wet pavement, to bursts of music, to laughter and breaking glass—and you fell asleep thinking of a sniggering wretch on his way now to Bremen.

§

At Johnson's suggestion, you put up where he did, at the Hotel de France et Choiseul in the Rue St. Honoré off the Place Vendôme. He was in Paris, he'd told you, to pass the Christmas season with his niece (or had he said ward?). You met her only once, at dinner the evening before they left on a motor-tour of the valley of the Loire. You recall her as tall and thin, not yet quite finished by her finishing-school, and pretty only because she was still under twenty—*He like young girls, nein?* you thought. You missed their departure in the morning and never saw either of them again.

§

You knew no one now in Paris, and alone amid crowds, you felt the invincibility of divisions. You went about (where? to what churches, galleries, gardens, landmarks?) thinking of agates you'd played with as a child, each with its own hardness, each with its own dimensions and color, each the container of its own design. You remembered trying to compress them into a mass, but when you opened your hand, there they were, a little warmer than before, but still divided by themselves.

What churches, what galleries in the year-end rain? What paintings did you see, what windows of various glass? Images appear to you in a confusion of stills, like an album assembled by strangers, and you stare at yourself out of sequence in nameless places doing indefinite things. You'd come with letters of introduction—to Samuel Putnam, Stuart Gilbert, Richard Thoma—but after a meeting or two, you knew you were an invasion, and you kept yourself away. Thereafter, you spent solitary hours at the Dôme, the Select, and La Coupole, even at the Closerie des Lilas, so long out of fashion that all you could've enjoyed there was the ghost of Apollinaire.

§

You remember a day when you were coming out of the Palais du Luxembourg into the Rue Vaugirard, and seeing a name in blue and white enamel on a wall—Rue de l'Odéon—you felt that somewhere you'd seen it before. You crossed over to follow the little street, and at Number 12, the vague became the known: there, on another wall, you found another name—Sylvia Beach!

Sylvia Beach, you thought, the publisher of *Ulysses*!

Years later, you'd write:

Above the windows of the shop, a sign read *Shakespeare and Company*, and she sold books there, books in many sizes, many shapes and colors, many languages, and, bound or *en brochure,* anyone's imprint could be found on her tables and counters and in the stacks that piered the walls, in tiered racks and rows that started at the floor. Until then, therefore, she was merely a seller of paper, a chapman who'd quit the streets and settled in a store . . . but there came a book in Ionic blue, its title in white letters, *Ulysses,* and she, in wandering her aisles, wandered the isles of Greece. How much life there is in books! she may have thought, and scanning the tapestries they made around her, she knew, she must've known, that there was none like her own publication, the one by the crooked Jesus, the writer in the sky. . . .

If she'd glanced at the windows, she'd have made out little through the vapor on the panes and the vaporous rain outside, cars, perhaps, huddled people, stars of light, but she'd not have noted one of the many passersby, seen him stop before the bookshop, and look down at a propped-up copy of *Ulysses.* Her mind was on other things, and she was unaware when the shape moved and came inside. If it drifted past her, if it asked a question and got a reply, if it paused to gaze at the black stove, the brass urn, the ceramic bust of the Bard, if it slowly flowed back to the door, she hardly knew it was there, never knew it had gone.*

§

A letter from your Cousin Melvin informed you that his wife had settled in Menton for the winter, and a few days later, you were on a night *rapide* on your way to the south of France.

§

Late in January 1931, you wrote to your father that you'd left Paris on the evening of the 12th and reached Menton at midafternoon of the following day. There, you said, *for the modest sum* of 38 francs, the Hotel Palais du Soleil in the Rue Piettra Scrita was providing you with a room and two meals a day. *For 7 francs additional,* you claimed, you'd also be given the missing meal, lunch, but you elected to take that where you found it—*every once in a while I walk to Italy, which is two kilometers away, or motor to Monte Carlo or Nice.* Your room opened into the garden, and from where you sat as you typed that letter, you could see date palms, magnolias, and *a huge cage containing wild canaries.* The mountains crowded the shore, you told him, rising behind the hotel to nearly a mile against a sky the same *colour* as the sea. It reminded you of a lake the two of you had seen on one of your jaunts (Otsego,

---

*From *To Feed Their Hopes,* University of Illinois Press, 1980.

was it?); its *colour* too had been turquoise blue. And you said that from an autobus on the Grande Corniche, you'd looked down on the port of Monte Carlo at the White Star liner *Brittanic,* and you were so far above it that *it seemed to be no more than a plank,* and you said *Take care of yourself, and think of your son, who loves you and wishes you well.*

Who preserved the letter? you wonder. There it is, a few sheets of gray paper in a matching envelope that bears a cancellation seemingly as fresh now as it was then—*Menton Alpes Maritimes 23.1.31* But did your father open it one morning at breakfast, did he read it aloud, laughing at your bombast, your two-cent observations, your affected spelling, or did he let it lie where your sister may have placed it and read the *Times* instead? Did he never see what his son had written, his son who loved him well?

§

Right now, you wrote to your sister, *I'm working exclusively on the novel,* [*] and you try to see back to yourself in the room that gave on a garden, on *date palms in full bloom,* on magnolias and a cage of wild canaries, and beyond all these the sea. But though you can recall the room, you always seem to be outside it, as though you were standing in the hall, peering through a doorway at someone else. And you wrote *I heard from Sam Putnam that he likes the second article I gave him, and it will go in the second issue.* [**] *Its purely descriptive—scenes on the deck, the voyage over, the trip to Oxford, the night at Plymouth, the voyage back. In the actual novel, these scenes are spread out over a couple of hundred pages.*

That second issue lies before you, and looking at the black type on the tan cover, you note for the first time the credo of the magazine, *Semper Africa novi aliquid apportat,* which you take to mean *Out of Africa always something new.* You stare at *Prose,* a paragraph four pages long, an unbroken wall of words, and you wonder what you gained by leaving out the doors. There's no way in, you think. From Africa this time, nothing new.

§

The villa rented by the Perrins lay on one of the slopes of the Vallée du Carei, a long climb from the Palais du Soleil on the floor. On your only visit,

---

[*] *The Water Wheel,* Dragon Press, 1933.
[**] "Prose," *The New Review,* Paris, 1931.

you remember counting steps to nearly five hundred before your mind ran out of breath. Arriving, you found that their villa, like your hotel, had been extravagantly misnamed; one was merely a pension and the other a *comme ci comme ça* cottage largely in disarray.

Apart from a brief meeting aboard the *Statendam,* you'd never before spoken to the mother. She proved to be quite fluent, glib, even, and despite a knowing manner, she seemed only to be covering uncertainty with it, as if she hoped to talk away what silence might reveal, a life on the fringe. The more she went on, the more such phrases rose in the mind—a thin-ice life, you thought, a sail too near the wind. All through her chatter, Anne, the younger daughter, was a silent presence occasionally passing from room to room, while Olivia sat in a deck-chair staring out over the town, the port, the sea.

No word of the almost one-sided exchange comes back to you, but you recall very clearly your sense of having strayed into a region that was both unfamiliar and inhospitable. You recall too that you wondered how it was for your Cousin Melvin—and how it would be one day for his mother and family. But you knew, you knew even then—how could you not have known?—that it would not go well.

§

Save for a Briton or two, the clientele of the Palais du Soleil was French, and knowing no one, French or British, you sat alone at meals, and after dinner, you took your Paris *Herald* to the salon to sit alone again and read. From a nearby chair one evening came a curse in English, and you looked up to find your neighbor brandishing a paper of his own.

"Damn it all, look at this!" and he shook the pages at you and then read off a bold headline. "RUSS ARMY OF 8,000,000 AT THE READY!"

There were half a dozen others in the room, but they paid no attention because, as you thought, they didn't understand the language.

"The bloody scum!" the Englishman said. "What do they need an army of eight million for?"

"Maybe they don't want to be invaded again," you said.

"Invaded! Who'd invade that filthy country?"

"My country would," you said. "And so would yours. After all, we did it before."

He rose and glared down at you, saying, "Sir, you talk like a traitor!" and then he strode from the salon.

You were watching the door close behind him when someone spoke to you through the fronds of a hanging fern. "You made a good *réponse*," the voice said.

You leaned forward and saw a young woman seated near you. "You speak English, then," you said.

"Not enough, *j'ai peur*. But what the man said and you said, that I comprehended."

You laughed, saying, "An army of eight million—all of them Jews, I suppose."

"You are *politique*?"

"I political?" you said. "No. I'm a writer." You thought of your little pieces in *Tambour*, of your four-page paragraph in *The New Review*. "Trying to be a writer."

"Of what nature is your writing?" the young woman said.

"I began by contributing to the literary magazines—*revues*, I suppose you'd say. At the moment, I'm working on a novel."

"*Très intéressant*," she said. "And on what subject is the novel?"

It was hard to say that the book was about you—what had you done that was worth the telling? And then you thought of *A Portrait of the Artist as a Young Man*, and it came to you that the telling itself was the deed. "It's about me," you said.

"And you are . . . ?"

"Julian Shapiro."

Her name was Simone Dykmann, she told you, and her home was in Paris. An uncle of hers was just then recuperating from an illness, and to look after him, she'd accompanied him to Menton.

"Shapiro," she said. "A Jewish name, is it not?"

"*Oui*," you said. "*Je suis un juif.*"

And she said, "*Et moi, je suis une juive.* And now I must go."

After she'd gone, you walked in the garden, and what you thought of in the night-time exhalation of the lime trees was the deed of the writing—the act that did not need to be explained.

§

A reply postmarked Hartford, Conn.:

Julian, sweetheart,
    You have made me happy. I want to tell you many things but I am fearful for us. Love and marriage have changed so radically for me I no longer trust my heart. I am a destitute tramp who can make no promises—and a person unfit for love and marriage. One thing only I am certain of—that of all men I have known and know, you are the only one for whom I still have "feelings" (for lack of a better

word), and these were stronger and more beautiful the last time we met. Please keep me informed about yourself and I shall do the same. No matter what I have said—or almost say.

L.

A line had been drawn through the last nine words.

From her refusal, you try to recall your offer. When had you written it, you wonder, on what gray day of winter rain? And where, at which counter or table or leaning against which wall? and how had the proposal been put— unadorned or with floral decoration, with pedantry or passion? *Sweetheart,* she'd called you, and you stare at the epithet noun, there for one spangled moment joined with *Julian.* How had you addressed her—*Beloved,* had you said, or merely *Dear* before or after her name? What avowals had you made, how had you laid to rest the cross-purpose past, and had you brightly argued that you'd had to go away in order to look back? What had *Julian, sweetheart* said, and why had she refused him?

§

March 5, 1931

Leave Menton early in a.m. Change for Italian train at Ventimiglia. Meet a Bersagliere and treat him to an orange and a Lucky Strike. Reach Genoa middle afternoon. Visit Cathedral San Lorenzo. *Why? Because it was consecrated by Pope Gelasius II in 1118? Because in its treasury there was an octagonal bowl that was said to correspond to the Holy Grail? Were you awed by the sacred basin, did you cross yourself in your mind?* An espresso at Chez Vous Dancing.

March 6

Visit Palazzi Rosso and Bianco. *Why? Was one really red and the other white, and what paintings were in their galleries, what tapestries, what antiquities from Rome? What thing or things did you see, what can you remember that you saw?* Visit birth-place of Columbus. Visit birthplace of Paganini. *Why?* Walk in the Via Venti Settembre.

March 7

Go to an exhibition of Japanese art. Two monkeys on a branch before a water-fall. A bird among blossoms. Cranes in reeds that match their attitudes. Deer embedded in leaves. Carp making oil-like ripples in a pool. Screens, fabrics, weapons, jewelry, bronzes—and names! what a registry of names! Goshinobu, Ignoto, Togken, Toyokuni, Myagawa Chosun, Hokusai, Setzuvan. Take the train to Pisa. There at the Nettuno meet Wm Graveney, young English sculptor. We dine together (remember *tagliatelli verde*).

March 8

Graveney and I set out from the hotel for a look at Pisa in the rain. Through winding streets, we find our way to the Piazza del Duomo and its four attractions—the Cathedral, the Baptistery, the Camposanto, and the Tower. *Do you remember del Sarto's Santa Agnese? Without your notes, or with, can you describe the colors she wears, her eyes (aspiring?), the lamb she bears in her arms? And what of the bronze doors you made so much of then—can you still see the basreliefs in the twelve or fourteen panels?* We hear a guide say that the Tower is 180 feet high and 15 feet off the perpendicular at the top. We climb it, making an outside circuit of each tier. And then the Camposanto with its murals, its statuary, and its dead. *Do you remember the poplars at the four corners, do you remember the flowers you wrote of, daisies, pansies, violets, and how the sun broke through to shade the frieze?* On a wall in the Baptistery, a sign reads: It is strictly forbidden to Ladies indecently dressed the entrance. We return to the hotel, and after dinner, we go to see *The Mark of Zorro*, still good despite the years.

March 9

Before leaving for Rome, one more look at the Santa Agnese *Why? What did it mean to you?* and a visit to Byron's house on the Lungarno *What had you read but the* Don Juan *(illustrated)*. At Rome, Graveney and I put up at the Albergo Saturnia. In the evening, a beer at Bffi's.

March 10

Taking photos as we go, Graveney and I cover *Cover?* the Colosseum, the Forum, the Public Gardens, the Pantheon, the Zoo.

March 11

To St. Peter's with Graveney, where we climb to the top of the dome *What were your thoughts up there, gazing down on Rome? Where are the musings on history, the new conclusions, the visions peculiar to you?* We see the Pietà, the Pope's jewels in the Sacristy, the Cellini candelabra, the tomes illuminated by Giotto and Pinturicchio, the gowns once worn by Charlemagne *Why does Rome read like a letter to those at home?*

March 12

Away from New York three months today and wouldnt care if it were three years *Or so you say.* To the Vatican again, this time to the Sistine Chapel and its sky of angels, and then to the Sala Raffaele, where I forget everything *Which means what—that you were carried away, and if so, why by the School of Athens and not by God's finger so near a finger of Adam's?*

March 13

Visit St. John Lateran, highest ranked church in the Catholic world, then, with Graveney, a long ride in an open carriage on the Appian Way, then the Termi Caracalla, where I'm photographed inspecting a Corinthian capital, and then the Pinacoteca, and San Pietro in Vincoli, and the temples along the Tiber.

March 14

Graveney comes to the station to see me off for Venice—sorry to part company with him. An all-day ride through Florence *No stopover there? Nothing worth seeing, visiting, covering?* to the Hotel Europa on the Grand Canal.

March 15

In the morning St. Mark's, then the Palazzo of the Doges, the Bridge of Sighs, and the Great Council Hall *You remember the Tintorettos, of course? and the Veroneses?* A ride in a gondola and then an espresso at Florian's in the Piazza, where, as a man tosses corn to the pigeons, I hear him say to his wife *Just as pretty as amber, but if I had it strung, you wouldn't wear it, would you??*

March 16

For God's sake, no more churches, palaces, galleries, houses where the illustrious lived! Go for a walk, watch the people, read a book—leave the mystical experiences to other Americans of the second generation! An espresso at Florian's.

March 17

Walk where, watch whom, read what? *Not the poems* Pansies, *for Christ's sake! And yet there it is in your hand on the flyleaf: Venezia March 16!*

March 18

By train through Padua *the shrew*, Verona *two gentlemen*, Brescia, Bergamo *snuff*, and Genoa. *Did you think of what you'd seen and wonder what you'd not? Would you remember colors, faces, rooms, names?* And then you were back in Menton.

§

It seemed quieter on your return. Winter being over, sojourners were no longer coming, and many were going away, Mlle. Dykmann and her uncle had already gone, and in the diningroom of the Palais du Soleil, there were fewer seatings, and in the salon, there were fewer of the strait strangers you'd seen there before. In the *place* near the Promenade, the hawker of *Le Matin* was more subdued, as if he knew the paper would remain on hand, and there were thinner crowds walking or watching small waves break on the shingle at their feet. You were put in mind of the season's end at the Jersey shore. There, even before the dispersal began, it was in the very air; and here too you felt that all were merely awaiting some agreed-on hour before going their numerous ways.

Within the week, you were headed for Spain.

§

Marseilles, 3 . 24 . 31, a postcard to your sister:

Had to stop here to get a Spanish visa, and a bad train connection makes me sit around for only 6 hours. Reach Nîmes tonight.

Julian

Barcelona, March 26th, 1931, a letter to your sister on the stationery of the Hotel Oriente:

its just what I expected and yet nothing like my expectations its gay and lively and theres lots of nightlife and noise and joking and arminarm walking sitting around parading doing nothing more important than enjoying life and crazylookingdreamsoldiers and singing and children run through your legs and ask for five centavos and hurdygurdies playing thumping spanish melodies and beggars and merchants with stock spread out on the pavement and students talk of revolution and monuments adorned with women as large as horses and horses as large trolleycars and hussars uniforms and carpetslippers and women with lightbrown skin that looks dusty and eyes that are wet black buttons and hair that shines like strings of beads and streets full of flowerstands and there are stands of birdcages canaries parrots in perfect design parokeets cockatoos birds that warble birds that twitter and birds that chirp cheep and trill and birds pink and birds green and black and red and the trees above them are filled with free sparrows that can be heard above the traffic and there are lotteryposters and posters for prizefights and bullfights and jack hylton is playing the mavra of stravinsky here *What is the mavra?* and lillian gish is in a picture here and the streets are wide and lined with trees in blossom and granite benches and loitering sauntering people and babycarriages and horsedrawn vehicles with coachmen and footmen and markets are crammed with meats and cheeses and leeks and bottles and bread and grain and peanutroasters and chestnut stands—and it is Barcelona!

Julian L.

Barcelona, April Second Thirtyone, to your sister:

No more toros, even though the meet the day after tomorrow is one of the best of the year, a windup for the Holy Week. I enclose the programme. Hemingway wrote about Villalta, pronounced Biyalta *there would be eight bulls, ocho toros, and two would be fought by Nicanor and two each by Joaquin Rodriguez (Cagancho), Francisco Vega (Gitanillo de Triana), and Jesus Solorzano*

and then you detailed a bullfight for her in your embarrassing wit of the day. You spoke of the crowds, the costumes and bearing of those in the procession, the dashing entrance of the shit-plastered sacrifice, the ritual of his killing, and only at the end did you write a passage that you allowed to live:

The toreador draws his sword and gives a last invitation, and the bull is bullheaded enough to accept. He runs square into the blade, the force of the charge ramming it home to the hilt. He sinks, all the while looking wonderingly up at all those confusing people and, I thought, pleadingly. No use.

Madrid, 4.9.31, a letter to your sister on the stationery of the Hotel Gran Via:

At the Prado, I saw a blind man being led around by a woman who was reading to him out of a Baedeker.

At almost every streetcorner, theres a Chinaman selling cheap jewelry.

I heard the Madrid Symphony, Arbos conducting, play the César Franck, Cherubini's Anacreon Overture, and Handel's Water Music.

I heard the Orquesta Iberica, strings only. Some of it very fine, especially parts of a Bach suite and a dance by de Falla.

I took tea at Satouska (swank place) and stared at the prettiest girl Ive seen in Europe.

Spanish waiters serve you from large platters. They serve you as much as they think you ought to eat.

I went to the horse races this afternoon and stared at the prettiest Tomorrow Toledo.   Julian L.

Madrid-Toledo, April 11 (a note):

The autobus is moving toward Toledo at eighty kilometers an hour. The wide road is a dipping strip of grey metal. On the lightness of the sky, a brownish blot suddenly stains southward. A flock of wild geese shoots over the machine as easily as it passes a tree. As though to flaunt their speed, they circle twice around the big object below them before disappearing over a ploughed rise to the west.

Of Toledo, all you can see now as you peer through a blur is the El Greco in the Iglesia de Santo Tomé — *The Burial of the Count Orgaz* — or do you see the reproduction you bought at the door? The city is gone, and its winding river.

§

The Puerta del Sol is the largest square in Madrid. There the eastern gate once stood, the Gate of the Sun, but ten main streets converge on it now, and wherever you start from, whatever calle or carrera you happen to take, always you seem to wind up in that great open area at the heart of the city. Being there often, you come to know it well, and one of its attractions is a bookshop that stocks literature in foreign languages, one of these being English. If it weren't for inscriptions in your own hand, you'd hardly admit to the miscellany you buy: the *Selected Poems* of Browning, Shakespeare's *Songs and Verses,* Joyce's *Chamber Music* and *Pomes Penyeach,* yes, and a translation of *The World's Illusion.* A curious assortment for the novice reader — are they *titles,* would you say?

A day comes when, as you're crossing the square, you hear the pound of running feet, so many that they make an unbroken sound, like that of a falls, and you look about you to see people by the thousands pouring into the square, a torrent of people who seem to be heading only for you. When they're almost upon you, you turn and run with them, a leaf on a wave, and then for the first time you hear the roar of voices above the flood, and what they're saying is *Muerte a Alfonso!* and *Abajo la Guardia Civil!* and *Revolución!*

No notes remain to explain why you left Madrid that night.

Between Madrid and Avila, a cold began to come on, and by the time you reached Valladolid, you were sitting in a corner of the compartment pressing your head against the chill of the window-glass. You were hardly aware of Burgos, but there was no going on beyond San Sebastian, where you were forced to break journey and lie to. A hotel bus took you to the Maria Cristina, but all you remember of it is a huge room and aspirina washed down with hot tea and rum.

In the morning (the next, was it, or the one after that?) you were awakened by the din of celebration, by song, shots, and the explosions of breaking bottles. You looked out at thronged streets, and everywhere in the churning crowds, you saw the red, black, and yellow of the republican flag: Alfonso was gone. Still, you did not go below to join in the rejoicing. Instead, you picked up one of the books you'd bought in the Puerto del Sol (Browning? Wassermann? the Bard?), but you could've done no more than turn pages and stare at smears of print. You were wondering why you'd decided to leave Madrid—or whether, in truth, you'd simply fled.

As your train crossed the bridge between Irun and Hendaye, you said (and your notes show it!) *Adios, España.* In God's name, how could you?

On reaching Paris, you did not return to the France et Choiseul. At someone's suggestion (whose—a passenger on the train, le contrôleur, or the driver of your cab?), you put up at a hotel in the 8th arrondissement. Its name, as you recall it, was the King George, and it stood somewhere between the Seine and the Champs Elysées. For a day or two, you knew little of it but your room, where you sat or lay drinking grog américain until your cold went away. On your first descent to street level, you turned to watch a woman obtain a key from the concierge. In the evening, you encountered her again, and on that occasion you spoke to her and were spoken to, and soon you were seated beside her on a banquette in a cafe called Le Moscou *Paris April 18 At a nearby table theres a woman alternately consuming food and picking her teeth with a long pin that she keeps in her veil.*

At a guess, your pickup was within a year or two of thirty—no longer a girl, at any rate, nor as yet passé. She was Icelandic, she told you, and a concert singer, having studied first at Reykjavik and later on in Denmark, where she'd made her debut. Only her occupation put you in mind of the other: she gave off a different degree of warmth, as if her place of birth had banked her fire. She was tall, and she bore herself well, but her bearing struck you as assumed, rather like the attitude for *Poise*. It was beyond this one, you knew, to sing you Schumann in a doorway, and it would've been beyond you to remember the hillside where she slept. Still, the other one was in Jersey and three years dead.

On the way back to the hotel, you bought a bottle of Chambertin. You'd never tasted the wine before, but somewhere you'd read that with ortolans, Oscar Wilde would have nothing else. In prospect for you was no feast on fattened buntings, only a night of making the beast with a lymphatic soprano. As you drank, more and more the room seemed to come free of its floor, and by the time you lowered the lights, it was swaying as if suspended, and of the rest of the night you remember nothing but a flesh-colored expanse. You woke in the morning to see the sun come to flinders on the sloping shoulders of a bottle. The woman was gone, and later in the day, when you asked the concierge for the number of her room, you were told that she'd departed for London.

how to know and check the spread of, you thought, and in a complex way, you became uneasy at once. Until then, you hadn't been troubled by the veneriana of the night before, but now, you somehow regarded the woman as your only security against what she herself might've caused. What was it that you supposed—that the carrier was the cure, or, better, the preventative, and that once she was out of sight, you could only watch for signs of disease? Many times a day—hourly, it seemed—you examined yourself for the gonorrheal leak, the genital or labial lesion. Was that a burning in the urinary tract, was that redness on the glans the beginning of a sore? While awaiting doom, how did you pass the time? Did you see more sights, did you write something new from Africa, did you read the books you'd brought from Genoa, Venice, Rome—the poems of Whitman, say, *The Enormous Room* or *Memoirs of a Fox-Hunting Man*?

For a small sum, the concierge revealed the singer's address in London, and you took a boat-train as soon as you could pack.

§

In London, you took lodgings in Queensborough Terrace, a few doors away from Bayswater Road. By the same reasoning—reasoning, you called it—that had brought you across the Channel, you felt more secure with the Channel behind you. Glancing about at what a pound a week had procured—

Birmingham furniture, lace curtains made by machine, you drew comfort from being near what you were afraid of and were able to lessen the fear. You made no effort to see your listless singer—if not Schumann, Schubert, Brahms, what *did* she sing?—and in passing her hotel each day, your only intention was to assure yourself that, if needed (for what?), she was still within reach, that she was *there*, just across the park. The knowledge seemed important, as if, having been bitten, you knew where to find the snake.

For all that fruitless absorption, you appear to have continued writing. In a letter to your sister early in May, you spoke of a short story called "The White Cassock" that you'd submitted to *The Criterion*, the quarterly edited by T. S. Eliot. Staring at the letter now, half a century later, you're aghast at such proof of your brass. All you can remember of the story is that it was a parable based on 1 Corinthians 13, but what book it was once a part of is forgotten, and forgotten too what impelled you to Russell Square. But you seem to have had brass to spare then, and a few days after mailing the story in, you called in person to learn its fate.

Met Eliot, you wrote to your sister, *but he hadn't read the story when I saw him, so we had a talk of about twenty minutes.* Nothing much was spoken of, you told her, and you described him as *a gauntish sort of chap,* and after pronouncing him *ugly,* you noted that he was dressed *like a professor of botany,* as though a science, like a regiment, wore distinctive garb. *His voice is smooth,* you said, *and his words careful—they come out like flowers, ever so slowly.* While with him, *I tried to tell myself that I was in the presence of a great man,* only to find that he was like someone you'd met once and hadn't remembered. And you signed yourself *Brother Julian.*

But Brother Julian was wrong. He was in the same room as

> grimy scraps of withered leaves
> and
> the troubled midnight and the noon's repose
> and
> thoughts of a dry brain in a dry season
> and the
> côtes brulantes de Mozambique.

They were there, but you did not know them that day in Russell Square.

§

Two second cousins of yours, a brother and sister, were coming in on the *Europa,* and you journeyed to Southampton to greet them from the tender. At Customs, watching them across a barrier, you saw that the brother was being detained. Suspicious of the bulging pockets of his trenchcoat, an Inspector had requested that he empty them. Dozens of pairs of silk stockings came to light, all apparently omitted from his declaration. Subjected then to a body-search, he was found to be carrying a loaded revolver. For a time, it was touch-and-go whether he'd be allowed to land, but in the end, he was let off with a fine of £50; the stockings and revolver were confiscated.

On the train to London, you said to the sister, "Next time, declare your stockings," and then to the brother, "But why the rod?"
"England is a foreign country," he said.

§

On the 11th of May 1931, a letter was delivered to you at your digs. It was on the stationery of *The Criterion,* and it read:

Julian Shapiro Esq.
72 Queensborough Terrace
W. 2.

Dear Mr Shapiro,
    I have read your interlude with much interest. It seems to me very well written, with a slight suggestion of George Moore about it. I feel however that it is a little too artificial to stand by itself. In your book, no doubt, the contrast of this and the other interludes with what I imagine is the close realism of the story, is very likely, I feel, to be highly effective; and that, I imagine, is at least partly your purpose. May I say, however, that I should very much like to see the whole book when it is completed, even though you yourself may think that it is too local.
    I am afraid that as you are leaving so soon I may not have another opportunity of seeing you, but if you should be near at any time when I was here, I shall be very glad to see you again, even if only to say goodbye.
Yours sincerely,
T. S. Eliot

§

Later on the same day, you wrote to your sister that you'd seen James Joyce in a restaurant near Piccadilly Circus. *Spotted him from photographs,* you said. *Sent a waiter over to snoop and verify. But the bastard made the mistake of ASKING Joyce! Joyce owned up, but requested that no one disturb him as he was with his family.* That made two rejections in one day, you said, without a hope that you could say *I've been turned down by better men.*

§

In the middle of May, you sailed from Plymouth on the *Deutschland* of the Hamburg-Amerika Line. To give your sister a chance to meet the ship, you sent her a radiogram the night before its arrival. You thought it dashing to send it in code, and on the receiving end it read *Agfa Deutschland Bofum.* By the time this was deciphered to *Coming Deutschland Twenty-second,* the ship was in port, and you were on the dock alone.

SCENE 20

PARENT AND CHILD (May 1931)

From wherever you'd been in Europe, you'd written at length to your father. From the south of France, from Italy and Spain, from Paris and London, you'd sent him accounts of your doings and plans, always as though your travels had been undertaken with his approval and almost at his suggestion. You'd told him where you'd been and whom you'd seen, furnished him with itineraries and mailing addresses, made observations of the ways of the Old World with all the shallow wisdom of the New: it was as if you were sending back dispatches to the sponsor of an expedition. In the half-year of your absence, though, never once did he reply.

On seeing you for the first time, he greeted you customarily, as one from whom he'd been parted for perhaps as long as a day. Of your extended absence, he took no notice whatever, and you knew he'd not acknowledge that you'd ever been away. It would've been futile to ask him for forgiveness: What is there to forgive? he'd've said. But when you rose to leave the dining-table, where the usual round of subjects had been covered, you went to his chair and kissed him, and then you stood there for a moment and smoothed his hair, and he did not shake you off.

94

SCENE 21

THE PARTNERSHIP (Late May 1931)

On the morning after your return, you accompanied your father downtown to the offices in Chambers Street. Through the windows of the subway car, you stared at familiar mosaics on the station walls—Columbus Circle, Astor Place, City Hall—and soon you were crossing the familiar park where you could still hear the words of another year, *All the difference in the world*, and you wondered whether she ever heard them too.

Just before you entered your father's suite, he said, "You'll find some changes, Julian."

You were greeted well by the office force, the stenographers, the telephone operator, the bookkeeper, and as you moved toward your room, you read your name and that of your partner on the translucent glass, and then you opened the door. At a glance, nothing seemed to have changed. There before you was the oaken desk (*The Hudson River*, you'd written, *was a quarter of a mile from his window*), and there stood the tall bookcase that held your first editions of Lawrence and Huxley, your mother's set of Shakespeare, your Marlowe and Jonson, your Wycherley and Steele, and there, in their places on the wall, were your Homer prints, your da Vinci drawings, your flowers by Demuth, and on a nearby table, the telephone held its receiver at arm's length, as if it were a child. There were no changes.

You seated yourself at the desk and ran your fingers over the varnished grain, you opened and closed a drawer, you made the swivel-chair turn a little to the right and then a little to the left, and in your mind, you placed Marlowe next to Massinger and Dryden next to Middleton. When your law partner arrived, he'd say—what? what would he say?—and slowly you began to know (how? why? with what sense?) that he wasn't going to arrive.

Rising, you went to your father's room. "Where's Herb?" you said. "What happened to Herb?"

"Sit down, kid," he said. "He came to me about a week ago—you were halfway home—and after thanking me for the use of the room, he told me he was moving out. Some day, he said, he'd pay the rent he owed, but I told him to forget it."

"I don't understand," you said. "Why was he moving?"

"He didn't say."

"And you didn't ask?"

"No."

"Why not?"

"I didn't want to pry. I felt it had something to do with you."

You shook your head. "We're friends, we're partners, and all of a sudden, he packs his briefcase and clears out."

"His mail is being forwarded to an address on East 43rd Street, in care of Ira Holley."

"Ira Holley!" you said.

Obtaining the precise address from the office manager, you went uptown at once. In a building between Fifth and Madison, a wall directory listed Ira Holley and the number of his suite, and there you were shown to your partner's room. He greeted you in a warm manner, but you felt that the warmth was manner only, the reflection of candle-light.

"Why did you move away from my father's office, Herb?" you said.

"You answer your own question, Jules. Because it *was* your father's office. With you away, I had no right to stay there. I stayed too long as it was."

"But for Christ's sake, we're partners! Where I'm welcome, you're welcome."

"I couldn't pay the rent."

"Were you ever asked for rent?"

"No, but only because of you. I was getting a free ride."

"With our colossal practice, we *need* a free ride, and we'll never get that from Ira Holley."

"I hate to tell you this, Jules, but it isn't *we* any more."

"What does that mean?"

"Holley made me an offer: I give him some legal services instead of rent. There was one condition, though—he doesn't like you, and he said you couldn't come along."

You went to a window and looked down seven flights at hats that seemed to be walking, at toys of traffic, at smoke, commotion, and almost visible noise, and after a while, you said, "And you agreed?"

"I had no choice, Jules."

"Sure, you did. You could've told him to go fuck himself."

SCENE 22

NOVELIST AND NOVICE (June 1931)

On your return from Europe, among the first of the friends you sought out was Nat West, now managing the Hotel Sutton on the east side of mid-Manhattan. You found him in his top-floor rooms, which looked southward through the rifts and haze of the island. His quarters disclosed only his literary occupation—a few dozen books disposed at random and a table holding a pile of manuscript and a log-jam of pencils.

"Welcome home, O Lost Generation!" he said.

"I was your traveler in Tyana," you said. "I presented my letters of introduction, and I was shown the rectum. But, damn it, I never saw the serpent."

"You got there too late, Scotty. It was all over before you arrived."

"The truth is, I got there too soon. I wasn't ready; I had no purpose. And having no purpose, I learned nothing. I just wandered around, showing my letter from brother George."

"Who'd you meet?"

"Sam Putnam, editor of *The New Review,* Stuart Gilbert, Hilaire Hiler in Cagnes, and in London a queer cove named Thomas Stearns Eliot."

"You met T. S. Eliot! How?"

"I submitted something to *The Criterion.*"

He gazed at you for a moment, and then he said, "*L'audace!* What did you show him?"

"A piece from the novel. An interlude called 'The White Cassock.' "

"A child of the lamp! And how did he receive it?"

"He turned it down."

"*Merde alors!*"

"When you come to the house, I'll show you his letter," you said, and you indicated the work lying on the table. "*Lonelyhearts?*"

"What else?"

"How about *Balso?*"

"At the binder's," he said. "Be ready any day." He went to a window and stared out at rows of lights in the streets, at those in building silhouettes, like holes in punchboards. "I was only assistant manager at the Kenmore. Here I'm manager, and it's eating me up. I get about an hour a day for the book—if nothing happens, and it always does. There's always some fucking deadbeat I have to throw out on his ass. I've got to get away, God damn it, or I'll never finish the book!"

"Get away to where?" you said.

"Anywhere," he said, and he turned back to you. "You and the law, me and this whorehouse. Why don't we *both* do what we ought to be doing—finishing our books? A summer of writing, Scotty! What do you say? Here's your chance to find a purpose."

"Tell you something funny, Pep," you said. "I think I know where to find it."

You told him about Beakbane, the game-warden you'd met at Long Lake the year before. You told him about Lalo and the *Symphonie Espagnole*.

"Write to him at once," Pep said. "Say you're a friend of music. Hell, say you're a relative."

Beakbane responded from his home in Glens Falls, saying that he happened to know of a suitable place for "a summer of writing," but he told you that you might lose it unless you applied before the end of June. The month having begun, the two of you had only a week or so to make your arrangements. Not the least of these was the purchase of a car, and after spending a day at the work, you found what you were looking for. On a small sales-lot on 125th Street near the Fort Lee ferry, you spotted a 1930 Ford, a Model-T roadster. The owner of the lot gave you and Pep permission to try it out, and taking the wheel, you drove it up the hill to Grant's Tomb, where you turned northward with the light traffic of evening. As soon as you were on the Viaduct, you called on the car for speed; halfway across, you were doing a mile a minute.

"Son-of-a-bitch runs like a scalded dog," you said.

"To coin a phrase," Pep said. "The Bard would've written *swifter than arrow from Tartar's bow*."

"Let's buy it."

Returning to the sales-lot, you were told that the price was $195, surprisingly low for a car in such good repair. "We'll take it," you said to the proprietor. "Make out a bill of sale."

He reached into the car, removed the keys and began to walk away. "The deal's off," he said through a chewed cigar.

"Why is it off?" you said.

"I don't give no bill of sale."

"If we don't have one, how can we prove we own the car?"

"You own it if you got it," the man said. "That's nine points of the law."

"Pay him," Pep said, and he moved you toward the dealer.

"But it must be a stolen car!"

"Stolen from whom?"

"How the hell do I know?" you said.

Pep indicated the dealer, saying, "I'm sure he doesn't know, either. If he did, being an honest man, he'd give the car back to the rightful owner."

Again the man spoke through the masticated cigar. "You got sense," he said to Pep. "Your friend here is a schmuck."

From the fund that you and Pep had put together, you counted out $195. The keys were handed over, and you and Pep drove away.

"You know something, Scotty?" he said.

"What?"

"You *are* a schmuck."

§

Your stepmother—Aunt Jo, as you called her—invited Pep to dinner on the eve of your departure for the Adirondacks. He was no stranger to the household, where he appeared often and was well thought of, not only for himself, but also for his father, known to your own since the early days in Harlem.

After greeting the guest, your father said, "I hope Max is well."

"He never changes," Pep said. "Thin, quiet, sad."

"Why do you say sad?"

"That's the way he strikes me."

"He's a warm-hearted man, the only kind I like. Give him my regards."

"I will," Pep said, and turning to you, he handed over a small flat package. "A gift for Yonkel."

Removing the wrapper, you found a hard-cover copy of *The Dream Life of Balso Snell.*

"One of fifty," he said. "Take note of your number."

Your number, you discovered, was 2. "An honor," you said.

During dinner, your sister leafed through the book, smiling at passages you could not identify from across the table. At one point, though, she read aloud, saying, "Bromius! Iacchus! Son of Zeus!"

Embarrassed, Pep said to your father, "You're a real estate lawyer, Mr. Shapiro. Did you ever handle any matters for Max?"

"I represented people who had dealings with him," your father said, "but I was never his attorney. When we met for the first time, though it wasn't in a law-office. It was at a hotel in the Catskills in the summer of 1905. At Hunter, I think, or it may have been Tannersville. Max and I were there with our families, so I guess that's when you first met Julian. He was one year old."

"I was two and a half at the time," Pep said, "but I was a keen judge of character. I'm afraid I found him rather childish."

"He's twenty-seven now," your father said, "and he's still rather childish."

"Childe Julian, they call me," you said.

"About Max," your father said to Pep. "Did you ever notice a certain characteristic of his? When he shakes your hand, he uses both of his. He's a friendly man—and you say he looks sad."

"It's like he was looking out at a black world."

Your father indicated the book, lying closed now before your sister. "What made you decide to become a writer?"

"He loves that question," you said. "It gives him a chance to say he wanted to improve literature. The family bookcase was filled with sets, and he read all of Tolstoy by the age of nine. If pressed, he'll tell you he found him long-winded."

"That was Dostoevsky," Pep said.

"Dusty Evsky, he calls him—claims he can improve him by tearing out alternate pages."

Turning to you, your father said, "And what's your reason for becoming a writer, kid?"

After dinner, you and Pep retired to your semi-subterranean room at the rear of the flat. There he spied the letter from T. S. Eliot, which you'd placed in an old picture-frame and hung above a chest of drawers. He leaned toward the black type and red heading, and after a moment, he moved away.

"You oughtn't to display that, Scotty," he said.

"You think not?" you said. "How so?"

"It isn't a good letter."

You read a few lines, less from the framed sheet than your memory of it. "He doesn't exactly spit on my gaberdine," you said.

"Don't you know when you're being let down easy?"

"Usually."

"He was merely being civil," Pep said. "Take my advice and put the letter away."

"The only bad word in it is *artificial,* which you take to mean feigned. But it doesn't have to be bad: it can mean made by art. There's nothing wrong with an artificial flower."

"Try sending a dozen to your girl."

"A better writer than I'll ever be wrote that after reading a piece of my book. I don't think he was dusting me off. He didn't have to. He could've sent the piece back with a *Thank you, but.* Instead, he offers to look at the whole book when it's finished. . . . But if the letter offends you, I'll take it down." And that was what you did.

Your sister appeared in the doorway long enough to say, "Get his autograph."

"What would be appropriate, Ruthele?" he said, but by then she'd gone. To you, he said, "How would you like this: *From one horse's ass to another?*"

"I didn't know there were two in the grass around Troy. How about something like *Affectionately,* you miserable bastard?"

He inscribed the flyleaf and handed the book to you. In his gangling hand, he'd written:

> For Julian
> Affectionately,
> Pep
> Nathanael West
> July 10, 1931

You laughed. "It happens to be *June* 10th."

THE COLOR OF THE AIR, V

RIP VAN WINKLE—1788
IN THE KAATSKILLS

Even to this day they never hear a thunder-storm of a summer after-noon, but they say Hendrick Hudson and his crew are at their game of nine-pins.

—Washington Irving

It would've been better not to wake. It would've been better to sleep on, dead, deep in that glen where the Kaaterskill rose, and the bitterns hid, and the watersnake sunned when the sun was overhead. It would've been better there, where none came but the queer conjured crew of the *Half Mon,* and they but for a day of nine-pin thunder every twenty years. It would've been better to stay, to lie forever between two wales of dust, one a bygone gun and one a keg of Hollands, without a dog, without a wife, himself dust and by all forgot.

He wasted time well once. He built fences for others and let his own stock stray. He fished in the rain and fowled in the shine, and though weeds grew and slates fell, time went by on a one-way tide. He flew kites for children and told them tales of witches, ghosts, and the Iroquois, and their lurchers knew him and suffered him to pass. He ran errands for the village wives, never wondering who odd-jobbed for him, and holding it better to starve on a penny than live on a pound, he laughed at those who wound their watches.

Now some new do-nothing flies the kites and spreads the fictions, and some new pack trails him on his back-door rounds. There are

101

new wives and new errands now, and new hounds drowse while time ticks by. Even the old Rip is new. Gone the free favors and the love of child and beast, gone the squanderer, sowing the hours where they yield the least. He has learned to think, and to all who'll listen, he sells his story for a drink of gin. He kills no time now: he's like the many, and time is killing him.

SCENE 23

MEMOIR OF A SUMMER IN THE WOODS (June-September 1931)

Lying before you is a rifle-case of green canvas. The edging, the straps, the muzzle-guard, all of these leather, are dried out and friable, and at a touch they shed a part of their substance, a yellow powder that looks like pollen. From the pockets of the case, you extract the two sections of a slide-action Winchester .22, and fitting the walnut stock to the blued-steel barrel and magazine, you seem at the same time to be joining the present with a season half a century downstream into the past.

You and Nat West are in a sporting-goods shop near Madison Square. Davega's, it was called, and on a counter before you rests the rifle-case, its canvas unsoiled and its leathers limber, and stacked beside it are little boxes of ammunition, five thousand rounds! and there are packets of paper targets, a pair of trout-rods, and a book of flies, and you remember still their magic names: Silver Doctor, Royal Coachman, Parmachenee Belle. And now to this mass of wonders, your companion adds two books on Camp Cookery, one by the trapper Nessmuk and the other by Horace Kephart, huntsman and guide.

Fired long ago, all those copper rounds, and snagged somewhere those vivid flies. The trapper's book has been lost and the rods of split bamboo. Only the rifle survives, that and the Kephart with its treatise on dressing game. You glance at the pages, and for the first time you note that a few passages have been underlined in pencil (by whom—you, was it, or Nimrod Weinstein, Nathanael West?):

hang it by one hind leg and begin skinning at the back, peeling the legs, then the body, and finally the neck

Had something been shot, you wonder, and if so what, when, and where? Or had the interlineations been made in advance, with the killing to come,

102

with some rabbit or gray squirrel still feeding, still flicking an ear on its last living day, and who would hold the .22, would it be West or you?

following the middle line of the chest, slit upward to the cut around the neck. Then reverse, and continue the slit backward to the end of the tail, being careful not to perforate the walls of the belly

Was some two-pound creature still chewing leaves?

open the abdominal cavity, taking care. . . .

§

At six o'clock in the morning, you drew up before the Hotel Sutton, where you found West waiting for you on the sidewalk. Near the curb lay a safari-bag, a satchel-like piece of luggage all of five feet in length. Across some dark Afric plain of your mind, a celluloid image passed, a file of Nubians balancing impedimenta on their heads—guns, whisky cases, camp supplies, and that selfsame cowhide bag—and bringing up the rear was West, dressed as now in a vested suit.

"Nate," you said, indicating his getup, "we're supposed to be heading for the wild."
And he said, "One never lets down."

He heaved his gear athwart the rumble-seat, and after adjusting his feathered Alpine hat, he climbed in beside you—and then in a stolen Ford roadster, two Harlem Jews set out for Glens Falls, fifty miles above Albany in the valley of the Hudson.

Crossing the island, you headed north, and from Spuyten Duyvil onward, you followed the river road. It was a fine day, you remember, and as you went, you may have thought your way back into history to redcoats marching through the wilderness toward defeat and surrender at Saratoga; or you may have sought a finish for an unfinished novel; or did you dwell on the friend at your side, his nature, his habits, the trend of his mind—or were you bent on the wide green river you descried through the trees?

At Tarrytown, the monument to André's capture, and there as well the Hollow where the Headless Horseman rode, but if such things concerned you in passing, others too turned in your head. You were leaving the past—family, friends, and daily ways—and you did not know where the new days would end. But every man his own Columbus, you thought, and then you were passing the gray granite walls of Sing Sing and, within them, the Chair, the edge of the earth for other headlong sailors.

Meanwhile, what was being said at your side? Were you hearing of Barbey d'Aurevilly and his *romans licencieux*? Was there mention of Persse at Poughkeepsie, of Barnabooth and *Ubu Roi*, and by Rhinebeck had you learned how the nickname Pep had been earned? Did he take the wheel at Red Hook, and after five wild miles did you take it back? Did you watch him use both hands to light a cigarette?

"The two-handed Weinsteins," you said.
"I've always had the shakes," he said. "I sometimes light my nose."

Soon after ten o'clock, you reached Albany, a hundred and fifty miles from New York, and by noon or thereabouts, you were in the outskirts of Glens Falls, another sixty miles further north. There you asked for directions to Beakbane's address. In his dooryard, a Gordon setter came to inspect you, and as Pep stooped to rough up his coat of black and mahogany, the game-warden appeared on the porch.

You presented West, who said, "Mr. Beakbane, my friend here tells me that he met you last year over at Long Lake."
"That's true," Beakbane said.
"He also says that the meeting came about because he happened to recognize the music of an obscure French composer."
"That's true too. It was Edouard Lalo."
"Pep," you said, "the time has come for you to say, 'I'll be damned.' "

Beakbane led you through his home to an office at the rear, where the walls were largely hung with geodetic surveys of his domain, the southern half of the Adirondacks. Their scale was small, an inch to the half-mile, and in the density of their contour lines, you could read the ups and downs of the earth. At the confluence of two streams, the Schroon and the Hudson, Beakbane inserted a push-pin.

"That's where the village of Warrensburg is," he said, and then he moved a finger across the chart to a black dot at the edge of an irregular patch of blue. "And this is a cabin owned by a friend of mine named Harry Reoux. It's six miles into the woods on a dirt road one car wide. There are no houses after you pass Fannie Bennett's place a mile or so out."
You said, "Where can we find this Harry Reoux?"
"He's a member of the State Assembly," Beakbane said. "Unless it's in session, he'll be at the Warrensburg Bank. He owns it."
On the way out, you stopped before a framed watercolor near the doorway. "A Homer," you said.
"Only a print," Beakbane said. "It's called *North Woods Club*, and it's dated

104

1892. The club is a private reserve about twenty miles over the mountains from the Reoux place. I sometimes fish there."

When you were on the road to Warrensburg, Pep said, "Cabin — to me, that connotes a rude structure of one room. How would I shut myself off from you?"

"Go outside," you said.

"Assemblyman and bank president. Scotty, I think we're in over our heads."

"My guess is Beakbane knows what he's about. He wouldn't bring us all this way for nothing."

"Don't bet too much on Lalo," Pep said. "People like to see people take a fall. The banana-peel. The mud-hole. Laurel and Hardy."

"Not this guy," you said. "There's something about him."

"I hope you're right," he said, "but I won't be surprised if we get pissed on." And then he glanced at you, saying, "But you will, won't you?"

And you said, "Yes."

Nearing Warrensburg, you passed a sign painted on a barn; it was an ad for a brand of gasoline known as Pur-ol Pep. Your companion read it off as, "Poor ole Pep!"

At the Warrensburg Bank, you were directed to the Reoux home, a large frame house set far back from the main road behind a screen of trees and shrubbery. There, on a broad verandah, you were received by a middle-aged woman who informed you that Harry Reoux was her son.

"He won't be back from Albany for several days," she said, "but he told me you might be coming, and I'm authorized to speak for him."

You said, "I suppose the sensible thing is for us to look at the cabin first."

"I was going to suggest that," she said, and she offered you a key.

Following her directions, you drove to a bridge across the Schroon and then climbed Harrington Hill to the Bennett farm at the summit. From there on, the way lay through wooded country, and you wound with it among groves of birch, white pine, and copper beech, and here and there you rounded a huge walnut that stood alone, as if it had drawn away from the touch of other trees. Grass grew between the wheel-tracks, and where these dipped to ford a brook, sometimes you saw cress swaying in the run. A partridge fled from covert to covert, and chicks fled with her like a gust of leaves. Merely to listen to the woods, you brought the car to a stop, and what you heard was the silken sound of the wind, and on it at intervals came the same several notes of a thrush.

"Turdus aonalaschke pallasii," Pep said. "The water-dripping song of *The Waste Land.*"

You drove on into the late afternoon, and coming at you now through the top of the forest, the sun broke into crystals of light, making a great stained-glass window of the trees. At a bend in the road, you began to run past a marsh that lay behind a thicket of reeds, but these soon thinned, and you found that you were rimming a pond showing a quarter of a mile of open water. On a rise at the far side, looking down on a small dock, stood the Reoux cabin. Again you stopped, this time staring, and Pep stared too, and now there were no stately observations, no allusions in Latin or otherwise. One of you might've said *Jesus Christ* very softly, but that was all.

The cabin contained six paired rooms, three suites in effect, one of them opening into another until the kitchen was reached; this opened into a long enclosed woodshed with a two-hole privy at the further end. The suites held iron beds and hair mattresses, old Morris chairs, and bookcases filled with bygone magazines. You and Pep made your way through the house from the ground-level porch to the two-seater at the rear, and then you came back to the kitchen, where, on shelves above a corner table, squads of crockery stood at attention; in a large glazed bowl below them, among its own shot-like droppings, lay the stiff little shrivel of a mouse.

From the kitchen door, a two-step stoop led to a path that ran down a slope past a windlassed well and ended at the dock you'd seen from the road. Standing on its weathered planks, you and West watched the sun skip across the pond, and from a spillway somewhere near, you could hear water pouring into water. Beyond a ruff of reeds, lily-pads rode the ripples, and far out in the clear, something broke and flashed.

"Trout too," Pep said.

You walked back along the path to the stoop. There you sat down and lit up smokes, and for a while you grayed the air in silence.

"What do you suppose the rent would be?" you said.

"Out of sight," Pep said. "I wish I'd never seen the place."

"Not me. I wouldn't've missed it, whether we get it or not."

"I'm not much on self-torture. What I can't have I don't want."

"Does that apply to girls?"

"Particularly to girls," he said.

"Tell that to Sweeney among the nightingales."

"That's good, Scotty. You mind if I use it?"

You spun your cigarette away, and then you quickly rose to grind it out in the grass. You looked at the cabin's shuttered windows and its roof of galvanized iron, and then you looked at the pine-jagged sky over the pond, and you said, "Pep, we've simply *got* to have this place!"

"Reoux'd want five hundred a month for it. I know a thing or two about rents. I manage a hotel."

"Let's go back and talk to Mrs. Reoux. We wouldn't've been sent out here if we didn't have a chance."

"Shit, then, Scotty. We'll give it a try."

The sun was behind you all the way to Warrensburg. It shone past your shoulders, sometimes making a mirror of the windshield, and you saw flashes of what you'd left behind instead of what lay ahead. Coming down Harrington Hill toward the Schroon River bridge, you ran through shadow, and you felt the cool of evening. Turning in at the Reoux driveway, you stopped the car under the porte-cochère, and as you mounted the steps to the verandah, you were spoken to through a screen in a dim doorway.

"Well, what did you think of the cabin?" Mrs. Reoux said.

"It's swell," Pep said. "Thanks for letting us see it."

"My friend is backward, but I'm forward," you said. "Speaking for the two of us, I want to say the place is perfect. All we're afraid of is that we can't afford it."

"Come inside, and we'll see," Mrs. Reoux said. She led you through a hall to a gun-room where, displayed in glass-fronted cabinets, rifles, shotguns, and small arms gleamed against a backing of baize. Taking in the weapons with a gesture, she said, "My son's."

Pep peered at a pair of over-and-unders, saying, "These are very fine fowling-pieces."

Mrs. Reoux said, "The cabin was built thirty years ago, when Harry was a boy. At first, it was only for family use in the summer, but after he grew up, we turned it over to him for his hunting parties. Up to now, it has never been let to anyone."

You and Pep glanced at each other, but you said nothing.

"It's good deer country around Viele Pond," Mrs. Reoux said. "A little too good, I'm afraid, and a certain amount of poaching has been going on up there. Nobody from Warrensburg, but that road runs on to Stony Creek, and that's where they come from. It was Mr. Beakbane's idea, and Harry agrees, that having someone on the place might keep them away. You two look responsible. You can have it on your own terms."

"Good Lord, Mrs. Reoux," you said, "we wouldn't know what to offer."

"How about twenty-five dollars a month?" she said.

Again you looked at Pep, this time with eyes wide, and likewise he looked at you, and then, only a fraction out of sync, you both said, "We'll take it!"

"It's too late to go back today," she said. "Better start in the morning, but come here first, and I'll give you some bedding."

You offered to pay then and there for the entire summer, but she shook her head, saying, "There's no hurry."

And at the door, again she spoke to you through the screen. "The pond—Viele Pond, it's called—belongs to us, and it goes with the cabin. And so do two square miles along the road."

§

After a dozen hours on the road, neither you nor Pep had much to say over an evening meal at Hall's, a diner on Route 9, the Montreal pike. Nor later, when you were lodged at the Warrensburg Inn, did you find that you could speak of the miles you'd put behind you or of the journey's cloudless end. Pep may have felt as you did, that what lay in prospect could only be savored in silence, and he soon took it with him into the second silence of sleep. For you, there were a last few illuminations, and in one of them, you saw the luckless mouse at the bottom of the bowl. This time, though, it was still alive, still rushing at the vitreous slopes, still sliding back among its minute defecations; from the shelves above, other eyes were on it, other mice were watching their brother die. Within your mind, you heard yourself say *Fowling-pieces,* and then you too were asleep. . . .

During the following forenoon, you made two round-trips to the pond, once with your gear and a bundle of bedding and once with a load of provisions. Pep lugged his safari-bag into the cabin and dropped it in the first room he set foot in, one of the pair that opened on the porch, and with that act, he established possession. You took the adjoining pair, setting yourself up in quarters that were back-to-back with his. On opening the shutters, you exposed nothing you were inclined to change, and such order as you found remained throughout your stay. Soon your typewriters appeared on tables separated by a wall of papered plaster, and with them were your binders holding manuscript and your pads of Manila ruled in blue.

You'd been told of a crockery cooler in a brook that crossed under the road, but some freshet had buried it in pebbles and silt, and you failed to find it. Instead, you filled the water-bucket with food that might spoil and lowered it away into the well, where it seemed to bob on the sky. *There's a hole in the earth,* you thought.

And so the summer began.

§

On his side of the wall, West worked on a revision of his second novel, *Miss Lonelyhearts*. He'd never offered to show it to you, but he'd told you of its origin and quoted from its dialogue until, even without a reading, its attitudes and intention had become familiar. In the character after whom he'd named the book, West was possessed of an enviable central position: every letter addressed to the columnist became a letter addressed to the author; every incurable ailment became his, every abuse suffered, every hopeless cause and predicament; and standing as he did near the focus of force, he seemed able to experience all the anguish of his anguished creation, even his hero's death. But however close he stood to Miss Lonelyhearts, he did not make the error of merging with him and thus becoming the very object he was trying to observe.

On your side of the wall, you were trying to complete the final part of your first novel, *The Water Wheel*. Long before, as far back as the opening line — *The Hudson River was a quarter of a mile from his window* — you'd made the mistake that West had avoided. Your champion, though you called him John Sanford, was always and only you, grandson and legatee of a Litvak match-vendor, and you were never free of him, never able to shuck him and join the world outside, and therefore when he spoke, your voice alone replied. You could never see him, for you were he.

§

There was no running water in the kitchen or anywhere else, and no power-lines ran to the cabin from North Creek or Lake George. When you needed light, you used a coal-oil lamp, a glass jar in which a wick lay coiled like a tapeworm in formaldehyde. All meals were made on a woodstove, a squat broadly-planted monster that reminded you of a Japanese wrestler. Apart from providing you with stews and fries, it was relied on for warmth after sundown. At the cabin's elevation, a little over two thousand feet, the sun made only fall days at best, and there was an empty-house chill in the shade. At night, it was cold and sometimes freezing, and you and West would cock your chairs near the stove, blowing cigarette smoke at an open lid and watching the heat reject it.

What was said in those evenings at two thousand feet, what was read in those saffron coals? Did you see a day nine years ahead . . . but how could you know what was coming, how could you hear a skull splinter and glass go to smash, how from so far away?

109

§

One day you'd write:*

The road went through a wild-looking stretch of woods and they saw some red squirrels and a partridge. . . .

He'd just written the sentence, you supposed, or just revised it, and he was reading it aloud, trying the leanness of the prose, the sound, the rhythm, and through a partition of two thin coats of papered plaster, you could hear him phrase in the next-door room. You could almost see the sheet he read from, ascrawl with that lurching hand of his, half script, half printing, and downhill all, the same letters formed in different ways, with gaunt caps and lank descenders, ungainly, spasmodic—like him, it was. He seemed ill-assembled, you thought, a morph made of spare parts and odd sizes, each with a will of its own, and he had a plural way of going, as if he contained a brawl. You heard a match strike, and you heard it flare, and you called up his cupped and quavering hands, and you saw smoke climb his face and gray his hair, and then he read aloud his words for a scene that might've been mounted on his windowpane.

. . . Two deer and a fawn came down to the water on the opposite side of the pond. . . .

In his grasp, a pencil became a sixth finger hostile to the other five, a stiff and sullen balking thing—held by him, all objects were grim and intervenient, and he was ever at odds with a cigarette, a hat, a shotgun, a knife and fork, a steering-wheel. There were many hazards in his world, many enemies, and on a day still nine years off, one such would prove ineluctable, and he'd die in a debacle of metal far from where he was now, in a cabin on Viele Pond, six miles west of Warrensburg on the way to Stony Creek.

. . . It was very sad under the trees . . . in the deep shade there was nothing but death—rotten leaves, gray and white fungi. . . .

Death would wait nine years for him to reach a certain road crossing three thousand miles away, and when he got there, it would break into his brain and expunge its pictures of a summer in the woods. There'd be no scenes showing him a spring-fed pond in a cattail ring, there'd be no wind, no cowlicks on the water, no reeds that seemed to run: where such memories had been, there'd be extravasated blood, spalls of bone, a great and pulsating brilliance. His heart would fibrillate for one more hour, and he'd die, and thereafter it would lie with you to make that summer live.

. . . The water was so cold that they could only stay in for a short time. . . .

---

*In *View From This Wilderness*, 1977. The italicized lines are from West.

110

Sitting there at your window, staring at the same view he had from his, you couldn't know that each of those summer days should've been set down as it went—each day, with all that was said and done. You couldn't know that he'd be gone so soon, giving you custody of that part of his life, you couldn't know that they might matter, his sayings and doings, his ways, his likes, the holes you found in his coat and the ones he found in yours—there'd be time to remember, you thought, and what you forgot you could always get from him. There were jots in the journal of your mind, notes of the bass you took from the Hudson, the paper and living targets you fired at, the woodstove meals, the smoke sucked into the coal-oil lamps, the talk (what did you say to him, for God's sake! and what did he say to you?), the do-nothing afternoons, the scrivening sessions on opposite sides of a wall. You'd remember it all.

> . . . *The new green leaves hung straight down and shone in the hot sun like an army of little metal shields. . . .*

Of that summer, buried under forty-five years, the only hard tokens are a spread of snapshots foxed now with age. In them, two figures stand, sit, lounge, two faces are fixed (on what? on whom?), hands hold sticks, a magazine, cigarettes, and an old car can be seen, and a porch, a doorway, a basin near a bench, and there are brown trees, sepia grass, and a tan sky. You have only to wait, you fancy, and you'll hear sound and witness motion: the cigarettes you hold will burn to the end, pages will be read and turned, the day will wear, and to something that one of you has said, the other will make a reply—you need only wait.

But it won't do! it won't do! There'd be no change though you looked and listened forever. There'd be the likenesses of that single moment, stock-still and silent, and they'd tell only what they told before, one particular time, like a stopped clock.

> . . . *Somewhere in the woods a thrush was singing. Its sound was like that of a flute choked with saliva.*

§

When you think of him now, as you often do, when his image comes to mind, it's always with his biography in numerals: 1903-40. In that Adirondack summer, though, he had nine more years to go; in that summer, he was still alive.

§

In one of the Viele Pond photographs, he's bare to the waist and wearing gym pants secured either by a necktie or a length of rope. Reposeful, he's standing against a porch-post, tall, lean, and unmuscular, a dangle of legs and arms, a loose and rhythmless man. How harmless he looks, faded by time and still! You know better, though. Something had been left out of him, or something extra put in; he had a function too many or one too few, and as if wires were crossed in his brain, he responded wrongly, answered bells that hadn't been rung; he was impeded by his feet and betrayed by his hands; he misjudged speeds and distances, and in passing through a doorway, he'd collide with the jamb. In motion, he was like a complex and amateurish invention, lurching, sidelong sometimes, and always about to explode.

§

During your first week at the Pond, Harry Reoux donated some equipment and sent it up by truck: a little flat-bottomed rowboat, a double-barreled 12-gauge shotgun, and several boxes of shells. After the boat had been put into the water, Pep loaded the gun and then poised himself, waiting for an imaginary bird-dog to find, and acting as if something had broken cover, he swung quickly and fired twice.

"Got one with each barrel," he said, and, pleased with his shooting, he propped the gun against a tree; it slipped and fell to the ground.
"One of these days," you said, "you'll blow your ass off."
"Or yours," he said.

§

A few years earlier, at a boys' camp on Paradox Lake, Nat West — or Nat Weinstein, as he then was — had begun to fancy himself as the heir of Leatherstocking, as another Natty Bumppo to the life. In truth, however, he was not at all like that bold and neat-fingered pioneer, for it taxed his powers to cut a slice of bread. Deft with words, he was inept at everything else. The entire world of objects opposed him, but those composed of two or more parts seemed to conspire to bring him down. A razor, a telephone, a pair of scissors — such things were in a fell scheme to make him fail. Unlike his exemplar, the Deerslayer, he could do little with his hands and nothing whatever without trembling: poor Natty Weinstein, he couldn't even build a fire. He'd bunch paper lightly, delicately (*you don't crush it, Scotty; you leave it filled with pockets of air*), and then he'd carefully crisscross it with kindling (*you don't just stuff it in; you place it, so,* and finally he'd touch off the little

112

pyre at all four corners—and it'd blaze brightly for a moment and go out.

And you'd say, "I get the idea."

§

You were there to write, both of you, and write you did, but you found at once that there was no unbroken road to that end. No Grandma Nevins would turn up at the Pond, no Anna Weinstein, no little mick housekeeper like Ellen Lang. No one would redd up the cabin, no one wash a dish or make a bed, and what you threw aside would lie where it fell until it got in your way: you'd have to do for yourselves what others had done for you—put in order what you'd put in disarray.

You remembered wash-days at your grandma's, with Ellen churning up steam from a huge tin boiler on the stove, you remembered the smell of kitchen soap and the stunning blue of bluing. There at the Pond, you did your own laundry or you wore your own dirt; and no grandma, no Anna, no Ellen brought hot food and took cold orts away. There was garbage to dispose of, not in a pail that went down a dumbwaiter and somehow came back emptied; you buried it in a hole you dug at the edge of the forest, and at night a raccoon or a bear would come to root up the cardboard containers and play sharps and flats on the tins and jars.

You ate, of course, but you still wonder what. You shot red and gray squirrels and prepared them—adroitly, as you thought—à la Nessmuk or Kephart, and you caught bullheads in the Pond and bass in the Hudson, and Pep brought down a partridge that died a bad second death in the pan—fried partridge! But not by fish alone could you have lived, nor by the bird *Perdix* or rodent game. What of the fruits and grains and roots of the earth, what of the egg, the nut, the curd, what of the sweet and the herb? Of course you ate—how could you not have eaten? But *what,* when all you remember is the coffee you made three times a day and the cakes that were baked by Fannie Bennett?

§

Along with the rowboat, Harry Reoux had sent a note saying that in addition to bullheads, there were game-fish in the Pond, and he told you where to find them. In two or three places, he wrote, there were flues of cold water rising from springs, and there only would the brook trout strike, half-pounders with olive backs and speckled sides. That afternoon, the two of you set out in the rowboat and located two of the springs by lining yourselves up as directed

113

with certain trees along the shore. From the dazzling lures in your hatbands, each of you drew his preferred cluster of fluff and feather, and happily you fell to whipping the water all about you. Alas, your midges, moths, and nymphs attracted only bullheads, and soon you merely sat there trying to shake them off.

"Pep," you said, as one whose opinion could be taken on faith, "there are no trout in this pond."

"You know why?" he said, as one who relied on reason. "Because the bullheads feed on their fingerlings."

Harry Reoux came up from Warrensburg the next day and took six trout in half an hour—olive-backed with speckled sides.

§

Just as Robert Cohn had read *The Purple Land* too late in life, so, perhaps, had Pep read *Huckleberry Finn*: he proposed the construction of a raft. In the woods near the cabin, he'd found the mossed-over ruins of a barn, and he planned to use its boards and timbers to achieve his aim. You were invited to help, and for some days you both worked hard and long—*schwer und bitter,* your father would say—on the Mississippi Scheme. When finished the raft was towed to the middle of the pond and anchored, but it would never support both of you at once, and even one would set it awash.

§

It was a habit of Pep's to stand with one foot cocked, like a horse.

§

Pep shot a sharp-shin, a small square-tailed hawk with a chest crossbarred in rust and white. He wanted to have it mounted, and you drove him to the nearest taxidermist, thirty miles away in Chestertown. One week later, you drove him there again to pick up the trophy. Sad to say, it called up no fancy of its life in the wild—it was merely a feathered carcass stuffed with kapok. Perched on a varnished branch, it glared through glass eyes with glassy ferocity.

Pep said, "It looks dead, God damn it!" and thereafter he'd have nothing to do with it.

You kept it in one place or another for many years, and finally you realized that you'd lost track of it.

§

A two-day rain made the road to Warrensburg impassable, and during that period both of you ran out of cigarettes. They were so essential then that you smoked dinches retrieved from the ashtrays, but when these too were gone, you were cabined six miles from the village and yearning for the lovely weed—and it was still raining.

"How'd we get into a fix like this?" Pep said. "I'm going crazy."
"I've looked everywhere," you said. "Even in the garbage."
"Scotty, we're out of shag."
"What about that safari-bag? Did you climb in and search there?"
"There," he said, "and under my bed, and in the toes of my city shoes."
Continuing the hunt, he lurched away into the kitchen. A hunch impelled you to his room, and in the breast-pocket of his three-piece suit, you struck gold—an unopened pack of cigarettes.
You called out to him through his doorway. "Hey, Natty Bumppo. . . !" you said.

§

He was one of those who woke slowly, and for a long while after rising, he'd remain in a state very much like a stupor. To surface, he'd fill a basin with cold water and sink his face in it until he ran out of breath. He'd repeat the treatment once or twice, and finally he'd be satisfied that he was wide awake. Actually, he kept on stumbling around for another hour.

§

He did almost no driving. You'd give him the wheel only on the state pike; over the hill-and-dale between the Pond and Warrensburg, and on all your expeditions for bass and pickerel, he always sat on your right. His hands and feet were not to be trusted to respond to his brain: he'd think right and turn left; he'd signal for the brake and tread on the gas. For him, all things mechanical were ungovernable, for he himself was beyond his control. Watching him on the rare occasion when you let him drive, you realized that he wasn't steering or shifting gears—he was holding on, he was trying to stay aboard a monster that meant to buck him off. You always wondered what dodge he'd used to obtain a license. Had it been denied him, he'd not have been at those crossroads that day, he'd not have been precisely there three thousand miles away. . . .

§

"Scotty," he said, "did I ever tell you about a meal I had in a Providence restaurant? I ordered a dish I'd never had before—roast raccoon. It was good, once I got the fur off."

§

He invariably pronounced the word *miss-hapen.*

§

He liked to kid you; he did not like to be kidded.

§

He may have brought several books with him from New York, but the only one you recall is Fowler's *Modern English Usage.* He'd spoken of the work before, but you saw it for the first time at the Pond, and all in a moment you were lost. At night, you'd read it in bed, skipping from one attractive heading to another (Wardour Street, Worn-out humour, Twopence coloured, Cast-iron idiom), but finally you settled down to reading it alphabetically, from *a, an* to *z, zz.* What did you not pore over by the light of your kerosene lamp? Avoidance of the obvious, Battered ornaments, Elegant variation, Pride of knowledge, The split infinitive—and, *mirabile dictu!* you found a split in the text.

You broke in on Pep to tell him of your discovery. "I was just breezing through Fowler," you said, "and, *mirabile dictu!* I spotted a split infinitive." "*Mirabile* has four syllables, Scotty."
It would've been a good time to tell him that he'd misspelled Apollonius, but you had yet to learn that yourself. "Fowler split an infinitive, I said." "You're pulling my leg."
You showed him a page. "There she is—'to wrongly give.' "
"How are the mighty fallen! Scotty, you've got to do something about that." "What?"

"At the very least, you must write to the man and point out his error. You have no choice. You owe it to future generations."

You fell for it. In care of his publisher, the Oxford University Press, you addressed a letter to H. W. Fowler, Esq., and to the joint author of *The King's English*, *The Concise Oxford Dictionary*, and *The Pocket Oxford Dictionary*, you cited his violation of the grammatical code. In Warrensburg some weeks later, the postmaster handed you a letter cancelled in Somersetshire. You took it out to the car and read it to Pep:

To wrongly give

Dear Sir
   The splitting of the infinitive was undoubtedly either deliberate or what is better — unconscious but instinctively right. I have no respect whatever for the prohibition when there is anything to be gained by disregarding it; & here it is clearly important that the two contrasted phrases — 'wrongly give' & 'wrongly fail to give' — should be made noticeably parallel by both having 'wrongly' immediately before the verb.

Yours truly
H. W. Fowler

Pep laughed. In some ways you were simple.

§

You remember an afternoon when you fared as far as Brant Lake to try for pickerel. Pep soon took two, each of them a good sixteen inches, but in an hour at the work, you had no luck at all, not even a strike; your spinners simply splashed and sank. Putting your rod aside, you lazed against a tree-trunk and lit a cigarette, and through its blue-gray smoke, you watched Natty Bumppo lay his lures before the reeds. For some reason — the smoke, it may have been — the deerflies did not disturb you, but around Pep, they were like smoke themselves, a swarm that dinged the air. Using one hand to cast with and the other to slap at the flies, he endured the torment until, bitten times without number, his face and all its features began to swell. His brow bulged, his lips thickened, his eyelids expanded and very nearly closed. His swollen head made his hat seem smaller, as if it belonged to a child, and finally (thinking of H. W. Fowler, Esq.?) you laughed.

He turned on you, flinging down his rod and saying, "What the hell's so funny, Scotty?"

It was Fannie Bennett who told you what to do to draw the poison. She gave you a large box of bicarbonate of soda, and when you reached the cabin, you made a thick paste and plastered Pep with it wherever he'd been bitten. It had a cooling and astringent property, and after several slatherings, the swelling subsided.

"Why the hell did you laugh?" Pep said.
"It was the hat," you said, but it might've been Fowler.

§

Lying before you now, wrapped in its green and yellow dust-jacket, is a copy of your first novel. Opening it to the front flap, you read:

> *The Water Wheel* recounts both the real and imagined-real adventures of one John B. Sanford in New York and London over a short period in 1927. The novel is completely dominated by Sanford, a self-assumed individualist—and self-styled "*law-clerk, sinner, ex-convict, adolescent, grandson and legatee of a Litvak matchvendor.*"

Facing that plaster wall at Viele Pond, you were still living in 1927, still in the midst of those adventures real and imaginary, still without the printed words. John B. Sanford was only a name in an incomplete manuscript. He'd trifled with his girls, L. and Olga, he'd railed at the world, he'd voyaged to nowhere and voyaged back, and there he was, waiting to be moved to a further page, another stage. Sounds came through the wall, but they were made by a different book.

§

You wrote to your father more than once during your stay at the Pond, but he did not answer.

§

After supper one evening, you and Pep were sitting alongside the stove, warming your moccasins on the shelf below the grate. Behind its mica eyes, you watched flames pleading, and your mind was somewhere else when Pep spoke.

118

"How's the book coming, Scotty?"

"The book," you said, and coming back from wherever you'd been, you realized that he meant *The Water Wheel*; it was the first time he'd shown an interest in it. "I've got about three hundred pages of manuscript, but I have no ending. I know what I want to do, but I don't know how to get there."

"You mind if I read it?"

"Why would I mind?"

In the morning, he returned the manuscript with only one comment: you'd so written, he said, that it was possible for a reader to identify one of the two girls you'd been close to. By any canon, he said, that was impermissible.

"It simply isn't done," he said.

§

Several times while in Warrensburg, you'd seen an autobus marked, within a ring of pines, *Green Mansions: an adult camp for moderns.** You were told that it was on a lake some miles north of the village and that it drew its clientele from city and suburban areas all over the state.

"An adultery camp," Pep said one evening. "Let's drive over and watch the Yiddische cowboys and their *schönes* from the Gilded Ghetto."

On the way later, you said, "I'm afraid some of your best friends are Christians."

"What's that supposed to mean?"

"You don't care much for the Jews."

"I'm a Jew myself!"

"That's what the guide says in *Balso*."

"He was speaking as a character, not as the author."

"In your mind, maybe. But a character can only come up with the author's ideas — and prejudices. Take Balso. He coins names he thinks are funny, Hernia Hornstein, Paresis Pearlberg — Jewish names. But it's really the author who thinks they're funny: Nathanael von Wallenstein Weinstein."

"If you don't think a character can be independent of an author, you don't know how to read."

"Melville is Ahab."

"According to you, he's also Moby Dick."

"Right, and he's Queequeg and Starbuck too."

"Let's get out of the Indian Ocean and into the Red Sea."

"Answer me something," you said. "If you'd been born in Louisburg Square, would it have been funny to write Hernia Hawthorne and Paresis Pickering?"

---

*Called Thoreau's Walden in *Adirondack Stories*, 1977.

In the cold mountain night, dew dripped from the trees and smashed on the windshield, and the road ahead glistened in the long light thrown by the lamps.

"If you're going to be literal," Pep said, "of course whatever's on the page came out of the author's arm. But no good writer is limited to one way of thinking, one way of seeing, and the better he is, the more ways he shows you. Joyce shows you Dedalus, no great trick, because he *is* Dedalus. But he shows you Bloom and Molly too, and he's neither, and through his imagination, they tell him what to do."

Green Mansions, you later wrote,* was "seven miles north of Warrensburg. Over the driveway leading into the grounds, a large signboard bore the same garland of pines that decorated the autobus. After twisting through the woods for about a mile from the turnpike, the side road ended in a circular enclosure where many cars were parked. When Mordecai** stopped his motor, he heard the tinsound of distant music coming faintly through the trees. The joints of a spine of light jiggled on the surface of a lake that bordered part of the enclosure. Tracing the music, Mordecai followed a footpath along the lakefront.

"The music had stopped by the time he reached the dancehall, and a crowd of men and girls were standing in the doorway. They surrounded him with their bodies, and with the odor of face powder and alcohol. When the music began again, he entered the building and took a stand near the rim of the dancefloor, watching couples bob around in front of him like the wooden animals of a carousel. Dozens of girls skated by in voluminous silk pajamas of green, yellow, pink, baby-blue, under the slatting sleeves of which moist halfmoons now and then appeared. The men, too, were dressed in what seemed to be a regulation uniform—moccasins, bright woolen socks, corduroy pants, and lumberjack shirts. Many of them carried nickel flash-lights in their hip pockets."

You and Pep did very much what Mordecai did. You watched others dance until you found partners for yourselves, and then after a turn or two of the floor, you wandered off over the grounds, lost to each other in the fragrance of the pine-tree dark.

"On the way to the boathouse," you wrote, "Rose stopped at her cabin for a coat. The outside of the cabin was covered with slabs of untrimmed birch from which, here and there, postcards of bark had been peeled. When the girl turned on the electric light, Mordecai saw that the inner walls of

---

*In "The King of the Minnies," one of the *Adirondack Stories.*
**The story's central character.

120

the cabin were decorated with a green and blue design representing pine trees silhouetted against an evening sky. He was surrounded by sunsets. On one wall of the square room, four suns were disappearing behind a stencilled ridge; on another, they were going down behind a washstand and a three-quarter bed with a box spring."

Later, when you were driving back to the Pond, Pep said, "Well, Scotty, how was *your* little *Madel*?"
And you said, "Oddly enough, she wasn't Jewish."

§

Both of you were serious about yourselves, and each of you pretended to hold the other lightly. A good deal of nettling talk passed between you: there were small displays of special knowledge, there were utterances in italics (do you get it?), and even compliments seemed to leave a sting. You'd sometimes wonder why that was so, and gradually it grew on you that you were vying with him, that despite the little you knew, you were trying to appear as wise — as *next* — as he. One day, please God, maybe he'd vie with you.

§

Among the magazines the shelves were stocked with was *Smart Set*, an almost complete file from 1907 through 1909. You'd never before seen a number of the old publication, but you were familiar with its name, which was much in use in your mother's day. Turning some pages idly one night, you soon found that you were idle no more; you were glimpsing her again as if she were alive. Here were the styles of her time, here the cars she'd ridden in, the soaps she'd used, the stays she'd worn and her shoes; here were the candies and perfumes of 1907, the wines and revues of 1909. It was she you saw in all the pen-and-inks, and hers were the eyes above a fan. That was her face, her figure, her thigh . . . and you caught yourself staring at a leg emerging from a carnation of skirts, at a slippered foot perched upon a chair, at an arc of words that read *Removes Excess Hair Without Undue Stench*.* You shivered, as if you'd dropped her picture and broken the glass.

---

*Related by West to S. J. Perelman, who used it in a scenario-sequence for *Contact* magazine, Vol. 1, No. 3.

"You cold, Scotty?" Pep said.

"No," you said. "I just came across this."

He took the magazine from you and read the caption for the depilatory. "That's rich," he said. "Without undue stench!"

It took a little while for the shivering to stop.

§

Among the photographs taken at the Pond, there are several of your sister Ruth. In two of these, she's high-heeled, and, dressed as for the city, she wears a band of pearls. In another, she's seated on a tree-stump alongside the propped-up Winchester and the Harry Reoux shotgun, and in the fourth, she holds a half-grown cat.* *Ruthele,* Pep liked to call her, and gazing at her grave face, you try to remember how she'd come to be there. Was she on her way to somewhere else, or, without a destination, was she merely on the roam? But it won't come back, and she sits, stands, leans against the guns, displays her pearls and a cat.

§

Along with an assortment of trout-flies, each of you wore in your hatband a tail-feather from Pep's partridge. It was too late to take the hats off when a car with New York State insignia drew up while you were firing the Winchester at targets across the road. Two game-wardens stepped out and gave themselves names—Lemmon and Robbins.

It was Robbins who spoke first, saying, "Harry Reoux said to look in on you."

And Lemmon said, "To find out if you saw or heard any goings-on in the woods."

"Not a thing," one of you said, and "All quiet," the other.

"What do you people do?" Lemmon said.

"We're writers," you said.

"I mean when you aren't writing."

"We fish, mostly," Pep said. "Or like now, shoot at the little rings."

You noticed that neither of the wardens seemed to look you in the eye; their sights were set higher.

Finally Robbins indicated Pep's hat, saying, "Except I miss my guess, that thing next to the partridge feather is a Silver Doctor."

Pep removed the hat to examine the fly. "Gray Hackle," he said.

---

*The cat of "Jasper Darby's Passion," *Pagany,* Spring 1932.

Then all of you fell to talking about—what? what did you talk about?—and when you admired the side-arms they carried, .38 Colts—they let you fire some rounds at an old stove-lid, at tin cans, at the knots in a plank, and after a time they drove away.

§

In a letter from London dated 18 September 1958, you'd write:*

. . . There were other afternoon occupations, and one of these was shooting off that Winchester .22. God knows how many rounds we fired at paper targets, but there was a tree about fifty feet from the cabin porch that we damn near cut in two with lead. I'd never handled a rifle before, and I never was sure that West had either, though he was full of pointers and carried himself with what he thought was a knowing air. In any event, as far as marksmanship went, we stood each other off—I was as good as he was, or he was as lousy as I—but in the matter of handling the weapon, I have to say that there was no more dangerous man to be in the woods with than Pep West. It wasn't that he didn't know guns were meant for killing. It was that he was too bloody fumble-fingered to put the knowledge to use. He was not only capable of handing you a piece with the hammer cocked; he was also capable of nudging you with the barrel. He did that to me once with a loaded shotgun. I'd been carrying the rifle for a while and West the double-barrel, and finally he called for a switch. When I failed to respond, I felt a poke in the back, and I turned, thinking he'd touched me with his hand. Instead, it was the shotgun muzzle. That was bad enough, but the safety was off. . . .

§

"What kind of publicity is *Balso* getting?" you said.

"Damn little and mostly bad," he said. "The Liebling piece and a few other mentions—but you know about those."

"Maybe I can get you something better."

"You? Where?"

"In *The New Review,* Sam Putnam's thing in Paris."

"What makes you think he'd spread himself for me?"

"Listen, you sorry old cock. Don't you even want me to try?"

"Try," he said.

---

*To James Light, a West biographer.

In a letter* from Warrensburg dated August 9th, 1931, you wrote:

To the Editors,
The New Review,
Paris—

A few months ago, Contact Editions published *The Dream Life of Balso Snell*, a first novel by Nathanael West. Since its appearance, Ive read several notices and reviews of it in the New York press; the hacks have generally misunderstood it, or made statements about it that usually swamp a book out of circulation. If it came to the attention of those who know more about a book than its price, I think it would be very much liked. This is the story of the novel:

Balso Snell, *a lyric poet by trade*, while wandering in the tall grass outside the ancient city of Troy, discovers and enters the wooden horse of the Greeks. Inside, he has a series of adventures.

(here an account of those adventures)

One of the reasons why the hiredmen, or the tiredmen, have failed to understand is because West used parts of the book to fling handfuls of dung in their faces. That may have been an error on Wests part, not because the critics didn't deserve it, but because the stuff probably got in their eyes. Mr. Pound recently wote in one of your issues that Mr. Joyce had complained that no reviewer had ever said he enjoyed *Ulysses*. Well, the sames true here. Wests book is at least funny, but no one has written about that. Its a good sort of literary fooling, a nonsense both above and below what the critics sweat for, what they go after with tongues hanging out, *solutions and answers; ah, saviour, you've given me the why of it at last.* This book doesn't try to explain anything: all the way its fooling and funny, but with plenty under the nonsense to offend those who always have *the high seriousness.* Sometimes the book gets hard and what the critics call *daring,* and whenever that happens they remember the bum novels theyve got stuffed away in their trunks, the rejection-slips and the earnest advice to try another profession. Then they rear up hollering about *young* and about *the lad will grow up.* Theyd say that about satire even if they knew the man who wrote it was a hundred and four. For them, *The Dream Life* isnt a needle: its a club. Its funny to hear the hired-tiredmen say *fine talent but perverted.* Let us pray for them in the words of Balso Snell:

---

*Printed in the Winter issue, Vol. 1, No. 4

O Beer! O Meyerbeer! O Bach! O Offenbach! Stand me now as ever in good stead.

Cordially yours,
Julian L. Shapiro

§

"Thanks, Scotty," Pep said.

§

Lying before you is an envelope of the Western Union Telegraph Co. It is addressed to N. West, Box 15, Warrensburg, N.Y., and it bears a Lake George cancellation for Aug. 30, 1931. The envelope contains a picture postcard written to West from somewhere in Canada by William Carlos Williams, and it reads:

> We started out to see you that Sunday but the rain was so heavy that we gave it up and came on through. This trip along the north shore of the St. Lawrence has been great.
> Yours. Williams.

You try to recall how the card came to your hands and why it was never shown to West.

§

Day after day, on went the writing on both sides of the wall. Where you were, the pages grew, grew, and presently, on the table before you, a pile of paper held the ending that had so long refused to form for you. And as you stared at your completed novel, once more that trial-by-recitation began in the room next door. For West, it wasn't enough to see the words; he also had to hear them. In sight and sound, he found their truth. And as you thought of the ordeal *Miss Lonelyhearts* was enduring, your mind came back to *The Water Wheel,* and taking up the last of what you'd written, you spoke it aloud—and then you too were hearing *you.*

It was a test you did not let yourself pass, and straightway fifty sheets of paper went with you to the kitchen stove, and there they fed the fire. You still had no ending, you thought; no water turned the wheel.

§

Beside the kitchen doorway, above a towel-rack, hung the shaving mirror used by Pep and you, and one morning, as you were about to lather your face, you noticed what seemed to be a rash near a corner of your mouth. Ivy, you thought, or sumac, and you put the razor away lest you break the vesicles and spread their serum. By the following day, though, you saw that what had seemed to be a rash was several separate eruptions, each of them red, raw, and beginning to suppurate. What the hell did you have? you wondered. You'd never seen anything like the outbreak—and suddenly your mind spoke *never seen* again, as if someone else were in your head. You'd *seen!* you thought, you'd *seen!* Two memories rushed at you—the booklet sent by your Uncle Dave and the singer in Paris—and crushing you between them, they came together in a silent crash.

"What've you got there, *mon brave?*" Pep said. "The blue tattoo of love?"
"Damned if I know," you said.
He named de Maupassant, Tchaikovsky, and Gauguin, saying, "They'd be able to tell you."
On the way to Warrensburg, he added Stendhal and Flaubert, and after a brief period of thought, Nietzsche and Strindberg.

At the office of a Dr. J. E. Cunningham, a sample of your blood was taken, and you were told to return in several days for a report. Of a low week, you remember only the lowest point:

"What'll you do if it's the pox, Scotty?" Pep said. "Shoot yourself?"

At the time appointed, you presented yourself to Dr. Cunningham, who handed you a printed form with the blanks properly filled in:

Division of Laboratories and Research
New York State Department of Health
New Scotland Avenue, Albany

Lab. No. *37726*   Date *Aug. 18, 1931*
In the examination of the specimen from
Name *Julian Shapiro*
Address *P.O.Box 15 Warrensburg*
Date taken *Not given*
Rec'd. *Aug. 14, 1931*
Dr. *J. E. Cunningham*
Warrensburg, N.Y.

No complement fixation was obtained with either of the
antigens used in the complement-fixation test for syphilis.
Augustus B. Wadsworth, M.D.
Director

"Probably just the barber's itch," Cunningham said.

On the way back to the Pond, you crossed the Schroon and climbed Harrington Hill, and you were long past Fannie Bennett's when Pep said, "Were you scared, Scotty?"

"Pissless," you said. "How about you?"

"Me? What did I have to be scared of?"

"Well, *mon copain,* if I'd turned up with a chancre, so would you. We were both using the same towel."

It was late in the afternoon now, and through the trees, the sun came straight at you, spraying the road with light. Suddenly you stopped the car, and making a sweep with your hand in mock declamation, you said, "Out of this nettle, danger . . . !"

"To coin a phrase," Pep said.

"Out of this nettle, I pluck a flower! Pep, old father, old artificer, I now have my ending!"

You started to write it the next morning. You didn't have to read it aloud, and when you finished it, you didn't have to throw it away.*

§

And the day came, finally, when your stay at the Pond was over, and you drove away. Neither you nor Pep had anything to say as you went slowly along the bank, passed the open water and the ring of reeds, and then paused for a last look at the cabin before leaving it behind you in the woods. It had been a fine summer, you thought, and you knew, as you know yet, that it was one you'd forget never.

§

Before you now the rifle-case and the Winchester .22, and as you gaze at the canvas, the wood, the gun-metal, you wonder whether Pep ever wandered his mind back to that summer, whether in his nine more years he remembered the little green Hudson River bass, the Brant Lake pickerel, the partridge

---

*It became Part VII of *The Water Wheel.*

feathers, the nights you blew smoke at the kitchen fire and talked of all things imaginable except a certain crossroads a few miles out of El Centro.

A roll or two of photographs, the Kephart book, and a Winchester .22—they're all that remains of a summer in the woods.

THE COLOR OF THE AIR, VI

GEORGE WASHINGTON—1793

A CONSTITUTIONAL IN PHILADELPHIA

> *In speaking to men of Quality do not lean or Look them full in the Face, Nor approach too near them.*
> Washington, *Rules of Civility*

To see him in those days, you didn't have to climb a tree or pry apart a crowd; you'd simply laze around at Front and High, and come noon (he was the punctual kind), he'd show up to regulate his watch at Clark's standard, after which he'd nod, once up and once down, and walk his presence away. He liked the sun, they say, and when out for air, he'd keep to the warmer side of the road, making the pace for that tag-along pair—a bodyguard, one was, and the other Mr. Lear, an all-purpose sort, clerk, candleholder, sander of signatures, purse-string, less than kin and more than minion.

They stayed a step or two behind their man, and they'd do nothing if you overtook him or, having gone on by, stopped to scan his lines: you were free to look, every day if you liked and twice on the 4th of July. He'd raise his hat now and then, to a face he knew, to a cap or ribbons in some upper window, and even, if you behaved, to you, but try to shake his hand, and you'd be there yet, a block of ice somewhere on High: he could stare you stiff without opening his eyes. The lurchers of this world—he knew how to deal with that stripe. Martha called him *Pappa* (good God, what if someone heard!), but to the populace he was *General*, and you bowed when occasion allowed you the use of the word.

It wasn't the worst, it was two of the best that he couldn't curb— the first was that West Indian bastard, that pack-saddle child, a hard-headed little beggar, a flint, and the second, and direr, that turncoat squire, a sage, an *illuminé*, a sniffer of books. They'd craze him with that feud of theirs, they'd put him in his grave! He'd listen while each attacked the other (how much could he bear!), and he'd read the vile gazettes they backed (a scandal, those scurrile rags!), and late or soon, in trying to divide his favor, he'd tear himself in half.

And so out along High he'd go, drawn by his mind toward the Schuylkill and the Forge. It was fifteen years back, that bad winter, but the cold was stunning still, the hunger untold, the chances of winning nil. All the same, they *had* won, and now what! The gentlemen crying up the myriads, and the upstart the few! A landed lord, Jefferson, a phrasewright, a violinist, a skirtraiser debonair, a Mister, he'd been born to be, and a Jacobin he ended, a votary of faction, *egalité,* and the guillotine, an overturner, renegade and odious, an incendiary puck. And against him the foreign-born Hamilton, bred in any kind of bed, a clever one with a cool and ready tongue, more genteel than gentle, an untarred Tory, kiss-ass of Kings and puller of strings for the rich. They'd be his death, that yoke of opposites!

You didn't have to smell or spy him out. Almost on the dot of twelve, he'd come along High, and at Clark's standard, he'd take out his watch and wind it. He wasn't hard to find. You only had to wait. . . .

SCENE 24

LONG VIEW (Fall of 1931)

Near the parlor window of the apartment on the Drive, two armchairs were so placed that from either one, the park and the river could be seen, and beyond them the Palisades and the Jersey sky. Even when the sash was raised, as now, only the sound of tire-treads reached the room, and the deep-down cough of a distant train. In the last light of a warm day, you and your father sat watching smoke from a cigar and a cigarette join a current of air and drift out into the evening.

"I suppose I ought to ask whether you had a good time up there," he said. "But if you didn't at twenty-seven, you never will."

"You were twenty-seven once," you said. "What kind of time did you have?"

"At twenty-seven, I had a year-old son."

"That doesn't quite answer the question."

"Walking the floor with you was a good time."

"I wonder how I'd feel."

"Tell me," he said. "What does Max Weinstein say about Pep and his writing?"

"When I'm around, nothing. But Mrs. Weinstein goes on sometimes, and it makes Pep sore. She thinks he ought to quit *the nonsense,* as she calls it. Do you think *I* ought to quit the nonsense?"

"*Is* it nonsense?" he said.

"Not to me."

"What would it take to make you give it up?"

You flicked your cigarette through the window and saw it break into sparks on the sidewalk. "An order from you," you said.

"You'd do that if I told you to?"

"I would," you said, and then you added, "I think I would."

"Well, I don't give orders, kid."

"Why not? You're the boss."

"Nothing good would come of it."

"I'd never hate you, no matter what you made me do."

"You say that now," he said. "But you're only twenty-seven."

SCENE 25

THE SONS OF PHIL AND MAX (September 1931)

Alongside the wall and its sloping copestone, you walked through the autumn evening down Central Park West. In green and cream enamel, streetcars came and went, and in colors of their own, a varied traffic passed. Underground, a train reamed the gloom, and above you, stacked against the sky, bright and blind rooms both seemed to stare at the night, and before you, the shaft in Columbus Circle rose from a fountain of glare. Your destination was the Hotel Sutton, there to meet with Natty Bumppo, Leatherstocking no more now in his heather flannel or his olive gaberdine; in his quarters, you thought, no moths flew at the kerosene lamps, and in his twelfth-floor vista, no leaves shook, no water flashed.

And then you were there, and he said, "In all the time we were at the Pond, nothing ever went by at night. I never heard a wheel."

"I wish we'd stayed for the winter."

"We'd freeze our balls off," he said, and then he laughed. "I knew a girl in Paris, and one New Year's Eve, I sent her a cable, saying *Ring out, wild balls.* She wrote to tell me that as delivered, it read *Ring out, wild bells,* and that weeks later she received a correction notice: *For wild bells, read wild balls.*"

"The one about the roast raccoon is better," you said.

130

"Can you beat that? *For wild bells, read wild balls!*"

The tall-tale legend, you thought—he's living it while he's alive. "Let's go for a walk," you said.

§

You no longer recall where the walk led you—to the East River, it may have been, or the other way, to Grand Army Plaza, but somewhere you told him of the talk with your father.

"What was his attitude about this writing business?" he said.

"He didn't say," you said.

"I hope you don't think he approves. Your Phil and my Max, they watch us as if we had a fever. They're waiting for it to break."

You thought of a night when the two of you were taking the air on the deck of a Fifth Avenue bus. It was headed down the Avenue and passing Union Square when something made you speak of the day you'd met on the golf course.

"That was my birthday," you'd said.

And he'd jumped up, saying, "Jesus Christ, Scotty!" and then he'd stumbled down the circular staircase and leaped from the bus.

You were nearing the Sutton again, and you wanted to speak of the love you felt for your father, as he felt for Max, but you thought that if you did, he'd quit you in the street, flee as from some offense to a sensibility—a crude remark, a loud tone, an accent that might draw a non-Jew's attention.

To hell with his delicacies, you thought, and you said, "I love my father," and he turned toward the hotel entrance. "Stay you! This is about the two of us. What we're doing—this writing business—hurts a couple of people we happen to love. We're putting ourselves ahead of our fathers."

"All sons do that," he said. "The world faces forward. Life is lineal."

"One look back, and we fuck up the parade—is that it?"

"The way of man is hard," he said, and he made a slow semi-circular gesture that took in the way of man. "It's all a horny dilemma."

"You know something, Pep? You're funny as a bird shot in the ass."

He indicated the Sutton doorway. "Come on up, Scotty."

You followed him past potted palms and rubber plants, a dark diningroom, a reception desk, and a door with lettering on a metal plate: Mr. West, Mgr. In his rooms, he stood at one of the windows looking out at a punchboard building under a punctured sky.

"You know what all that is out there?" you said. "The Black Hole of Cal Coolidge."*

"That's not bad," Pep said.

"It came out of nowhere."

He moved to another window, and he too stood looking out at the night for a moment, and then he said, "How'd you like to live here at the hotel, Scotty? Rent-free, I mean. . . ."

SCENE 26

APT. C-6, 131 WASHINGTON STREET (Fall of 1931)

You'd written to L. G. from wherever you happened to be in Europe—Paris, Menton, Madrid, Pisa—and to three of your letters she'd replied. Since your return, though, you hadn't seen her until, on a late-September afternoon, you drove to Hartford and drew up at the address she'd inscribed on the flaps of three envelopes. In grayed ink, three times you may read her street and number, but you have no recollection now of the building—was it stone or frame?—and nothing reminds you of the weather, the time, the day of the week. You have a sense of space roundabout you, and you seem to see trees and shrubs and part of a lawn.

Not having been told of your coming, she was not at home when you arrived, and you waited for her in the car, watching for a sight of the gift you'd been offered nearly five years before. Were you there to accept it then? you wondered, and was it still to be had if you held out your hand? When you caught sight of her, she was some way off and moving toward your through scrims of sun and shade, the *sol y sombra* of the paved street—or was it an unpaved road? When she saw you, she neither paused nor hastened; she merely walked at the same pace until she reached your car. How did she greet you, how did you greet her, and what did she say and you reply? Did she permit a kiss or avoid your touch? Did she invite you in from the street or the dust of the road, or did she assume that you'd follow when she turned away? And when she came to a door marked C-6, did you say

"So this is where my letters went from Nîmes and Toledo and the Alpes Maritimes."

---

*Related to Jay Martin, who used it as a chapter heading in his biography of West, 1970.

Once inside, she cast off her hat and shoes and let herself fall into a chair, saying, "Would you like to see those letters, Jule? Would you care to reread your billets-doux from Nîmes and Rome? Or did you keep copies, do you know them by heart?"

"The carbons are in my mind."

"Pretty," she said. "You know what you wrote, then, from Padua, Venezia?"

"I know what I said, and I meant it."

She laughed. "Meant it in Tuscany, but not in Savoy—is that it, Jule?"

"You talk as if I left you at the altar," you said. "It was you who refused me, not I you."

"Jule, my ardent lover, you can't know this, but your proposal was delayed. It came by the same ship as your withdrawal. I read them in the proper order, of course, the first filling me with gladness, the second with—as your people say—cold noodles."

"My people say *kalte farfel,* but don't give me that stuff about *my people.* You don't hate my people."

"I ought to," she said. "One of them tried to give me away, and another looked in my mouth."

"I sent that second letter because I needed time to be sure I meant the first. What was wrong with that? You didn't know your mind, either."

"Will you ever know your mind, Jule?"

"Some day, maybe."

"You didn't know it the first time I met you. You didn't know it through two runaways to Europe. And you don't know it yet. You have a profession that you don't practice, and you chase after girls and then shy away. What are you after, for God's sake, or what's after you?"

The room was nearly in darkness, and it hid the things you hadn't seen, the pictures and books, if they were there, the carpeting, the furniture, all but that chair at the window, and you said, "I'll go, if that's what you want."

But she said, "No," and she said, "No, Jule."

SCENE 27

A HOTEL OF CHARM AND REFINEMENT (Fall of 1931)

Its advertising described it as being *in the fashionable Sutton Place district,* and for its *tastefully furnished rooms,* the rates were given as $12 a week for a single and $22.50 for a suite. In fact, however, the nearest point of that fashionable district lay a thousand feet from the hotel, whose actual neighbors were two long rows of brownstone tenements. With its *meals at moderate prices* and its *free swimming pool,* the Sutton stood tall and incongruous, a flower among weeds. Approached from either end of the block, it seemed to suffer from the proximity of inferiors, even to fear it, as if the crowd were closing in and making breathing hard.

The rooms (a suite!) assigned to you confronted a sheer of russet brick, six stories of windows that framed the action of silent lives. During the many months that you faced them, you saw no sign of *charm and refinement,* but did it occur to you, you wonder, whether they found such things in you? Did you ever transpose yourself, did you ever try to see what was seen from the other side of the street, or was there always only the side you were on, with its *meals at moderate prices* and your *tastefully furnished* suite?

SCENE 28

HOMAGE TO A CALL-GIRL (Fall of 1931)

You can see her still, a small and rounded woman with terra cotta hair—like pottery, you thought—and with freckled skin in every shade from brown to red (*pointillé,* she might've been, as if painted by Seurat). Naked, as she often appeared before you, she made you think you were seeing her through a transparent garment, and therefore her curves and concaves seemed covered after all.

"Jesus Christ, Julian! Don't you know what she is?"

But you hadn't known, not till you were told. If, as said, she spread for all, why did *all* mean *all but you?* Why draw the line at juvenile Julian? Was there some quality of yours that put her off, or was the quality hers—were you the reason, or was the reason she? What stopped her? you wonder. Was it self-regard or (how impossible!) regard for you?

SCENE 29

THE OLD MAN'S PLACE (Fall of 1931)

The incident on which the novel is based was related to you during your stay at Viele Pond. You may have heard it from Harry Reoux, from Beakbane, or from the wardens Lemmon and Robbins, but whatever the source, the occurrence took place in the wild and wooded country west of Thurman and south of The Glen. The road leading into the region was poor and travelled only by the few who lived along its windings through timber and outcrop. One of these was a man named Walter Pell, who, after his son Trubee went to war, had clung to a played-out quarter-section, and he was there to welcome him on his return in 1919. With the boy, though, there were two ex-soldiers from his company, and it was then, you were told, that the trouble began. What followed was a season of wrongdoing that Warren County had never before known: it began with poaching and highway robbery, and it ended in rape and murder.

The story was given to you unadorned, almost in outline, as if in view of its enormities, descriptives hardly mattered. The naming of the Pells and no one else did not change the quality of the episode; it seemed rather to make the myth more universal, to invite its ascription to other locales. Of anyone anywhere, you thought, the same tale might be told. In its lack of detail, it recalled a picture-frame without a picture that had hung in a grade-school classroom (*It's for your own picture,* the teacher had said).

After returning to the city, you thought about the story often and everywhere, even in the midst of work on something else. You'd be rewriting *The Water Wheel,* turning your mind back to its time and place, to what you had said through its people and what they had endured for you—and suddenly you'd find that you'd strayed to a later time and a different place, to three ex-soldiers waging a war of their own in the Adirondack woods. You'd somewhere added names to go with Trubee Pell—Martin Flood and James Pilgrim—and somehow they'd come by faces, voices, histories, particularity, and then, quite unexpectedly, you began to see them in motion, and at last you knew you had a picture for your frame.

§

In the fall of that year, on the roof of the Hotel Sutton, you wrote the first version of *The Old Man's Place.* From there, a dozen floors up, you could see the tip of Manhattan far to the south, the bow of a ship two miles wide and fourteen long, and you'd let yourself suppose that the island was about to sail, was sailing now, moving down-bay toward the Narrows and the sea outside the Hook, a ship of stone on the way—to where? you'd wonder, and then you were back on a roof, twelve stories up from the street.

You met the woman because of the sun. It was using you as a burning glass, you fancied, and at the point of convergence you'd find its image, a small sun on the tar beyond you, or on the parapet. You turned, but it wasn't the sun that you found, concentrated on some bright button, some round of glass: it was the woman, and lying at her feet was a sheet of paper, one of your pages blown away. Picking it up, you read what you'd written of Harrington Hill—"It was very hot and still, and there was little wind on the east slope. The trees moved only in great sections, slowly, like animals breathing"—and when you looked up, the woman was watching you.

You sat down next to her, recalling the notion you'd had, of the island under way, the city in motion, and you thought of a voyage on a sea without a shore, an endless crossing of a boundless main. You glanced at the glare of paper you held in your hand, and you were about to read aloud from it—*it was very hot and still,* you thought, *and there was little wind*—but in the end you said nothing and waited for the voyage to begin.

It never began. In the time that followed, you saw her every day and night. You walked bright and dark streets with her, walked streets and parks in the rain. You spoke of things seen and things remembered, of books read and to be written, of the dead you'd loved and the living, of envies, resentments, desires, of yourself and other heroes, and she suffered your talk and listened, as if all you'd said were new. But she never let you touch her, and one day, when you tried to call her room, you learned that she was gone.*

§

At the hotel desk, the clerk refused to reveal her forwarding address, and when you pressed him, he referred you to the Manager.

You said, once you were in West's office, "Your clerk won't give out any information about Miss Paterson."

"I know," Pep said. "I told him not to."

"Why? What's the big idea?"

"Do you know what she is, Scotty?"

"She's my friend—that's what she is. I've been seeing her for weeks now, and all of a sudden—an empty room."

"I put her out."

"What!"

"Your friend Rosa Paterson is a call-girl. Anyone can have her for fifty bucks, and just about everyone has."

"How can that be? I've been with her every night."

"She works the graveyard shift—12 to 8."

You thought of your wanderings, your declamations in dark streets, your calling a call-girl your girl.

"Tell me," Pep said, "Did she sell you any?"

"No, or give it away—and that's why I don't believe what you say."

"A babe and a suckling," he said. "You'd believe it if you ever had the clap."

---

*From *To Feed Their Hopes,* 1980.

SCENE 30

ONCE AGAIN, THE WANDERING JEW (December 1931)

He'd write to you from wherever he lit, *der ewige Jude,* or from wherever he was going: always he'd be in some faraway place or heading for a further. *Now in Java,* he'd inform you, and soon he'd be in Sumatra. Singapore was hot, you'd hear, which would explain *Just leaving for Tangier.* On a postcard, he'd declare *Moscow is a revelation,* only to follow with views of the cherry trees in Idibiya Park and a veronica performed for a Mexican bull — and then he'd say *Am staying in Shanghai for a while,* but you'd know the stay would not be long.

He'd send you old lottery tickets, outlandish playing-cards, snapshots of shrines and sampans and naked natives and once a beheading in a Chinese street. And there'd be clippings with printed wisdom (*One horseshoe may bring you luck, but a load of horseshoes is junk* — Elbert Hubbard), and there'd be requisitions on his funds, which you handled, and there'd be orders to fill — for Blue Boar pipe tobacco, for I-O-Sil, his contra-venereal lavage. And endlessly you'd read his fumings against the running dogs of capitalism, against the lackeys and the lumpen — and against you for being unable to collect a bill from his debtor. *After reading your last letter,* he wrote, *I no longer wonder who put the phew in nephew. Don't tell me that I can kiss the money goodbye — do something about that lying s.o.b. If I were there, I'd settle his hash* — ah, but he wasn't there; he was in San Francisco and about to leave for somewhere else.

SCENE 31

THE LUCKLESS ONE (January 1932)

Her health beginning to fail, your Grandma Nevins had been invited to Long Island to reside with her daughter Ida. Before removing, though, she desired to see her misfortunate boy Romie for perhaps the last time, and you were chosen to escort her to where he was incarcerated, a state institution about a hundred miles from New York. Borrowing a car, you called for the old lady one winter morning and set out with her on the bitter-herb journey.

It was clear and cold, you remember; it had snowed a few days earlier, and though skiffs remained in the woods and fields, the road was dry all the way to Napanoch.

You hold a letter addressed to Sister Ruth:

> Dear Neice Ruthy;
> I hope you answer this letter as soon as possible, as I would like to hear from you.
> The last letter I received from you, was dated July 21st, 1931, in which you mentioned that you were smart, and were happy to hear from me, also you thought I had forgotten you, which is not so. I don't forget anyone in the family as long as I live. I have a very long memory, please remember it.
> Please send me a picture of your self, your father, and Julian.
> My dear please sens me 1 #61 Parker Pencil $10.00 and i box of hard leads 10 cents.
> Received a 42 single pages (typewritten on one side only, dated Paris) and entitled "A Journey Round The World," and the author is your Uncle Dave. It is very interesting, read every word of it, hope he sent you one. From what I read in it, he surly and truly is having a swell time.
> Now to let you know about my self, and to begin with will say that I feel well, still work at the old job, and hope to secure my freedom soon.
> My love, and regards to your Father and Julian.
> The Parker address is 149 Broadway N Y C
> > Your loving Uncle
> > Mr. Jerome Paul Nevins
> > #528

I hope to secure my freedom soon, you think, and you refold the letter and put it away, and you remember that day with your grandma as you passed fields and woods piebald with snow, and then there were walls, and within them there were fences and barred doors and finally a room where you were told to sit and wait for Jerome Paul Nevins, #528.

After a time, he was brought forth from somewhere, and as soon as he entered, he struck a pose and said *Ta-da tsing!* and then he grinned, as if with great daring he'd performed a breakneck feat. Your grandma said *Unglück, Unglück,* and Romie, taking the word as approval, gave an encore.

Ta-da tsing!

The luckless one, you thought, the poor misfortunate boy.

SCENE 32

FISH-SHAPE PAUMANOK (January 1932)

After the death of your Grandpa Nevins, your grandma had lived alone, looking after herself and getting about the city on her own. Her small flat had a bed to spare for visitors, and often you'd light there for a while, and so too your Uncle Dave on his headlong flight from where he was to some place else. When your grandma's health began to go, her daughter took her to Long Island, and to act as her companion, she also took Ellen Lang. Soon after the change had been made, you paid the pair a call.

Fish-shaped Paumanok, you thought as the train bore you through Jamaica and Hollis and Valley Stream, and you wondered whether Whitman had seen these same petite hills and trees and the rills that ran in the swales. Had there been snow on the ground when he started or only a sense in the windless air that snow was on the way? *The dweller in Mannahatta,* you thought, and you watched Walt's roads speed in and out of your windowpane.

Your grandma spent much of her time in her room now, and sitting over tea with Ellen, their chairs rocking slowly as if the chairs were rocking them, they talked of the ways of the present world and the better days of the past. Twenty years younger than your grandma, Ellen seemed to have used herself more, lived faster. Her red-gold hair had lost its gold to gray, her face clung to its bones (like hung clothes, you thought), and her lips, thick before, had thickened further—at barely fifty, the little mick was old. The fire of her spirit burned ardent still, though, and she seared you for your rare appearances, for your gentlemanly air, for the stink of your smoking weed.

"A real squireen he is, now! A boyo in a pink coat!"

And with scorn furling her upper lip, she turned to your grandma, and the pair conspired again, the old Jew and the aging mick, and the evils of this world were whispered away, and the good of the next brightened the windows of their faces.

CONTACT: AN AMERICAN QUARTERLY (Fall 1931)

One morning not long after you'd moved into the Hotel Sutton, Pep West joined you at breakfast (*Meals at Moderate Prices*) and told you of a new magazine in prospect. Quoting its slogan, he said that it would "attempt to cut a trail through the American jungle without the aid of a European compass." It was to be edited, he said, by William Carlos Williams with assistance from himself and Robert McAlmon. Contributions by each of them would appear, along with poetry by e. e. cummings and Louis Zukofsky, and to your surprise, you were invited to make a submission for Vol. 1, No. 1.

It was rash to run with such company, but you had the effrontery of ignorance, and your thoughts went at once to a story lying on your table upstairs. Based on the paternity suit brought by the hired girl Marjorie Brown against Preacher Peabody, it needed only a going-over and a suitable title before being ready for a reading. The revisions were soon made, and, taking a title from the text itself, "Once in a Sedan and Twice Standing Up," you delivered the manuscript to Editor West. Believing that critical notice would be taken of a publication so promising, particularly of its first issue, you were in the highest feather when told that your story had been accepted.

Inspirited, you set to work on a series of stories, all stemming in one way or another from the Viele Pond idyll. They proved to be unadorned and laconic recitals, usually of a city-dweller in exurban surroundings, and what talent they may have shown was occasionally betrayed by your faulty imagination, as when you described an encounter between a hawk and an owl, an unheard-of circumstance among Raptores. All the same, when they were offered to *Pagany*, an older quarterly, three of them were accepted and printed, a long one alone and two as a pair.* Your luminous hopes dimmed, however, when West told you of a decision by Dr. Williams to drop your story unless you changed your jaunty title to something less suggestive. You were mulish enough to refuse.

Within a day or two, Dr. Williams wrote to you from Rutherford:

---

*"Adirondack Narrative," in Vol. 3, No. 1; and "I Let Him Die" and "Jasper Darby's Passion," in Vol. 3, No. 2.

My dear Shapiro:

I don't think the value of the story depends on the title or that the change of that would detract in the least from the whole. To me it seems merely prevocative [sic] even misleading, if the quality for which I would use the composition should be the criterion. I wish you would reconsider your decision. Meanwhile I am sending back the story.

Yours sincerely
W C Williams

In a second letter, written only a few days later, it is clear that you replied to the first, arguing for the retention of your title:

Dear Shapiro

This is what happened. I read the story and liked it and the title appealed to me as snappy though it made me feel a little uneasy when I thought of publication — so I accepted the script, but I worried about the title.

At the last minute I decided that I just didn't want the emphasis your title gave to the sex phase of our first issue. I didn't want the casual but possibly favorable reader to believe that we were stressing the pornographic; God knows the issue is already too strong that way as it is. The story I was willing to use — but the title was a red flag that I had to sacrifice.

I'll stick to my original decision and use the story if you want me to, title and all — for you are the writer and must have the final word — but not in the first issue.

Yes, we'll meet some day soon — it will be a pleasure.

Yours
W C Williams

Soon after the initial appearance of *Contact* — without your story — West called you on the telephone one evening and asked you to come to his rooms.

When he opened the door for you, you assumed that he was alone, and you said, "What's on your mind, *boychik*?"

He nodded at someone out of sight, saying, "Dr. Williams wanted to meet you."

From behind the door, a presence manifested itself more in light than mass: you recall no face or figure, only a glint, as from refracting glass. You see still an outstretched hand, but for all you know, it never reached you, nor can you say what words were said, though you've wondered since whether you could've heard another stunner like the one he made for Eric: *Rather the ice than their way.* It was your first meeting, and your last. At most, you were there for fifteen minutes, and they were all you'd ever spend touched by that lustre—how could you have known that a quarter of an hour was to be your share?

——

SCENE 34

——

WHEN I BECAME A MAN (Early 1932)

I put away childish things, wrote Paul to the Corinthians—but you, you never outgrew them, and one such thing was a sense of injury. A slight, real or supposed, a hard word or look, a promise broken, an arrival late—any of these, because you felt it lessened you, was enough to stir resentment. You'd watched others endure the same and worse with never a sign of diminution, as if they fixed their own value, and no one else could change it, but always you seemed to wax and wane with the world outside you. When you became a man, alas, you spake as a child, understood as a child, thought as a child. You were a long-pants kid with a short-pants mind.

From his correspondence, it's clear enough now that it was Dr. Williams who ruled that your title must be changed; at the time, with no evidence to support you, you ascribed the ruling to West. Somehow you must've persuaded yourself that he'd merely looked on, that he'd said nothing when he should've spoken, or, at best, that he'd spoken indifferently instead of as a friend. Altogether mistaken, nevertheless you seethed, and only a few years hence, the friendship would end.

Your story, "An Adirondack Narrative," appeared in *Pagany* at the beginning of February, and on the 15th of the month, you heard again from Dr. Williams:

> My dear Shapiro:
>
> I've been very much impressed by your story in Pagany which is one of the best things of the sort I've come upon recently. That's putting it mildly too. I offer you my congratulations, most heartfelt.
>
> Damn it, I regret extremely our difference of opinion over the tale you sent us for Contact. Won't you put aside any feeling you may still have in the matter and send us something else at once for our second issue? So highly do I value what you are doing that I make no reservation in the matter but will print whatever you give me without question—tho I'd like another Adirondack story if I might have it. Really that was swell. . . .
>
> Sincerely yours
> W. C. Williams

You replied, saying that his letter had bowled you over (*youve stunned me, honestly*) and that although you had no story on hand, you'd do one especially for him. It was ready within a few weeks:

> Dear Doc
> Finished that story for Contact. On the advice of counsel — to wit, Pep — called it *The Fire at the Catholic Church*. He said he was sending it on to you. I hope you like it.
> Read the title story in *The Knife of the Times* and want to say it was one superb job. Best, as ever.
>
> Sincerely,
J. L. Shapiro

Two days later, he wrote:

> Dear Shapiro:
> Yes, *sir*, that's a story. Many thanks for it and my admiration to boot — all yours.
>
> Williams

Under the title suggested by West, the story was printed in the second issue of *Contact*. You were writing now, and others seemed to think you'd put away childish things. You may have thought so too, but you know now you had not.

SCENE 35

THE DRAGON PRESS DRAGON (Spring 1932)

Note: In my file for *The Water Wheel* is the original line-drawing of the dragon; from it, six times reduced, the cut for the colophon was made. On the back of the pen-and-ink is a typed inscription reading: *A Chavin "dragon," probably a conventionalized armadillo combined with insect features.* The substantive *Chavin* does not appear in the Encyclopedia Britannica and is doubtless a misspelling of *Chavante*. This word is given in the Webster International, where, along with *Chavantean*, it designates a tribe of Indians native to Brazil. There the armadillo is found. — J. S.

You remember many unimportant things about that day at the Sutton — the mild weather that seemed to air winter out of the world, the way you were dressed as you sat before *The Water Wheel* manuscript, the sounds that came up off the street, even a child watching you from a facing window until you watched it back and it ran away. Barefoot and wearing shirt and pants only, you stared at a page as if waiting for some word, some idea, to announce its defect and demand to be changed. . . .

"The Metropolitan Museum," you'd written, "stank of age, dust, mold, and preservatives. When he reached the Spanish section, he stood in front of a painting by Goya. He did not examine the picture closely, but imagined that under dark trees in the distance, there would be figures moving with scarcely any sound, dancing carefully and not touching each other, but all related in a mild and disinterested cruelty. Sanford sat down in a shadowed corner.

"A man and woman came into the room. The woman was holding an open book in her hand. When they were in front of the Goya, the woman read a passage from the book. The man stared at a small brass that was nailed to the base of the frame *Francisco de Goya y Lucientes*. He did not raise his eyes even when the woman closed the book and began to make a description for him. She stated the size of the picture, the number and position of the figures, the different colors. It was only then that Sanford began to wonder how long the man had been blind. . . ."

You remember thinking of the blind man you'd seen at the Prado, of transporting him from there to the Metropolitan, of making use of his affliction, of how writing, like the law, was no respecter of persons—and then you heard a knock on the door. Crossing the room, you opened it on what, for all you now can see, was an empty hallway. There comes to mind only a disembodied voice introducing itself as Angel Flores—Anhel, it said—and telling you it had been sent by Nathanael West.

"You're a writer, he told me.
"Trying to be," you said.
"May I ask what it is that you have written?"
"Oh, a few stories," you said, and you nodded at the table. "Also a novel."
The voice entered the room, saying, "A novel. And would you wish to say what it is about?"
"Me," you said. "Most first novels are about *me*."
"All novels are about *me*," the voice said. "I am an instructor in eSpanish at Cornell Universidad. I am also a translator from eSpanish into English and vice versa. And *finalmente*, I am a publisher—the Dragon Press."
You'd seen the imprint once only. "*The Knife of the Times!*" you said. "That's a damn fine book."
"Your book—how have you called it?"
"West suggested *The Water Wheel*. I lean toward *Among the Rocks*."
"What we have, then, is a choice between West and Eliot," the voice said. "*Con su permiso*, I would like to read the book."

144

"As a publisher?"

"*Que mas?*"

"At the moment, I'm trying to improve it."

"Ah! That is a good sign."

"Of what?"

"It is a new thing—a writer speaking of improvement."

You laughed, saying, "Of course, the truth is that it *can't* be improved."

And you permitted the voice to take the manuscript away.

SCENE 36

INSTRUCTOR, TRANSLATOR, PUBLISHER (1932)

It seems strange that you can't recall what he looked like. You had many a conference with him, he was a guest in your father's home on the Drive, and you were in his in Ithaca, but no feature, no dimension, no mark or coloration returns with the untranslated phrases you hear at the mere mention of his name. The man has disappeared, leaving behind him only his voice, four of his letters, and a drawing of a Brazilian dragon.

He accepted *The Water Wheel* soon after his return to Cornell. In a note dated August 6th and addressed to you at the Sutton, he wrote:

My dear Mr. Shapiro:

The Dragon Press offers to print, distribute, and advertise your novel THE WHEEL or some such title, during the Spring of 1933. After the deduction of the cost of manufacture, publicity, distribution, and advertisement—all of which will be submitted for your approval—the Dragon Press will be pleased to transfer to you 33⅓% of all the accrued profits derived from the said work.

Faithfully yours,
THE DRAGON PRESS
per Flores

These were Circean numbers, and having no Hermes to proof you against them with moly, you hearkened at your peril. On the same day, another note arrived from Ithaca:

Dear Scotti:

I don't think we have *the* title as yet. The one I liked best was AMONG THE ROCKS, but we must get away from Eliotite symbolism. In his poetry the word rocks have a decided (almost quintessential) value —not so in your novel. Don't worry about the matter, we'll find one: a short title is always impressive, or at least people remember it longer: Ulysses, The Fountain, Alexanderplatz, The Counterfeiters, The Edwardians, Mist, for example. But this is a stupid logic.

Doc Williams enjoys our enthusiasm and the idea of the Dragon publishing you and West. Give my very cordial regards to Mr. West and tell him how anxiously we are waiting for his mss.

Cordially,
Flores

On the 7th of September, he wrote to you from the Gran Via in Madrid, saying:

Dear Julian:

I have told all my friends in Madrid about you and they think I am a bastard for not finding some way of bringing you along. They are extremely excited to see your book in print. My encomium has led them to believe that perhaps you have Spanish blood. . . .

The Castellana, Recoletos, Alcala, keep on flowing, fraught with perfumes, gestures, and furtive glances. In these days of depression, my people are the only ones who do not give a hang & go on laughing & drinking manzanilla and sherry.

Salutations for West—I hope his novel is now available. For you the very kindest esteem and cordiality.

Angel

The fourth letter was postmarked Madrid and dated 14 September:

Dear Julian L.:

I am tickled to death by the splendid blurb with which the New Review homaged our chef d'oeuvre. Of course it sounds a trifle childish, their emphasis on *their* discovery: *any* intelligent critic would have done the discovery. The thing is the work! You have written something tremendously important. I have found a Spanish publisher for the Spanish version of your novel, and I have various influential cues leading to French and German translations.

I'm getting ready for a Paris sojourn. I may see Putnam, and I'll stay for dinner with F M Ford and Tate & his wife.

My very kind regards to Pep and Melvin & to your very kind family & for you cordial greetings.

Angel

But there were to be no translations into Spanish, German, and French, and your 33⅓% of the proceeds was to come to a third of nothing, and the kind and cordial greetings were soon to drain away, like your Spanish blood.

146

THE COLOR OF THE AIR, VII

THE DONNER PARTY—1846
WINTER CARNIVAL

A man is a fool who prefers poor California beef to human flesh.
                                        —Lewis Kiesberg

That's what they say he said, and since they're all dead now, the band that set out from Independence, it becomes the fact of the matter, or as near the fact as we're apt to get. They're all gone, those that died on the way of ills and Indians, those that made the summit of the pass and froze there in the drifts, and the rest, that ate the stiffs and lived to tell the tale—they're in hell now, one and all.

Hence, when you hear that this Kies- or Keysberg dined off the livers and lights of man, take it to be so, and credit too that he helped his meals to die, and for the fifty years they prolonged his life, hate him and call it a lie that he wasn't as black as painted: he was black, all right, as black as space. But if that's true, this is truer—there was damn little white in the party by the time it got through a winter in a dozen feet of snow. By then, who had not tried a slab of ass, or the tripes, or a kidney, or a fried brain, or a tit he'd had his eye on since Missouri?

They were human, the whole witch-held party, and they were up to anything going (name a deed, and you'd find a doer), wherefore, there being no Christ in the mountains, hungry Christians wafered-and-wined it off the body and blood of their kind. There was some stink about it afterward, but only among the meat-packers.

SCENE 37

THE VALUE OF A DOLLAR, I (Summer of 1932)

You took dinner at home one evening, and afterward you and your father went for a walk on the Drive. The sun was going down over the Palisades and, far further off, the long ridge of Schooleys Mountain. Your pace was slow, hardly dispersing the smoke ghost that drifted with you under the trees. *How he loves a cigar!* you thought, and as always you breathed its flavor deep, as if you were sampling him.

"Let me tell you a *Megillah,* kid," he said. "After the war, things began to go good for one of my clients, and within a few years, he was pretty well fixed. He had a brother, though, who could never make a dollar. A decent enough chap, but put him in business, and he'd lose his shirt. The truth is, he was something of a *Narr,* a foolish man. To him, life was a laughing matter, and whenever my client set him up—in a clothing store, a dry-goods store, even an ice-cream store—he laughed his way to ruin."

You wondered why he didn't use the man's name: he was talking about his own brother, your easy-come Uncle Charlie.

"But he had a wife and two children to support," your father said, "and for them it was *bitter Gelachter* when he went to the cleaners."

You remembered your uncle's dry-goods store. It was in Tarrytown, and the rear door opened on the tracks of the New York Central. How many times you went there just to watch the trains! And you remembered the clothing store and the black satin gusset he put in the back of your pants. And you remembered his ice-cream store in Harrisburg, where kids came for the two-scoop cones that he handed out free.

"After the fizzle with the ice-cream store," your father said, "something more had to be done, so my client built a block of shops—a taxpayer, it was called—at a cost of $65,000. He put his brother in charge, and all he had to do was keep the place in repair and collect the rents. But he laughed, he laughed, and the building fell into such a state that it had to be gotten rid of. The only way to do that was to trade up, that is, use the taxpayer as a down-payment on something bigger. What he did was buy an apartment house, throwing in the taxpayer plus $700,000 in cash, his life's savings."

"All this," you said, "because your client wanted to help his happy brother."

"When my client took over the apartment house, there were only two vacancies out of ninety flats. But then came 1929 and the bad days in the Street, and the two vacancies grew to be sixty, and with the rent-roll down, the mortgage couldn't be paid, and my client lost the building. Three-quarters of a million gone to the dogs."

"It's a good story, pop."

"Would it be better if I gave my client a son?"

"How would that improve it?"

"Well, at the foreclosure proceedings, the client could say, 'Son, there goes three-quarters of a million,' and the son could say, 'Yes—of my money.' "

It was growing darker, and the sky was closing down over Jersey—like an eyelid, you thought. "That would make it better," you said. "If you wanted to find out what your own son would say."

148

"And what would that be, kid?"

"I'm sorry you lost the money," you said, "but it was yours, not mine, and my regrets are for you."

"That would make you a good son," he said.

You walked on for a way, and then you said, "How do you know I didn't just make that up?"

"Did you?"

SCENE 38

THE VALUE OF A DOLLAR, II (Summer of 1932)

You spent a night at home, and in the morning, when you and your father left the apartment, he made a stop at the office of his landlord, a Scandinavian named Sandblom.

"Ah, Shapiro," he said as you entered. "What brings you?"

"The same old story, Mr. Sandblom," your father said. "I can't pay the rent."

"I hear that every month."

"I'm afraid you'll hear it next month too."

"What can I do about it, Shapiro—throw you out?"

"I wouldn't blame you a bit."

"Would *you* throw *me* out?"

Your father laughed. "On a rainy night," he said. "And I'd distrain your furniture."

"Do you know why I let you stay?"

"I have no idea."

"Because you don't cost me."

"I don't understand."

Sandblom said, "Right above you, on the second floor, there's a tenant that *does* pay his rent. For being so kind, I have to provide him with steam and hot water. The pipes go through your flat, and the same steam heats you, and with the same hot water you shave."

"What will you do when *he* stops paying?"

"Throw you both out."

SCENE 39

THE VALUE OF A DOLLAR, III (Summer of 1932)

Going downtown in the subway that morning, you stared at the ads near the ceiling of the subway car—for collars, cigarettes, Dodge trucks (Dependability)—while your father looked through the pages of the *Times*. In the inner pocket of your jacket, you carried a quarterly remittance from the Nevins Estate—a check for $180. It remained hidden there from 96th Street to 72nd, and it was hidden still at Times Square, but somewhere between Penn Station and 14th Street, you thought you felt it stir, as if it were trying to work itself free. You tried to suppress it by thinking of what the money would buy you—clothes, a weekend in Hartford (or had she returned to Boston?), a free and easy month of spending. You thought too that you didn't have to spend it at all: you could convert it to cash, smooth out the creases, count it daily, and put it away. When such thoughts ended, you took out the check and handed it to your father.

"What's this?" he said.
And you said, "I was hoping you knew."

SCENE 40

AUNT JO (Summer of 1932)

It was almost three miles from the Sutton to your home on the Drive, a ride that cost but a dime on the Fifth Avenue bus, but to save the fare, you'd often walk all the way for an evening meal. Along your route, for the most part on Broadway, you'd pass restaurants inviting you to eat your fill for 35¢, but the price was beyond your means, and savoring cuisines as you crossed them, you'd head for the table where you'd be fed for nothing. There your sister would sit facing your father, and you'd sit facing his wife, to you Aunt Jo, and all through some spontaneous agenda—observations of the day or week, questions and answers, family rumors, *scandale*—you'd find that some part of your mind was on the Painted Woman.

Two years had passed since the long estrangement between you had ended,

150

and in that time, you'd come to know that she was no more a painted woman than your Aunt Rae, who'd given her the name; indeed, you thought her less. There was no guile in her mouth, you'd learned, and what arts she employed were not for gain. All she ever seemed to aspire to was recognition of her presence, membership merely, and she'd seek it in ways that were open and stunning displays. Plumes were made for her, and décolleté, and with her fine-favored features she'd always appear to be the one moving picture in a collection of stills. She'd gleam, she'd glitter, and, knowing she was seen, she was satisfied. "Everybody thought I looked beautifully today," she'd say.

For your nine-year denial of her membership, she bore you no resentment; her nature was such that she couldn't stay angry long. To put out a blaze, all you had to say was, "Aunt Jo, the dinner tasted deliciously," and her rancor would be gone.

SCENE 41

STEPSISTER LEAH (Summer of 1932)

When you knew her first, in 1913, she was five years old, a doll-size replica of her mother. Her dark-hued skin was an inheritance, and so too the color of her hair and eyes, a brown so intense that it verged on black. Passed down as well was her voice, uncommonly deep for a child, almost a contralto, and seemingly frightened by its tone, she'd seldom speak. When she did, it was someone else you heard, the mother through the daughter's mouth.

She was a playmate of your sister's then and later, and sometimes she'd be at your grandma's when you returned from school, and you'd utter one of the sounds supposed to mean hello and then hurry off to your compelling sidewalk games. And thus, though only in glimpses, you saw her grow until she no longer appeared to be her mother at a distance; she became her mother young, another tawny beauty.

"When she got married," your father said, "I did a little something for her, more than a little, but it wasn't enough."

"For her?" you said.

"For me. I had too much to make up. I wasn't ever unkind to her—but I guess that's only another way of saying I was."

"If there's any fault, it's mine. She was in your house, and I wasn't."

"I can't let myself off by blaming you," he said. "I was cold to her, and it troubles me, it troubles me sorely," and then he shook his head, saying

"It's odd. The family objected to a stepmother for you and Ruth, and I turned out to be a stepfather to Leah. My own I sent to summer camp, to boarding-school, to college in Virginia. I sent Leah nowhere. She always pretended not to mind, but she did, and I knew it. And she was as good as gold all the time. I'd hope for rudeness, deceit, anything that would justify me, but nothing did, and nothing does."

"A father doesn't usually own up to a son," you said. "Not in our religion."

"It's a hard one, kid," he said. "There's nowhere to go for forgiveness."

SCENE 42

THE WATER WHEEL (Summer of 1932)

Designed by your cousin Mel Friedman, the book would soon go to press at the plant of his employer, The Haddon Craftsmen, in Camden, New Jersey. Until such time, however, you used the manuscript to elicit comment from the literati you were acquainted with, among them Dr. Williams, Samuel Putnam, and novelist Manuel Komroff. From a reference in one of Flores' letters, it would appear that you even had a hope of assistance from Edmund Wilson, whom you did not know, and from T. S. Eliot. If so, the hope was abandoned.

Komroff's response kept his enthusiasm at less than a deafening pitch. He wrote:

> Your book is a lively protest. I wish it were a revolt, but that would be wishing for another *Don Quixote* or a *Dead Souls*. The difference is that one is personal and the other has in it a tinge of sacrifice that I think your writing will achieve. I have been forced to read on in spite of myself. This force is something that makes fiction alive. It is a power that few writers acquire. Some will envy you and others will say that you will have to write more, for they will want to read more.

At first, you were inclined to regard the statement as backing and filling that managed to say nothing in opposite ways. But once you'd overcome your chagrin at not having been found to be another Gogol or Cervantes, you saw that the appraisal was not quite as unserviceable as you'd thought, and for the good it contained, however hedged, you decided to use it on the book-jacket, and you did, word for word.

Sam Putnam said rather too much than too little. On his magazine letterhead, he wrote from Mirmande now, in Drôme Dept.:

> The New Review likes to claim, and is, I believe, fairly justified in claiming Julian Shapiro as a discovery of its own. I personally regard Shapiro's novel as the sort of thing that has to come after Joyce, Stein, Surrealism and all the rest. In other words, it is *chronologically right.* But this is far from being all. It is as fine and sensitive at times — if the word were not so utterly damned, I'd say "beautiful" — as Virginia Woolf at her best. This on the more instinctive side. In addition, Shapiro is a highly conscious and finished craftsman, which is to say that he is always exceedingly readable.

This statement too, with its disquieting reference to Virginia Woolf, was reproduced on the jacket.

Dr. Williams' response to the book was expressed in two long letters that seem to have flowed hot from his mind onto the page. Nothing suggested a rough draft or any other attempted ordering of ideas: he could've been more direct only if, instead of writing, he'd spoken his fifteen hundred words of criticism. Not all of them were favorable. Many, in fact, took exception to the book's structure: *Writing gets its full flavor,* he wrote, *only from the complete organization which the writer imposes upon it. There can be no part in a work which seems to crumble into bits of brilliance.* Of your use of the particular word, however, he said much that you found to your purpose, and you chose the following passage to accompany those from Putnam and Komroff:

> I can't say that I have ever seen better work. It is really written, it moves, it has the quality of a novel. The story as a story bites in — it becomes serious, a matter of serious concern to anyone who can think and feel. It is excellent.

Read now, fifty years after they were written, Dr. Williams' letters appear clearly to be more than an opinion of *The Water Wheel.* Beyond doubt, they're the statement of a literary belief: that a work cannot be truly significant unless its *sweep of form* includes its incidental forms. *A work of art,* he says, *is a small machine. It must have as perfect an internal economy as a machine has, not a flick of grease too much, every word, every part pared down to geared essentials.*

At the time, though, you were not concerned with theory. Through a principal character named John Sanford, you were bent only on revealing the thoughts and experiences of yourself, Julian Shapiro, during a few decisive weeks in the summer of 1927 — and you'd done that in a pell-mell of language that carried him through two overlapping loves and a round-trip to nowhere.

You undertook to dispute the "sweep of form" tenet with Dr. Williams, writing that while you hadn't dwelt on organization, the book nevertheless possessed it by reason of the fact that it so unfailingly centered on its protagonist. *There is no part of the book,* you wrote, *which is not completely Sanford. Even the so-called objective descriptions are Sanford. Sanford wrote the book, as it were. Sanford acted in it. Sanford arranged it and all its parts.*

But Dr. Williams would not allow the claim. In such concentration, he held, the inner tension had sometimes been lost, letting the book, which should've been a whole, "a small machine," break into parts. Good though they were (*You have done as fine writing and with as great an integrity in it as anything I have encountered. Really enviable to me. You make me believe once more in the honorableness of a craft as writer.*), you had not succeeded in making the parts hold together.

Taking the praise along with the dispraise, you thought you were getting less than you deserved. You know better now. A writer only by virtue of a few modest stories and a poured-out first novel, you'd been taken seriously by a poet even then of great distinction. Hardly realizing that you'd been honored beyond your worth, you picked over his comment and glumly lifted a paragraph that, on the contrary, should've lifted your spirits high.

SCENE 43

HELL TO PAY (Late Summer 1932)

At breakfast one Friday morning before Labor Day, your father proposed a visit to the family home in West End. He hadn't seen his mother or his sister Sarah since their exodus from the city in June, and if he hoped to remain in good standing, he said, if he valued his filial and fraternal good name, it behooved him to put in an appearance before the summer's end. Knowing that he was only mocking himself, you took pleasure in his inflated periods; no one could've been less self-important than he, and therefore you enjoyed his sham floridity, his ready-willing-and-ables and all the other jargon he despised.

"I'll go," you said, "if you lend me the fare."
"I'll blow you to a ticket," he said, "and the same goes for anyone else."

For their own reasons, Ruth and your Aunt Jo declined the offer, and when you left the apartment with your father, you carried a valise with a change of clothing for both of you. At his office, he disposed of a few minor matters, and after grabbing a sandwich (you ate a meal, he said; you grabbed a sandwich), you caught the midday Jersey Central boat for the Highlands. You placed a pair of carpet-covered camp-chairs near the lower deck gangway, and within moments you were watching the river flow past in a great smooth surge that looked like pea-green paint.

You hadn't taken note of the boat you were on—it could only have been one of three, the *Asbury Park*, the *Sandy Hook*, or your favorite the *Monmouth*— but all were much the same, white twin-screw steamers with two black stacks, and all were fast, good for twenty-two knots at company speed and even better when pushed. There was a time when you knew the name of the shipyard that had built them (was it Harland & Wolf on the Delaware?), but you can't be sure now, though you still can see a plaque above the engine-room bulkhead and, within, the beautiful complication that steam set in motion.

Seated close to the water-line, you could feel the reciprocation of the pistons, the turning of the propeller-shafts, but for all that, it seemed to be the shore, the docks, the harbor islands that were steaming by while you were standing still. You stared out at Jersey passing, at the haze of Bayonne, at the entrance to the Kill Van Kull.

"I'm glad no one else came with us," your father said. "I want to talk to you about something very particular."

You lit a cigarette and spicked the match at the river. *Spicked*, you thought; there was no such word. "I'm listening, pop," you said.

"It's about your cousin Melvin."

"Then I know what you're going to say. You're going to ask whether I knew he was married."

"Wrong. I was going to ask if you knew he *intended* to get married."

"There isn't much difference, is there?"

"A great deal, I think," he said. "If you knew about it beforehand, then you did something unforgiveable in failing to talk Mel out of it, or at the very least, in failing to inform his parents. In case you've forgotten, I'm talking about two people I idolize—my sister Sarah and my brother-in-law Harris. I want the truth, Julian—did you know what Melvin meant to do?"

"I did not," you said.

He hesitated, and then he said, "Well, I've put the question, and you've answered it. I can't doubt my own blood."

"All the same," you said, "I can see that other questions remain. Am I right?"

"Yes."

"Ask them."

155

And now St. George was going by, and after it went the cardboard cut-outs called Tompkinsville, Stapleton, Rosebank, and then you were in the Narrows, reading for the hundredth time the warning on Ft. Wadsworth: CABLE CROSSING—DO NOT ANCHOR.

"First," your father said, "I want to tell you the effect all this has had on Sarah and Harris. I hate to say it, but they've said prayers for Melvin. To them, he's dead."

You stared at him. "They must be living in another country," you said. "Another century."

"It's hard to credit, but they've actually sat *Shiva** for him."

"Would you do that if I married a Christian?"

"No," he said, "and I begged *them* not to do it. They wouldn't listen."

"Uncle Jack married a Christian, Aunt Helen, and she's as much in the family as I am. Why didn't Aunt Sarah sit *Shiva* for Uncle Jack?"

"Jack's her brother. Melvin's her son."

"And here I am, going to her house for the weekend. I'll be as welcome as a pogrom."

"When did you get wind of Mel's involvement with this girl?"

"I was with him the night he met her. It was back in '27, when I was living at the Fifth Avenue Hotel. He took to her at once, and she to him. From time to time, he'd ask me for the key to my room."

"And you gave it to him?"

"Yes."

"Why?"

"I didn't see any reason for them to do it under a stairway or on a roof."

"But by making things easy for them, you abetted their marriage."

"That's unfair. If I didn't let him use my room, they'd've used somebody else's or found a dark street."

"It *was* unfair," he said, "but look at it this way. It must've been plain to you that this was no ordinary relationship, and you were the only one who knew about it. Only you could've averted this outcome."

"How?" you said. "I didn't know Mel's intentions till after he was married, and even that I found out by accident. What could I have done before the fact? Peach on him? Tell the Friedmans that their Melvin was fooling around with a Christian girl? They'd only have said, 'Better a Christian girl than a Jewish girl.' And as for Mel, he'd've shunned me for life."

Where was the *Asbury Park* now, the *Monmouth,* the *Sandy Hook?* Was she off Midland Beach, New Dorp, Crookes Point, where the shore began to bend toward Raritan Bay? Was the water iridescent, was there smoke over Perth Amboy?

---

*True spelling *Shibah.*

"Well, maybe it'll all be straightened out some day," your father said. "Right now, there's only sadness in the family. They're bewailing the loss of a son."

"I ought to stay on the boat when it docks. I ought to go back with her to Manhattan."

"That won't be necessary. Your passport to the household is me. Whether you know it or not, I always have been." He threw the remains of his cigar at the wind. "But take my advice, Julian. Steer clear of Harriet."

"Why?"

"She's never liked you, and now she likes you less."

Your cousin Harriet was an older sister of Melvin's and recognized by all as the future queen of the family. Her mother Sarah held sway, but as she aged, the daughter more and more ruled from the shortening shadow of the throne. She seemed only to advise, but since time and again her advice was decisive, in effect she reigned now, though the sovereign was still alive. You'd long been aware of her disfavor, for she'd never been at pains to conceal her lack of regard; nor were you an admirer of hers, ardent or otherwise. All the same, you knew her to be intelligent, open-handed, loyal, and winning in her ways, and moreover she was a beauty, indeed the most beautiful woman in the family, and there were times when, but for one other quality, she might've put you in mind of your mother: she was what everyone called "a good hater."

In speaking of sadness among the Friedmans, he'd badly understated the emotion. The precise word for it would've been grief. Here were a father and mother, here were sisters and brothers and even Rosie Ackerman, the long-time companion of your Grandma Shapiro—and all of them moved solemnly, spoke in dismal tones, dressed darkly and unadorned, quite as if one of their number no longer lived in fact. Their youngest, so full of promise, had been cut down in his morning, and they grieved for his undone years.

With the Friedmans at *schul* the following forenoon, the house was even quieter than usual. Your father had gone up to his mother's room, and there he sat conversing with the old lady and Rosie in Yiddish. Now and then you could hear their voices from the foot of the stair as you passed it while pacing the empty hall. What you were thinking about at the moment you've never been able to recall—it might've been anything, Mel, your writing, Hartford, the call-girl at the Sutton. Whatever your thoughts, though, they were shocked out of you forever by a sudden tirade from the landing. There, halfway down from the upper floor, your Cousin Harriet stood leaning against the banister and pouring a spate of hatred upon your head.

"You've got your gall to come to this house!" she cried. "You cost the family its dearest child, and yet here you are, as cool as a snake! I hold you responsible for what happened to my brother — you planned it, you egged him on, you killed him! You're heartless, you're evil-minded, you're a disgrace to your father and every other Jew!"

"You're raving," you said. "Why don't you ask me for the facts instead of filling the air with spleen? You're accusing me without knowing the truth, and therefore all you've said against me is a lie. I'm responsible for nothing that Mel has done, and if you don't believe me, you can go straight to hell!"

"Get out!" she screamed. "Get out!"

Still in a rage, she rushed down past you, pale and glaring, and slambanged from the house. Knowing that your ill-timed visit was over, you went up to the second floor to bid your Grandma Shapiro goodbye. Your father was standing at the head of the stairs.

"I hope you didn't hear that," you said.

"How could I help hearing?" he said. "Both of you were shouting."

"I wasn't looking for a fight, but I couldn't turn tail after what she said. She's dead wrong about all this. She doesn't know beans with the bag open."

"Don't be too hard, kid. To her, a sin has been committed, and she's looking for someone to blame."

"What am I — her *Shabbas goy*?"

"She's immoderate — I'll admit that. But do you have to be immoderate too?"

"Not everybody can be a Phil Shapiro," you said, "least of all I. So the best thing for me to do is kiss Bubbe and take off for New York."

Seated with your grandma was Rosie, less the old lady's attendant, you thought, than her everpresent friend: they were not unlike Ellen and your Grandma Nevins, a pair of ancient faithfuls praying in murmurs for this sinful world. Rosie could neither read nor write, in Yiddish or any other language, and your grandma, if she knew a little English after half a century in the land, made no use of it except to take in someone's supposedly safe aside. In her mouth, you were still Yonkel Layv, never Julian, but once in a while, to pinch you gently, she'd let you know she knew your name — Jula, she'd say, and her bright brown eyes would shine.

You bent over the bewigged and shrunken old lady (how could you have written of her as you did? you wonder, how could you have been so different from your father, so disloyal to your blood?), and in the aura of saffron she gave off, you kissed fingers twisted by age. You turned away then to take your leave of Rosie, but she'd gone below for the morning mail and was just coming back with a packet of letters. These she began to assort on the coverlet of the bed, and, absorbed, she hardly saw you go.

Your father was still in the hallway, and nodding back at Rosie, you said, "Tell me something. How does she figure who gets what? She can't read, but she's never wrong."

"I've asked about that," he said, "and nobody knows."

You smoothed his hair, saying, "See you in town, Shappie."

"Here's a fiver, kid. Unless you mean to swim."

From a bench at the West End station, you saw your Aunt Sarah and your Uncle Harris walking home from *schul.* They were the length of the platform away from you, too far for recognition, and you sat where you were and watched them move off.

SCENE 44

A DAY'S ABSENCE FROM THE SUTTON (Fall 1932)

You and your family were at breakfast around the diningroom table. Before you, a cup of coffee steam, its vapor mingling with the smoke of your cigarette. You indicated a basket holding two Vienna rolls, the last of the morning delivery.

"Eight for a quarter," you said. "How can a man bake a roll and bring it to your door for three cents? Seems to me he'd go broke at that price."

"Figure it out," your father said. "He must be making a profit, or the rolls wouldn't be here. Say he nets a nickel out of that quarter. If he delivers to twenty families, he makes a dollar on one hundred and sixty rolls. Of course, he needs more than a dollar a day to cover rent, supplies, gas, and a delivery-boy — say he needs fifty a day. That's only fifty times a hundred and sixty — or eight thousand rolls. I'd say he was in a good sound business. Of course, the mortality-rate is high."

"I've been writing for four years," you said, "and I've yet to see my first nickel out of it."

"You ought to bake rolls," your sister said.

You said, "Why are you up so early?"

"I'm spending the day with Aunt Rae."

You glanced at your stepmother, who seemed calm enough at the mention of the name.

Your sister went on to say, "And you ought to see her too. She's your aunt, and she hasn't been well. How long are you going to bear a grudge against her?"

"Ruthie is right," your stepmother said. "All that is in the past."

"You surprise me, Aunt Jo," you said. "Do you know what she used to call you?"

"The painted woman. I heard about that long ago."

"Everything is in the past," you said. "But not what the Perlmans did to me and Uncle Dave."

159

"That's dead and buried too," your father said. "Forget it."

"I must be among Quakers, not Jews," you said. "All I hear is turn the other cheek. What for? To get it kicked?"

"In one way or another, the four of us here have been injured by the Perlmans," your father said. "You're the only one who can't get over it."

You said, "I'm sorry Aunt Rae isn't well—I wish her no harm. But do I have to pretend I've forgotten the scheme against grandpa?"

"Now it's grandpa you're sore about. Before, it was yourself and Uncle Dave. When are you going to get sore about me and Jo? It was only your purse that was stolen—trash, according to a better writer than you. But Jo and I have been filched of our good name. If you're taking up the cudgels, at least pick a noble cause."

"What's the matter with Aunt Rae?" you said to Ruth.

"They don't know yet."

"She would be gladly if you called," your stepmother said. "You would do her good."

"If I ever go, should I say the painted woman sent me?"

SCENE 45

THE FIDUCIARY (Late 1932)

In an earlier year, as your Uncle Dave was about to depart on one of his transmarine emigrations, he came to your office and placed in your keeping all the money that he was not taking with him; in addition, he signed a power of attorney giving you the right to collect income when due from his father's estate. Knowing that he regarded mankind as joint and several thieves and himself as their favorite victim, you were pleased at being exempted from his scorn of the species.

"You're too dumb to steal," he said. And then he was off, and from time to time you'd have tidings of the whorehouses of Barcelona and those of Palembang.

Nothing now exists of what you wrote to him, but his letters, whether from Port Swettenham or Rangoon, were outcries against some lone larcener or some conspiracy of picaroons. It was his lot, it seemed, to be forever fleeced. Lying in wait for him was a world of pettifoggers, sharpers, flimflammers, and jacklegs, and whenever he wrote to you from a foreign strand, it was to egg you on against his deceivers—this swine or that swindler—to drive you to sue and pursue them, to corner one of his many knaves and retrieve their pocketed pickings. Thus flayed by him, you dunned them in his name, but as they'd been more than a match for him, so they were for you, and no sternness, no threat feazed them: they coughed up nothing. And when, as always, your efforts ended in failure, you'd hear from your Uncle Dave:

> When I get back to New York, he wrote from Barcelona, I'm going to can you as my attorney. Next trip I make, I'll have someone who can look after my interests properly. I'll get a good man—a truck-driver.

You used the Emigrant Bank as a depository for your uncle's funds, and for convenient access, you maintained the account in your name instead of his. For long periods, his only income derived from the trust-fund established by his father. It came to something less than a thousand dollars a year, but being a first-class traveller, he travelled second-class always, and his money seemed to take him far beyond its printed value, as if, when spent by him, somehow it bought more, bore him further, grew. He drew on you seldom, therefore, and with what you were holding for him, he was voluntarily generous:

> If you should need any of my money, he wrote from Shanghai, don't hesitate to use it. I know you will act with discretion.

> And from Paris he wrote: About the loan you made to yourself, do not think I am in the least excited. I told you a long while back that you were welcome as long as you exercised care, for as one is knocking about as I am, any emergency may arise.

> And, once again in Barcelona, he wrote: It is O.K. with me about the money you borrowed. Did you think I would raise a stink after giving you the right?

But he did not know that what you owed him had grown to nearly five hundred dollars, enough to support him for half a year, and instead of berating you, as you deserved, he was still erupting against his old enemies—Bernstein, Perlman, and *that swine Gordon.*

SCENE 46

L. T.: WHY DON'T YOU PRACTICE ON A WHORE? (December 1932)

Your shame deepened the more she hid, or tried to hide, her rage. For some reason, you saw her as a stream, dark Afton, but so far from being stilled by you, she seemed about to flood, to disturb a Mary's dream. She left the bed and crossed the room, but if she'd done so by design, it left her on the way, and she stopped and gazed around her as though to retrieve it from the air. She found nothing, and you thought again of Afton, of green braes drowned and your shame.

Why don't you practice on a whore? she said. Her nipples were hard, clenched, you thought, and they appeared to be raised in anger—pacifiers once, they soothed no more. And there was anger too in her private hair, a black and almost wreathing smoke, and there was anger almost as sensible as heat in the stare that flared her eyes, and she shamed you when she said what she'd said before: *Why don't you practice on a whore?*

You knew that if you ever saw her again, the words would still be there: they'd never be unsaid, never be withdrawn, they were as unredeemable as time, they *were* time, and having passed, they were forever in being. In the mail that night, you sent her two one-dollar bills, new ones you'd gotten at a store. You hardly knew what you meant. Surely she wasn't a whore. . . .*

SCENE 47

THE INSULTED AND INJURED (End of 1932)

In trying to account for your adversary bent, you always look to your Uncle Dave. By some lapse in descent, you fancy, you took your nature not from your line, but collaterally through him: nowhere else could you find those smolderings you knew so well in yourself, those coal-mine fires that never burned out. Once ignited—by the spark of a chance remark, by a slight supposed or real, an omission, any bright trifle—they seemed to become inextinguishable,

---

*From *To Feed Their Hopes,* University of Illinois Press, 1980.

162

and as if queered by their gases, you could only watch them eat endlessly into the drifts and galleries of your mind. How you longed at times for your father's moderation instead of your uncle's rage! But, alas, you were not so graced, and before the year closed, a friendship you prized went up in smoke.

§

Your story, titled as you'd wished, "Once In A Sedan And Twice Standing Up," appeared in the third issue of *Contact*. The company was very fast: there were contributions by Dr. Williams and Robert McAlmon, a chapter from West's novel, *Miss Lonelyhearts*, stories by Erskine Caldwell and James Farrell, and poetry by Louis Zukofsky and Carl Rakosi. but the third issue was not the first issue, where you felt it should've gone, and for a long while you'd lived with that fire of resentment slowly consuming some underground seam within you, nor was it doused by the facts, which were known and plain.

Letters from Dr. Williams prove beyond question that the decision to exclude your story was made by him. For some reason, though, possibly because of the way in which West apprised you of it, you persuaded yourself that the decision had been his. You'd just had lunch with him in a restaurant on upper Broadway, and through the course of an hour, nothing had been said that touched on *Contact*. Only on your way out had he spoken saying over his shoulder, "By the way, Scotty, Bill tells me your story will not be printed in Number 1."

It was as if you'd walked into a doorway that was only painted on a wall. You were so stunned, you recall, that the word itself came to mind: *stunned*, you thought. Following West into the street, you wondered why he hadn't told you the news at the table, broken it through coffee steam and the smoke of cigarettes. Had he wanted to avoid a scene in a public place, the embarrassment of anger, loutish behavior, being stared at by strangers—being taken for a Jew? But whatever questions you might've put to him, whatever arguments you might've offered, you were able to voice none of them, and, reaching the corner, where he paused, you could only walk away.

You were dazed with disappointment, and over a mile or two of wanderings, you could dwell on nothing but those offhand words—*By the way, Scotty, Bill tells me . . . Bill tells me.* You went far before they began to thin out and make way, and when they did, the first thought to suggest itself was that West had failed in some way to act the friend—and once you entertained it, you could not let it go. You saw him at best as saying nothing when Dr. Williams barred the story, and at worst as ruling it out himself. Whichever it was, you thought, it came to the same in the end—and the fire burned on, and you let it fume and even fanned its glow.

§

That s. o. b. Charley, your uncle said
That swine Gordon
Enemies, he said

SCENE 48

A RESTAURANT ON 34th STREET (End of 1932)

It was one of the Childs' chain, occupying the ground-floor of a building between the McAlpin and the Waldorf. White-tiled like all of its kind, it was brightly-lit and glaring, and even in recall, it seems to shrink the pupil of the eye. The place comes back to you with sound as well as sight, and you hear, now as then, the escaping steam of speech, the tones of china in collision, the chimes of silver coin. Seated at a long table, you see yourself with what you'd always called *the crowd*. You'd just come from a recital or some theatrical performance (or could it have been the Met?), and above the meager servings of food, the cups of weak coffee, there was a crisscross of comment, and tentative judgments passed. Faces that you were rarely to see so gathered again appear before you without change, as if the fifty years gone were only fifty days. *The crowd,* you think, and you watch George make some point in a passion of words, and Pete listens, and Erwin too, and Little Sam, and Pep hovers over a cigarette, letting smoke crawl up through his hair, and then Big Sam, known to all as the Chinaman, inserts a quip into a pause and draws a laugh—and you say nothing, having nothing to say. *The crowd,* you think, *the crowd,* a confluence like any other, brought together by a soprano, a play, a string quartet, and soon it'll be a crowd no more. It'll run, walk, ride, it'll go away from here—from this table under that chandelier.

With its points all made, George's lecture ends and small talk starts, and more smoke grows to gray Pep's hair. *The crowd,* you think, now about to come apart—but Big Sam is speaking, as always of his days on the Shanghai bund, and you hear still another of his occidental jokes about oriental quirks, still another story of the heathen chinee. His one claim to attention is that two-year stay in the foreign settlements along the Whangpo, but what had

164

he done there, how much had he seen from within those walls? The Chinaman, he'd been named, yet what did he know of dark ways and tricks peculiar?

Through the din and drone around you, you take in a performance that seems partly a plea for applause. It evokes none, and you're about to turn away from the dunning when you note that Pep has begun to heckle the act. Unequal to Pep's salt, the Chinaman falters, but Pep gives him no rest, baiting him with quip and question, with mock displays of learning in the art and history of Cathay, until finally you feel compelled to say

"Let him alone, Pep."

Sam was Big only as measured by his Little namesake; actually, he was of medium height, a pale slight man living in skin that seemed to belong to someone else, as if he'd donned the wrong suit of clothes. He was a lawyer, you believe, but you never saw him in the professional round; he turned up on concert nights, at this or that showing of the rage in art, and near the feet of Maestro George. How dependent he was on George! From George, he drew all his ideas, and at times you thought he drew breath as well. For him, George's say-so was the Word, the manifestation of the wisdom of this and every world. But on that particular night, the word was spoken by you.

"Let him alone," you say.

Why? you've often wondered since. Were you shielding Sam or picking a quarrel with Pep? Were you nobly for the underdog or meanly against the dog on top? What moved you—pity for Sam or the sleeping fire come awake?

Pep says, "A man who was in China longer than Marco Polo ought to be able to tell us about their calligraphy, an art they rate as high as painting. Don't you agree, Scotty?"
"No, I don't."
"Failing that, we have a right to know the chronology of the dynasties. As, did the Han precede the Sung, or was it vicey-versey? Who among us but Sam has these things at his fingertips?"
"Why don't you quit, Pep? Go after someone your size."
"Someone like you, do you mean?"
"Yes," you say. "Someone like me."
"But, Scotty," he says, "I'd be afraid to match wits with you. You might show me up for what I am."
"What you are, Pep, is a sheeny in Brooks' clothing!"
The table has been quiet during the exchange, but now it's as if the quiet has spread to other tables, as if the very crockery is careful not to touch and the cutlery to interfere.

"A sheeny in Brooks' clothing, Mr. West," you say. "I knew you when your name had two syllables."

No other word was said that you now remember, not even out in the street; *the crowd* simply parted and went its several ways.

§

Your days in *the Fashionable Sutton Place District* were over.

SCENE 49

CODA (End of 1932)

In the morning, you took your suitcase and your Royal down to the Sutton lobby and went to the Manager's office to say goodbye to Pep.

"I'm on my way home," you said. "I didn't want to leave without thanking you."

He said, "Nothing to thank me for, Scotty."

"I'll leave the key at the desk," you said, and giving him a half-wave, you turned to the door.

He let you reach it before saying, "You shouldn't've spoken as you did last night. It was unseemly."

"Well, not everybody can be a gent. Some of us have to be slobs."

"Before you go, tell me something. That sheeny business in Brooks' clothing—did it come to you on the spot?"

"I'm not that quick. I made it up in advance."

"And my name having two syllables once?"

"That too. I was laying for you."

He nodded, saying, "See you some time, Scotty."

"Sure thing, Natchie," you said, and with that, you were gone.

THE COLOR OF THE AIR, VIII

EDGAR ALLAN POE — 1849

IN BRONZE ABOVE A DOORWAY

Little home of a great poet
—13 West Range, University of Virginia

Did I live that life, the one just over, those forty years of dayless
days, and did I behave as they say I did, were such my ways, did
I write the hack and consequential work I signed, did I wear black
to match my blind-man's view of the world, a worldwide open grave,
was such my turn of mind? Did I stem from strolling players, did
my father cut and run and my mother die of lungs, leaving a few
ringlets and a miniature, so poor, so poor she sang and danced in
motley till a month before the end?

Was I given a home by Allan, and did he give or I take his name,
was I clever as a child, did I rhyme in Latin, recite to guests for praise
and watered wine? Did I love at fifteen, my first time and my first
Helen, and was she soon insane and dead and I insane alive? Was
it then I began dwelling on tombs and cinerary urns, on magical
radiances, compelling perfumes, ciphers and fascinations, dark-age
horrors, death gradual and intricate and sometimes by machine? Did
I know of drink then or learn its use at school (milk slings, they
say I took, and peach-and-honey — what was peach-and-honey?), and
while there did I lose three thousand at loo, debts of honor (whose?)
that Allan refused to pay?

Should I have starved when he cut me off, was it base to enlist
as a common soldier, a loss of face to eat my country's bread in the
ranks, and if so, why when appointed to the Point, did I dram it
till they drummed me from the Corps? Didn't it matter, didn't I
care, did I guess at twenty-two there'd be no forty-four — those sudden tirings, the troubles in my head, my shaking hands, and where
was all desire except when desire was safe, among consumptives,
among premenstrual misses and no longer bleeding maids?

Why did I marry my twelve-year-old cousin Virginia, whose
mother was nearer my age, and in the hovels we shared with a cat,
a bobolink, and a pair of canaries, did I ever see her naked, did I
surprise secret skin and shocking hair, and did I sink the sight in
opium when drink was slow to drug me? My aunt (Muddie, I called

her, and my bride was Siss), my kindly tireless uncomplaining aunt, did she beg for us in shops and on the road, did she take in laundry, mending, lodgers (and lodge them where, on what part of the floor?), and when I went away, did she tend my wife in her lifelong dying and send me the fare to come home?

Did we move from place to place, we three with cat and birds, always to a smaller space, always taking fewer things, and if, as the doctors said, I had a lesion of the brain, did that explain my presence at the Springs while Virginia bled the bedsheets red? Did I lift material, pretend to erudition, puff jinglers for puffs in return (*R. H. Horne puts Milton in the shade*)? Did I laud empty lines, woo lady poets with reviews, give them valentines, was I *not myself*, was I high cockalorum when Lowell came to see me, did I court the widow Whitman and still unwidowed wives? Did I rave in my drunken manias, did I take poison and puke it back, did I, that winter at Fordham, warm my virgin's feet with her cat?

Tell me, did I die in the street or a Baltimore room, and tell me lastly this—some day, somewhere, in bronze above some lintel, please God will it say *Domus parva magni poetae*?

SCENE 50

FIRST NOVEL (Early 1933)

This book is for O. B.
—dedication

Working alone in the half-light of your basement bedroom, you corrected four sets of galley-proofs in the course of a month. What little you knew of operational and typographical signs you'd learned while proofing *Balso Snell,* but it was rudimentary and incomplete, and now, in trying to mark changes, you found it necessary to spell out messages in the margins—to whom? you wondered, to what unknown in Camden? Deletions, spacing, alignment, transpositions—these and other print-concerns gave rise to a succession of epistles that were sometimes read and sometimes not, and coming upon an error that the printer had twice overlooked, you wrote *God damn it, get it right!*

The book had been written with scant regard for standard form. For many a reader, every page, with its aberrations of style, spelling and punctuation, would make strange reading, almost in another language. Dialogue invariably appeared in italics and without quotation-marks; no hyphens were used (tobaccosmoke, fiftyseventh) and no apostrophes (didnt, wasnt, couldnt); there were occasional archaicisms (as, in a long parody of *A Man Without a Country*, where the letter *s* was rendered by an *f*), there were neologisms (waterdry, dismalgay, detalia), and frequently large caps seemed to make the print shout.

The pages were set in Garamond, a French type-face somewhat on the bold side, with a distinctive italic almost as black as roman. It made an active spread, perhaps even overactive in view of the headlong pace of the text. There were no graduations of speed, as Dr. Williams had correctly said, there were no roundabouts, no pauses: the writing sprinted all the way. It drew breath never, not even at the obstacles you strewed in its path — columns of words, boxes, triangles, geometries of words, all the rocks and scoria of typography.*

In calling your principal character John Sanford, you'd had no thought of pretending that you and he were not the same. His origins were your origins in the writing and in fact, and so too his motivations and experiences and such of his thinking as might be worthy of the name. John and Julian were openly identical, but as John he spared you the vainglory of referring to yourself as *I*. In a sense, of course, it was impossible to avoid seeming self-important: after all, you were writing about you, an act that rather plainly fixed the place you held in your esteem. Apart from that, however, writing of yourself as if you were someone else gave you a less obvious way of showing the lining of your coat.

The novel contained only three other characters, all of them girls. The first two were approximations of actual people; the third, part real and part fancy, was used as a catalytic and brought in from a later time. All action centered on Sanford; indeed, since he appeared on every page, he was the book's solitary event. No thoughts but his were presented, no emotions, no preferences or aversions, and while the girls were permitted to speak, they spoke only to evoke his lines.

The life-span of the book was a few months in the summer and fall of 1927. Its opening scene, a fifteen-page étude of Sanford, took place in his office, where he was found to be gazing from a window at the Hudson River a quarter of a mile away. The intention of the scene was to exhibit his nature and character in whatever complexity they possessed, and he was shown to be a man of many minor antipathies and no great love, not

---

*The book was designed by your cousin, Mel Friedman.

even of himself, the law-clerk grandson of an immigrant peddler.

The contents of the room, its decoration in particular, did not cry out his profession. In lieu of tomes on the law—Coke, Kent, Littleton—his bookshelves were largely laden with Elizabethan drama and the French and Russian novel. Nor were the walls hung with the usual steel engravings of jurist and statesman; in their place was the aquarelle grace of Winslow Homer. These things, though, were only an outer show of inner contrariety: it was within his mind that he dragged his feet; there were the grooves and mars of opposition. Shown across fifteen pages of 12-point Garamond were the main forces he was trying to resist—a girl he could not bring himself to name, the law, and the country he lived in, by which he meant, though he hardly knew it, the country bounded by his skin.

Having established Sanford's kind and condition, the narrative proceeded to his second affinity, this one with the girl whom West, on reading the manuscript at Viele Pond, had been able to identify. Left unnamed like her predecessor, she was actually George Brounoff's sister Olga, and though the relationship failed to flourish, its effect on Sanford lasted long. Entering upon the experience with a limited understanding of himself and almost none of others, he was destined soon to wither it, and the rest of the novel was devoted to describing the yellowing of the leaf in detail.

The writing of the book was a distorted act of contrition: the intention was the extinguishment of your guilt by offering a surrogate to suffer for it, as if John's penance would atone for the sins of Julian. You spared Sanford nothing. All your posturings were transferred to him, all your rant and greenness, your natural proclivities and those you had assumed. Your fears became his, and where you had fallen, he fell too. You overrode whatever you encountered, rules, the rights of others, their preferences and ideas, their language, even—worse, you trod down their affections, strode on growing grass. On the page, the same railing as off, the same mistakes, the same injuries, and there John declined the gift even as Julian before him.

Written after the death of Olga, your book of redemption miscarried because its sole concern was you: never had you expanded, never as John had you gotten beyond Julian. You'd beaten your chest, but the sound you made was hollow, and Olga heard it and let you go. The Hudson began the book, and the Hudson ended it. *As he went down the street,* you'd written, *the lights on the river kept pace with him. . . . The waters were glistening.*

SCENE 51

FIRST REVIEW (March 1933)

Day after day you went downtown to the New York offices of Haddon Crafts-men in the hope that finished copies had arrived from the bindery in Camden. At last, on entering one morning, you found yourself facing a stack of books, vivid in their green and yellow jackets.* You took one up, turning it in your hands as if it were some incomprehensible object; you opened it, scanned lines you didn't recognize, tried it for weight, and finally, failing to realize its significance, you carried it away under your arm. You walked the city with it—with *your* book this time, not Melville's or Turgenev's, but Childe Julian's. And somewhere along the way, your mind moved to the Boy King's father: what would he say when he saw the book? how would he view your words? would he rue your leaving the law? It wouldn't do to have taken that green and yellow thing among his mournful clients, the case-reports you'd forsaken, the still battery of Royals. You had to wait for his coming home, and the afternoon seemed long.

It wasn't endless, though, and at his customary hour, he was there in winter's aura. You met him at the door, kissed his chilled face, and led him to the diningroom where, beside his place, lay a green and yellow shape that con-tained four years of you. As he examined it, you fancied that the painted water was about to pour.

"A nice-looking book, kid," he said. "Mel did you proud."

But dinner intervened, longsome like the afternoon, and all through its savors and commotion, you wondered how your father would receive your shrift in crown octavo and a green and yellow jacket, and you wondered too why his welcome meant so much. As far back as you could recall, you'd been headstrong and heedless—you'd listened without hearing, you'd acted without thought. Why, when you'd pleased him so little early, did you long to please him late? Would his approval now remove his disapproval then, and if not, you thought, what would it matter? . . . But it did matter.

When dinner was over, your father put a match to one of his favorite cigars,

---

*Reproduced from an original by Lester Rondell. Their colors seemed to flow over a black arc of letters formed by the title, like water over the buckets of a wheel.

a Hoya de Monterrey, and into its gray-blue emanation, he drew your green and yellow book. When he opened it and began to read (*The Hudson River*, you thought, *was a quarter of a mile from his window.*), you placed an ash tray on the cleared table before him and left him alone in the room. As though by agreement, Aunt Jo and your sister retired to some out-of-the-way area of the apartment. You seated yourself in the parlor, where you stared at a headline reading: ALL BANKS CLOSED BY F. D. R. Below it was the news that Carter Glass had refused to issue the presidential order and that his post at the Treasury had gone to William Woodin, and you remember thinking of *Woodin* money. You glanced out at the black river and its jackstraws of Jersey lights, and you thought *The waters were glistening.* . . .

From the diningroom came the sound of something striking the floor, and going to the doorway, you saw your book sprawled alongside the table. A shot bird, you thought as you picked it up, a green and yellow bird, and you inspected it as if looking for a wound.

"Damn it, Julian!" your father said. "Why write a book so that no one can understand it?"

Something just alive was now suddenly dead, you thought, and you said, "But, papa, why did you throw it on the floor?" That was all you could dwell on—the throwing away.

Punching the air with his cigar, he said, "There isn't a man alive who can make heads or tails of that. It isn't writing at all. It's nonsense."

But you were still gazing down at the dead book, its pages creased, its binding sprung. "I worked on it for four years," you said. "It wasn't right to discard it like that."

"Not everybody is as bright as your friends—Flores, Pep Weinstein, Dr. Williams. If they're the ones you're writing for, fine, but if you want to be read by the common run—by me, for instance—you'd better write in our language."

"You chucked four years of my life on the floor," you said. "How could you do a thing like that? How could you do it, papa?"

You put the book down somewhere, on a table, on a chair, perhaps even back on the floor, and taking your coat and hat, you left the house, quietly closing the door.

You'd walked far that afternoon, but you walked even further now. You were hours in the streets, at first in the bright and crowded evening and then in the dim deserted night. You passed buildings where friends lived, a cousin, an uncle, a girl, but there was no one you cared to see or speak to, no one who could've expunged your memory of the broken bird. You kept on walking, therefore, until you could walk no more, and it was almost one in the morning before you returned to the flat on the Drive. To your surprise, your father was waiting for you. Seated in the downcast of a standing lamp, he was holding the book that he'd earlier thrown away.

"I finished it," he said, "and I think I know what you were trying to say. It was wrong of me to do what I did. Don't mark it against me."

"I'd never charge anything against you," you said, and you kissed his always fragrant hair. "Next book I'll dedicate to you."

"I meant to ask," he said. "Who's O. B.?"

"The girl who followed L. G."

SCENE 52

THE HARLEM SCHOOL OF LITERATURE (Spring 1933)

Two years earlier, in adjoining rooms at Viele Pond, you and Pep West had labored all summer on books that were destined to be published within days of each other in the spring of 1933. *The Water Wheel,* your first long work, appeared in mid-March, and even before the almost immediate issuance of *Miss Lonelyhearts,* it had either been pronounced a failure by the critics or left to die ignored. In store for *Miss Lonelyhearts* was a far more painful fate.

It was received with great praise: if gods wear hats, they took them off. They uttered their approval in tones of wonder, as at a voice that had spoken from a pillar of fire—it was just such a paean as you'd dreamed of for yourself. Although Pep had read you the letters on which the book was based, the few chapters in *Contact* were all you'd seen in print. Seeing it entire for the first time, you thought back to the Pond and to words that came at you through a wall, and you knew now what you'd shut your mind to then—that his words had come from an expanded view of the world, flown on a rare kind of fancy; yours had grown no wings and never left the ground.

You knew such things when you compared the books—how could you not have known?—and yet of those days that spring, you remember almost nothing. The time is not so much a blank as expunged of memory, the memory of defeat. It's plain to you now that you'd been vying with Pep from the beginning, but you could admit it to no one then, least of all yourself, and yet there were the two sets of notices, one hailing an arrival and the other saying goodbye—and it must've been galling to read of glory from oblivion. How did you behave? you wonder, what did you say when only one of the names from the Pond was lauded? did you hide chagrin by adding to the praise? or did you take some away to your shame? And you wonder too why you have no answers.

§

Reverential reviews of *Miss Lonelyhearts* were still coming in when, with a potential bestseller to distribute, the publishing house of Liveright went into bankruptcy. The printer, still in possession of 2,000 copies from a first edition of 2,200, immediately refused all further deliveries until paid. By the time another publisher was found to assume the obligations of Liveright, demand for the book had ceased, and when the sequestered copies were finally obtained, they could be disposed of only through remainder bookshops.

Because of your quarrel with Pep, you saw nothing of him during that period, but you heard from others that he was well-nigh distracted by the misfortune: if a heart can be broken, broken his was. A book he'd passionately believed in for five years had been turned to paper at the very moment when the passion had proved to be justified.

And when told of his grief, what did you say, Julian, what did you do, what did you feel on your side of the wall . . . ?

SCENE 53

WITH THE COMPLIMENTS OF THE AUTHOR (Spring 1933)

You sent a copy of *The Water Wheel* to L. G. After a long stay in Hartford, she'd returned to Boston, and without understanding why, you couldn't stay away. What you expected to find, unclear then, is unclear yet. All you were aware of was the usual periodic yearning to see her, and it was in no way curbed by the book's failure or even what she'd written to you on reading it:

> Am forced to admit I like it very much & dislike it heartily. I admired more than I enjoyed, admired the writing in itself, enjoyed your words for their stimulation. Next reaction—consumed with rage and disgust with Sanford—and with you for showing him up. The morning after reading it every subway noise suggested words & I felt as tho I were in one of the past years, 1929, walking down streets with you, my ears filled with the sound of your words.

Bobby Raabe sent me a clipping of "An Unpleasant Egotist"—
from the book section of the Times, I imagine. Very good criticism.

Undeterred, you went to Boston. Employed by the law firm of Gaston, Snow,
Saltonstall & Hunt, she lived on Claflin Street in Brookline, and it was there
that you saw her for the first time in more than a year.

On the train, you'd wondered about her reception of you—would it be
cold, like the April day, or would she greet you dispassionately, as if passion
was up to you? And then you were at Back Bay, and later, with evening
coming on, you were at a door on Claflin Street—and there she was, holding
out her hands. She led you past the staircase (white newel, white rail, white
balusters—why always white?) to her rooms at the rear of the house. Their
only light came from a fireplace, where small feats were being performed by
gymnastic flame. You glanced at neutral upholstery, at noncommittal paper
on the walls, and amongst the rented furnishings, you found no personal possession of the tenant, no garment, no photograph, not even, crumpled in a corner, a childhood doll, one-eyed, soiled, but precious still—nor did you see
The Water Wheel. It was there, though, if only on the air.

"You wrote that you were disgusted with Sanford," you said, "and you
were supposed to be. But why the disgust with Shapiro for showing him
up? No critic saw it, but the purpose of the book was to show him up, to
confess him."

"Are you a Catholic these days, Jule?"

"What's wrong with disclosing wrongs?"

"Nothing, really," she said. "But it doesn't make the wrong go away, as
you Romans seem to think."

"Us Romans don't think anything of the kind. We know that confession
has do to with the sinner, not the sin." In the fireplace, there were red and
yellow somersaults and occasional vaults of blue. "The sin stays."

"What you mean, then, is that you wrote the book for yourself—not for
O. B. or me."

You rose from your chair and moved to the tile apron of the mantelpiece,
and there you stood gazing down at a bed of coals, live red chunks that seemed
to be acrawl. "Did I ever tell you that O. B. was dead?"

A moment passed before she said, "No, Jule, you didn't," and it took her
another moment to say, "Were you in love with her?"

"She asked me the same thing about you."

"You're not answering."

"After my stupid trip to England, we were just two people who knew
each other."

"In the book, you return to say you love her. In fact, you say it five times."

"Actually I never said it once."

"Maybe not, but the truth is. . . ."

"I don't know what the truth is. But if I do love her, is it for what she was while alive or only because she's dead?"

"Some day, Jule, it may come to you."

SCENE 54

FIRST LETTER FROM *CENTRAL PENSION* (March 1933)

La mas confortable y centrica
Para familias y viajeros

Barcelona 1 de Marzo 1933

Dear Julian:

"There is a great wheel. It is a water wheel: it turns round and round and it fills the empty vessel and it empties the full."

The above is a quotation from "Josephus" by Lion Feuchtwanger. Thus do I hope that your water wheel will fill your empty vessel, and as for emptying the full, you are well able to do that yourself with your champagne appetite. . . .

Your Uncle Dave

SCENE 55

AND LATER REVIEWS (Spring 1933)

In order to learn how *The Water Wheel* was being received by the reviewers, you subscribed for a service called Romeike, which for $5 agreed to provide you with one hundred clippings from literary pages of newspapers and magazines throughout the country. Soon after publication, notices began to arrive in the mail. The first two, both of them dated March 26th, killed your hopes at once. The more important of the two appeared in the New York *Times* under the caption AN UNPLEASANT EGOTIST:

This first novel has some effective, even brilliant scenes. It has originality in language, especially in the projection of moods. But, when it is all over, one is puzzled by what it all means. The book doesn't hang on any peg. Perhaps as a psychological study of John B. Sanford, the law clerk who is its chief character, it has meaning — but the rest is only pyrotechnics.

This Sanford, whose thoughts and activities for a few weeks in 1927 make up the story, is an egotist, an unpleasant weakling with a narcissus complex, and an aversion to dirt, and a fear and hatred of disease that is quite frequently to be found in this kind of psychopath. His thoughts, dreams and memories, his revulsions and attractions, are spread out before us, but Sanford is scarcely an interesting enough case to make his story important, and his quite uninspired, vain and silly thought processes seem not worth our while, although at certain times Mr. Shapiro renders them with recognizable truth and effectiveness. Sanford is one of the most objectionable of men; he is essentially a hateful creation. And that his creator does not see him as he has made him is one of the weaknesses of the novel.

Three women enter the story. A trip to England on the expectation of entering Oxford, a return to the United States in dread of a disease which he hasn't got, a sudden realization that he is in love, form the framework of Sanford's history as told in the novel. The rest is sensitive, neurotic workings of the Sanford mind, with its defensive egotism and masochistic pleasure in self-torment — a study in the immature egotist and his inferiority sense.

Mr. Shapiro, with his verbal brilliance, will do better work in a more objective novel.

The coup de grâce, though none was needed, was delivered in the Miami *Herald,* which headed its review SEX, SIN, SLIME:

> This is a first novel. It should be the last. Some critics quoted on the cover flap declare the story is fine, sensitive, beautiful, excellent. They must have been thinking of something else at the time. If a garbage can is sensitive and lovely, then this book may be. But it should be heavily sprinkled with lime to kill the odor.
>
> The author is a young man and so is his chief character, a person who can see only the gutter, even when the sun is shining. The form in which the story is told is different, somewhat in the nature of "Strange Interlude," with the unspoken thoughts given in italics. There is no conversation in quotes. It, too, is in italics. There is little action, the narrative dealing with the indecent and horrible sentiments and certain sexual experiences of our scavenger hero.
>
> While we are no friend of censorship, yet the publication of such bilge as this will call for a stop. Of course, we may be of the

babbitry class of Main Street and cannot appreciate this intellectualism, the bosh of literati, in which only dirt is realistic. It is a pity God's trees must be massacred to provide paper for printing this stuff, even though it is occasionally entertaining. It is without excuse.

H. Bond Bliss

You were at breakfast with your father and family when you read those words aloud, and at the end there came to mind what someone had said (was it Sumner?) at the death-bed of Lincoln: *The wound is mortal.* The silence at the table could've lasted no more than a few seconds, but to you it seemed infinitely prolonged, and through it you knew only black space and desolation. It was hard to face the others, and to avoid their avoidance of your eyes, you stared at the clippings as if, read again, they'd change.

"I'm no critic," your father said, "but the book deserved better than it got." Your sister said, "Maybe other papers. . . ."

"Once you're buried by the *Times*," you said, "not even God can resurrect you."

"Don't feel badly," your stepmother said.

During the next several weeks, another twenty-four clippings fell from the slot in the hallway door, but even as you'd said in the beginning, the book was in the grave, and in the grave it would stay.

Some of the comment was favorable. For *Esquire* magazine, James Farrell wrote: "It is apropos to mention a few books which deserve not to be forgotten. One such is *The Water Wheel* by Julian Shapiro, a first novel. It is a study of a late stage of what is called adolescence, and contains some scintillating and brilliant writing." And in *Scribners,* Alvah Bessie declared: "What is of importance is the genuine passion of his utterance, the presence, in this work, of a sensibility working at fever-pitch. If this novel retells a story now familiar to the modern reader, it ultimately throws a bit more light on the horrors of adolescence, in this instance the adolescence of a young Jew. Here is the perennial exaltation of the race, balanced by the inevitable descent into the abyss; here is the extravagance of emotion, the heightened intellectual sensibility, the self-abasement, the self-aggrandisement. Many readers of the same generation and, curious word, 'persuasion,' as Mr. Shapiro's here will recognize themselves in 'John Sanford,' and the at times pleasant and at times uncomfortable shock of the recognition will more than amply repay them for the purchase of the book."

And there were reviews from Boston and Spokane, from Oakland and Albany, from Providence, Pittsburgh, Omaha, but nowhere was commendation freely given; always it seemed to have been extracted, like coins from a niggard hand, nor, to your chagrin, were the coins always silver, and what read like favor seemed to ring like disesteem. No review was all good, but many were all bad, and in the end it went for naught that you were briefly taken note of in Wichita and Cleveland, in New Bedford and New Haven, and even by the readers of the Salt Lake City *Tribune*: you'd come and conquered not, and in no time you were gone.*

SCENE 56

BROOKS BROTHERS: MEN'S CLOTHIERS (May 1933)

The concern, in all its advertising, proclaimed its age. Founded in 1818, ever did it recall in chaste script the nobler era that saw the nation founded too, as though, both being institutions, neither could've come into being or survived in the absence of the other. Under high white ceilings, clothing was stocked in stacks on long tables of oak, and since salesmen approached only when summoned, merchandise might be *bought*, but never was it *sold*. In those spacious rooms, always there hung textile fragrances, the perfumes of felt and leather, the pressed-flower redolence of antiquity.

On Madison Avenue one day, you encountered Sam Ohrstein, Little Sam, near the 44th Street corner. He was about to make some purchases for a coming trip abroad, and at his invitation, you kept him company. You knew you'd made a mistake as soon as you entered the store. As it had so often done, the place cast a spell wherein you were persuaded that without a brand-new pair of shoes, you'd never live to reach the door. But you had no money, nor did a flush prospect loom, and in your extremity, you touched Little Sam for a loan. As to repayment, worry hardly made a mar on the surface of your mind, and yet all you possessed on any day was the small change your father left for you in his pocket, a few nickels, a dime, a quarter, only enough for carfares and a pack of cigarettes. But spellbound where you stood, you borrowed fifteen dollars, thinking *How beautiful are thy feet with shoes.*

In due time, which is to say seventy-nine days after the accommodation, you were served with a summons to appear in the Municipal Court, Borough

---

*Dragon Press paid no advance, no royalties were earned, and after a sale of fewer than five hundred copies, the rest were remaindered.

of Manhattan, Ninth District, to answer the complaint that Samuel Ohrstein, at your special instance and request, had advanced you the sum of fifteen dollars, no part of which had been paid although due demand therefor had been made. You did not appear—to what avail, with your small and silver change? Soon afterward, you received a letter from one Arnold Malkin, an attorney:

August 1, 1933

Re: Samuel Ohrstein
vs Julian Shapiro

Dear Sir:

Judgment has been entered in the above entitled action. Unless immediate arrangements are made to liquidate this judgment, execution will issue.

Yours very truly,

You paid the sum demanded. Possibly you bethought yourself of the more sanguinary meanings of *liquidation* and *execution*.

SCENE 57

THE 48th PASSENGER (November 1933)

> *Then, since the heavens have shaped my body so,*
> *Let hell make crook'd my mind to answer it.*
> —Gloucester, *Henry VI, Pt. 3*

You'd known Sam Ohrstein for several years, and though you'd never become friends, you did have friends in common. Among these—indeed, in any company—he was the equal of all, and you looked on him as so far your intellectual superior that you rarely spoke in his presence. He was profoundly informed in many fields—philosophy, music, literature, painting, mathematics—and when issue was joined in general discussion, you listened, rapt, while he sat reasoning the opposition into defeat.

But alas, when he rose from where he was seated, when he stood somewhere among others, in the Carnegie lobby, say, or at the corner of some street, there and then he ceased to be anyone's equal, for he lacked an inch of being five feet tall. In a group, he'd always be looking up, always be engaged on a plane above his level, and whenever you saw him so, you'd think of a child among elders, any of whom, a father, an uncle, might reach down to wipe

180

his nose. Little Sam—he seemed to belong on a playground, a child consorting with children.

His size was never alluded to, except, possibly, when you were brash enough to address him as Sammy, but if the matter was not to be mentioned, it lay all too near the surface of the mind. How otherwise, when his upturned face always met faces looking down? In the end, when his mental stature could not requite him for his physique, his agony must've been Gloucester's.

Late in the year, you found this reference to him in the pages of the *Times*:

DISAPPEARS AT SEA
Bronx Man Missing From
Ship Arriving Here

Samuel Ohrstein, 30 years old, a student of Islamic literature and Indian philosophy, who was a passenger on the steamship *American Trader* of the American Merchant Line, disappeared between 3 and 4 A.M. today while the liner was nearing New York.

He was last seen by his roommate, Frank Murphy.

The *American Trader* arrived here from London with forty-seven passengers.

According to the ship's manifest, Ohrstein lived at 321 East Tremont Avenue, the Bronx. He was reported by passengers to be a quiet reserved man who spent most of his time alone and seldom talked with anyone.

But for the missing man's name, your eye might've passed across the stark report to other matters of life and death—to book reviews, to boilerplate and racing charts, to art-world news and ads. Once seen, though, the name seemed to project itself from the page, as if it had suddenly turned from fine-faced type to bold. Samuel Ohrstein, you read, and when your mind read *Little Sam,* you found that you were staring at your shoes. *Little Sam,* you thought, now less than little, a skull and rib-cage on the continental shelf, and an embassy came to you from another such diminution only the year before: *the dice of drowned men's bones.*

You didn't know why you couldn't let him end in a hundred words of print. You were aware only of a need for something more, for last words, if any, for a last sight, even for the faint sound of his splash. Unable to let him die in the dark *between 3 and 4 A.M.,* you obtained the address of his cabinmate from the shipping company and wrote to him early in November:

Mr. Frank Murphy
c.o. L. G. Witmer
1402 Washington Street
Bloomington, Illinois

Dear Mr. Murphy,

For several years I was acquainted with Mr Samuel Ohrstein, your late roommate on the *American Trader*.

His disappearance was a strange one, and his friends would like to know more about the facts preceding the tragedy, for the newspapers were quite brief in their account of it.

Therefore, if you feel disposed to communicate with me, I should very much appreciate being informed of Mr Ohrstein's speech and conduct during the short time you knew him, and anything else you believe would help me and others who were friends of his to understand his act.

I enclose a self-addressed stamped envelope for your convenience, and trust that you will be kind enough to reply.

Yours very truly,
Julian L. Shapiro

Mr. Murphy responded through a firm of Midwest attorneys, one of them probably his brother:

Mr. Julian L. Shapiro
Miss Goldie Ohrstein*

Dear Sir and Madam:

Your respective letters addressed to Mr. F. W. Murphy relative to the disappearance of Mr. Samuel Ohrstein have been referred to me for reply. Since the subject of your inquiries is identical, I am taking the liberty of answering them jointly.

It seems that Mr. Ohrstein had been a student of Islamic literature and Indian philosophy and was returning from a foreign pursuit of those subjects. During the entire trip he did not exchange over ten words with Mr. Murphy but spent the greater majority of his time lying in his berth and smoked innumerable cigarettes. While lying on his berth, or often standing up, he would close his eyes and mutter to himself but outside of this evidenced no unusual actions in the stateroom. He was found one morning by several people on the

---

*A sister of Sam Ohrstein's.

boat sitting on a stairway, seemingly bewildered, but when someone tried to help him to his stateroom, he said, "Let me alone." His actions were reported by Mr. Murphy to the ship's physician on several occasions but the physician said that since he was apparently not ill and did nothing particularly peculiar that he could not interfere.

The night he disappeared there was quite a strong wind and the sea was very rough. He left the room about 1.00 A.M. but returned almost immediately for something and then went out again. Mr. Murphy was asleep and did not see him but simply heard him leave and return and then again leave. His clothing was on the chair in the morning and his bed had not been occupied, so it appears that he was not clothed at the time of his disappearance. In the morning one of the stewards mentioned the fact that he had seen him in the corridor with a shirt on but no trousers. That was the last that was seen of him, and the first intimation that Mr. Murphy had of his disappearance was when some of the ship's officers came in in the morning and said that they had looked the boat over and he could not be found. It might appear from this that someone else had information as to his disappearance, unless someone had looked for him in the stateroom before Mr. Murphy arose and had reported his absence.

Mr. Murphy was unable to form any more opinion of him than these brief facts indicate. If you have any specific inquiries that are within Mr. Murphy's knowledge, he will be pleased to give you that information, and I trust that these facts will be of some service to you.

Very respectfully yours,
Edwin B. Murphy

Murphy & Simenstad
1500 Rand Tower
Minneapolis

A specific inquiry might've been directed at the "ten words" of the exchange between Mr. Murphy and Little Sam, but you did not make it, and you wonder still what the ten words were. What was said by Little Sam, and how did Murphy reply. . . ?

And so ended Little Sam's thirty years of life, vaguely known to you while he spent it and hardly more so when it was gone. This time, *the dice of drowned men's bones* bequeathed no embassy, and even now, after half a century, you cannot fathom the way he lived or why he died. No imaginings have led you to his last lonely hour on the rolling deck of the *American Trader*. Closed to you the workings of his mind and the meditations of his heart, and for all you know of that forty-eighth passenger, you might be one of the forty-seven who'd lived to land and learned nothing.

SCENE 58

THE FLAT ON CENTRAL PARK WEST (November 1933)

You hadn't seen it in more than a year, and though you couldn't know it that afternoon, you were never to see it again. A first snow was falling, you remember, a slow downdrift, as in a saturated solution. The brown grass of the park had turned white, and there was a white copestone on the wall and piping on the branches of the trees, and on the black streets and road-ways, tire-tracks scarred the fall. On every bench, there were four strips of snow, a meringue, and it covered hats and cars and people's backs, and the sill outside the window. Inside—

The front room was the room of old, its piano dominating the spare sur-roundings like a monument in a square. You saw Platon Brounoff stare as before, and the same prints were there, Bakst, Soudekine, Repine (the painter of lavender snow!), and on books of music you read Schubert *Seventeen Songs,* Mendelssohn *Concerto in G minor,* Granados, Brahms (of the golden tone, George said). And dust as usual lay on the floor, and smoke was buoyant in the air, and though the portières were drawn, you knew as if they were open what the next-door room had contained.

You and George were seated near the windows, both of you gazing out at a grained world descending before you like a strip of early film. You'd been close friends once, with the same interests, the same sympathies, the same ardor for each other's company, but that time had passed, and with it had gone its spirit. In the hope that some trace of it remained, you'd come to see him with the letter from Little Sam's roommate on the *American Trader.* No sooner had he begun to read it, though, than his expression changed from indifference to displeasure, nor did it relent when he handed the letter back.

"You've got your gall, Julian," he said.
"Have I?" you said. "How so?"
"You didn't know Sam well enough to make him your business."
"Anyone is a writer's business, whether he knows him well or not."
"My God, Julian! Don't tell me you're going to write about Sam!"
"For the past couple of weeks, that's all I've been thinking about."

"First it was Olga, and now it's Sam!" he said, and he rose in agitation and moved about the room, stopping finally at the piano, where he played a discord. "Incommensurable," he said.

Without knowing whether he was describing the notes or the personal relationship, you said, "You didn't help me when I was writing about Olga. I've been hoping you'd help me now."

"With what? I don't have Sam's diary!"

"I never asked to see Olga's diary. I only wanted to know if it mentioned me."

"And when I said it didn't, you went right ahead and wrote what you wanted to believe was true!"

"*Was* it true, George?"

"That's all in the past," he said. "But *The Water Wheel* isn't. Olga's in it, and there she is for all to see."

"What they see is a fine girl that a fool let go of. Nothing more."

"My mother doesn't feel that way, and neither do I. We both think you degraded her."

"If so, you're both wrong. I didn't degrade her any more than Beatrice was degraded. God damn it, George, can't you see that I meant to degrade myself?"

"When Pep told you he could identify Olga, why didn't you listen?"

"Because it wasn't criticism," you said. "It was only a lesson in manners."

"You needed it."

"Maybe, but not from him."

"From me, then."

"How, when you never asked to see the book?"

"Why didn't you offer to show it?"

"Nobody offers himself like that! I've been writing a long while, and your interest hasn't been worth a pinch of bird-shit!"

"If you think I should've helped you to use my sister in your book, you're out of your mind." He indicated the letter, still in your hand. "And here you are with another appeal. Why this concern with Sam? You weren't a friend of his."

"He knew too much for me. I couldn't've kept up."

"But now that he's dead, you can. Is that it?"

You glanced back at him, saying, "That's kind of small for a big mind like yours."

"It is, I guess," he said, and he took his seat again. "I'll talk about Sam if you like, but I won't interpret him for you."

"Meaning you won't tell me what you know."

"Yes," he said. "When you wrote to that roommate of his, what did you expect to find out?"

"More than the fact that Sam smoked a lot of cigarettes."

"They were together for only a week. It takes longer than that to know someone."

"On a merchant ship like that," you said, "you never get very far from the other passengers. Some of them must've spoken to him, and he to them. How else would they have known he was a scholar? I think he even laid it on about that. I never heard him on Indian thought or Arab lit."

"Didn't you?" George said.

"I've read about suicide in the papers, and I've read about it in books—in *Sanine,* where it's treated seriously, and in *Zuleika Dobson,* where it's only a Pep West joke. But before Sam, I never knew anyone whose death was an act of his own. You ought to be able to understand why I can't turn away from it."

"I understand, all right," he said, "but I'd understand better if you cared about him living instead of dead."

"You're trying to make me out a grave-robber."

"What else are you? What were you once before?"

"You've developed some genteel notions about what's suitable for a book. You probably borrowed them from Pep. You'd've done better if you'd stuck to an earlier writer. In *A Raw Youth,* he talks about the greatest human sin—suicide."

"He also said that God alone is judge of it. That doesn't mean you."

"That's where Fyodor and I part company," you said. "If it's the greatest *human* sin—and what other kind is there?—then I *am* judge of it. I don't know a thing about Little Sam, and plainly you know a lot that you aren't going to tell. That's pretty tightminded of you, George, but you can be sure of this—I'll write the book anyhow."

You stared out at the snow for a moment longer, and then, crossing the room, you paused near enough to the portières to touch them. You didn't, though: you could apprehend through the material the room beyond and what had once been there. Then, nodding to George, you went away.

SCENE 59

THE NOVEL ABOUT LITTLE SAM (December 1933)

You began to write it soon after your disjunctive talk with George, and by the following summer, you'd have a manuscript, still incomplete, of several hundred pages. Though you couldn't know it then, it would always be incomplete: you'd revise what you had, refine it, add to it and take away, but another year would have to pass before you realized that you'd set yourself

186

a task beyond your powers. The book you'd conceived was to have been nothing less than the history of a madness. The manuscript, even as it stands, attests your belief that Little Sam was irrational, but you seem to have been unwilling to ascribe the dementia to his size alone. There was a deeper cause of alienation, you must've thought, and you sought it in his early years, where, when you failed to find the fact, fancy faltered too.

You had only one telltale to go on. During the final months before his departure from the country, he'd besought his friends to unburden themselves of sin, a heart's desire that they could achieve by confession—confession to *him*. You knew of these harangues at secondhand: you were not among those whose souls he was concerned with saving, doubtless because he held that your trespasses and redemption mattered little to the world or heaven. Taking this uncommon behavior together with his conduct on the *American Trader,* you evolved the theory that far back in his past, he must've dwelt in a climate of evil, that later living had stirred the dormant memory, that ultimately it grew to dominate his mind, to contain it, even, and in a darkness that he perceived as light, he became the Messiah. In the end, you reasoned, his compulsion was so overwhelming that even a recognition of evil was evil, and therefore he had to get rid of himself.

For a time, you called the book *A Lingering Illness,* a title you'd eventually change to *David Holloway,* the fictional name you gave to Little Sam. Lacking knowledge of his real occupation, you made him a teacher of history at a school appropriated from your own experience, De Witt Clinton, and you filled its corridors with your own recollections, voices through the transoms, music from the music hall, oak-framed pictures, trophy-cases, laughter, dust. Unacquainted with Sam's private life, you invented a woman to share it with him, a clerk in the office of the school, and ignorant of his actual nature, you supposed one to go with his craze, and on the page he became ill-tempered, impatient of stupidity, and caustic, all these characteristics being in evidence whenever the woman appeared in the scene. As presented, she was much troubled by Holloway's erratic and prejudicial ways, and as to herself, her affection suffered long from his capricious humors.

In the first half of the book, the only relationship developed beyond a mere encounter was the one between Holloway and the woman Evelyn Poole. Every other coming together was hardly more than a chance meeting—in the street, in a park or a store or Holloway's mind—and all were used, as the one important relationship was, for a display of his preferences and aversions. At bottom, though, all such were yours.

Early in the writing, you'd come to realize that you were cutting Holloway to your pattern; there were variations, of course, particularly in the regard you had for your parents, but to a large extent he wore your clothes. Like you, he'd been born in Harlem, and he too had attended the Model School, bought penny-candy at Pop Schorr's store, and skated and fallen on the Mere, and with your eyes and ears he'd seen and heard in Walla Walla and Rome. They were your measure, all these things and more, and, alas, they did not fit him.

You managed, in that first part of the manuscript, to advance one of your themes: the smallness of Little Sam. No word that he spoke, no reaction or recall, no moment in his classroom or with Evelyn his girl—nothing was free of his mindfulness of the five-foot level of his eyes. You wrote him no page where he was allowed to sit in the sun or lie on the grass, to enjoy colors and fragrances, to watch clouds and people pass. There were no such simplicities: all was wracked and skewed for a child-sized man in a man-sized world.

In the other section of the manuscript, you put forward your second theme—the true origin of Holloway's, of Little Sam's, messianic behavior. With only your imagination as warrant, you based your theory on an act of his mother's during his childhood, unseen but sensed—the act of adultery. Driven by his urge to purify the world, he journeyed to another state in order to confront his mother with her offense and to offer absolution through confession. In an interminable scene, he could only rail and rant as he had done with Evelyn, but not having witnessed the deed that had shaped his life, he failed to break down his mother's denial. The dispute spread over pages by the dozen, ever growing more diffuse, more involuted, and evolving ultimately into a pseudo-mystical collision of the Holloway trinity—his father, himself, and an unholy ghost called "the strange man," his mother's partner in adultery. There, in near unintelligibility, the manuscript broke off.

In later years, you'd pick it over for such value as it contained and use it elsewhere. As it stood, though, some sixty thousand words that ended in a ravel, it was shown to no one, and after several vain attempts to knit up the sleeve, you abandoned it.

THE COLOR OF THE AIR, IX

ABRAHAM LINCOLN — 1865
MARSE LINKUM

Tell fewer of the funny stories I told
And make no further mention of my plug hat,
My rolled umbrella, and my outsize shoes,
Bury the legend that I was a bastard deep,
Let my mother's sleep be that of the just,
And if you must be heard, speak briefly
Of my wife Mary and my wife's madness,
But speak not a word of my spoken-for Ann
Nor say that I loved her all my life.

Forget my arms and legs, my awkward ways,
And the guffaws I caused when I sat a horse,
Forget the catnapping pickets I pardoned,
Forget my Four-score speech, my Bixby letter,
And my six-mile walk to refund six cents,
Forget the first house I lived in (let it rot
And let all the others, but not the last),
And build me no more monuments, nor cast me
But as pennies for children, for small change.

Say not that I saw two faces in my glass,
One like my own and one strange, as if bled,
And dismiss my dreams of a terrible end
Such as many now dead dreamed of and found
Before the sunken road at Fredericksburg,
Make little of my anger at little McClellan
(Outnumbered! With two blues for every gray!)
And less of the lie that the slaves were freed,
Because you know better, and so do they.

Say naught of my high voice and my sad eyes,
Throw away my relics (the watch and key,
The muffler, the ox-yoke, and the rock
On which I scratched my name and Ann's),
And retain but a pair of my photographs,
A Brady for the hard evidence of my looks

And a Gardner for the books of learned fools,
And now that only my coat can be pilfered,
Stop moving my coffin from place to place
And let the ghouls unfrock these bones.

Such are the slight favors that I request,
Yet if it please you not, grant me none:
Get my old chestnuts off your chest
Should they still strike you funny,
And if you like, praise me as Honest Abe
And raise a log-cabin Christ with nails,
Re-engrave this grave and homely face
On your money, preserve the box at Ford's,
And make cold fact of the cool fiction
That my father's name was In- or Enlow,
Wring more tears from women on the floor
For bounty-jumpers and last-remaining sons,
And count the ones that kissed my hand,
And if your tongues are slung in the middle,
Then keep Ann and my love for Ann green
While you hail the hell I had with Mary.

Small favors, and done without with ease,
For I doubt there's much I much require
To lie decently dead save your living long,
And you will so live, and I will so lie,
If you know the truth: it was you, not I,
That Booth was hired to kill, it was you,
The Union, that he fired at in firing at me,
And since I died of what went wide of you,
Please remember all I stood for when I fell.

SCENE 60

WHAT ARE YOU DOING YOUNG MAN? (Early 1934)

Are you so earnest, so given up to
literature, science, art, amours?
— "Starting from Paumanok"

Were you so given up? Didn't you know, between your wordy amours, that she was sitting with her Ellen and waiting for the end? Wasn't there time, what with running from the American Room to the Met, from Marin to Courbet, to remember your mother's mother, rocking with her mick from the Moy and waiting for the end? Did you, young and earnest, scriven twenty miles away while she waited for the coming of the end? *Uremia,* your Aunt Ida said, and she said *The hospital in Woodmere,* and she said *Come soon, Juno,* and you went that afternoon.

You were only an hour or so on the way, but you found her already in a coma, and she didn't know you were there. Her hands lay still, partly open, and you thought of their untaught skill, how they measured quantities, subdued materials, soothed pain. Her face was a crisscross of wrinkles, crazed like cloisonné. Her breathing was irregular, from shallow to deep and then from deep to shallow again until it almost died away. You eyed Ellen across the bed and nodded at the door.

In the hall outside, she said, "The poor creature. Never a bad bone in her body."
"Or a bad word in her mouth," you said. " 'The devil shouldn't take you,' she'd say. *Shouldn't.*"
"It was grief you gave her, darlin' Julian."
"You knew her better than anyone. Didn't I ever give her pleasure?"
"When you was sleepin'. She'd look at you, layin' there nice and innocent, and she'd say, 'He looks like my Ettie.' "
You touched her hair, now gone partly gray, saying, "You unrelenting old mick."
"Get along with you, now. Take yourself for a walk."

It was a cold day, the kind that told of snow on the way. It would come from the south, you thought, where the wind lay now, off the sandbars and the sea, and it was into the wind that you walked to reach, finally, a broad and empty beach. The surf attacked the shore in a long dun-colored line that again and again the shore threw back. You stood watching the endless assault and repulse until, close to the high-water mark, you saw a small brown-gray shape; a willet, it might've been, and it was spearing for food with its up-curved bill. Wading at times to its breast, it mined the foam and sand for snails, fleas, pelagic worms. For some reason, or for none, you wanted to approach it, to see it more clearly and to let it see you without alarm, and moving toward it, you inched across the beach. If the bird was aware of your approach, it gave no sign, and if it marked your nearness, it was with a sidelong eye. Only when you could've fed it from your hand did it leave off feeding and fly to other ground. That was when the snow began to fall.

You never did think the bird had anything to do with your grandma, who died while you were away, with only Ellen of the Trinity at her side.

You so earnest, so given up to literature, art, amours. . . .

SCENE 61

FAREWELL TO AN OLDERLY WOMAN (Early 1934)

It snowed for thirty-six hours, and when it stopped, on the morning of the funeral, the weather set in cold and froze the foot-deep fall as it lay. From a window facing the Drive, you looked out at the park, now one long strip of white, and the iron river and the cotton Palisades. Your father joined you, and, side by side, you gazed at the last day of Leah Nevins.

"I wonder if the trains are running," you said.

"I can remember the blizzard of '88," he said. "I saw people walk out of their houses through windows on the second floor."

"You don't have to go, you know. Not at your age."

He was silent for a moment, and then he said, "When your grandma was my age, she took the three of us into her home—you, me, and Ruthie. Did you ever think what that must've meant to her—having my family there after hers had grown up and gone?"

"I don't suppose I did," you said. "I'm not very good at thinking about others."

"Nobody is. But every once in a while, a person does something so fine that it has to be honored. Your grandma gave us a place to live when I didn't have a dime. How could I fail to show my respect?"

"You're fifty-five years old."

"She was good to me," he said, and that ended it.

The trains were still running, and as far out on the Island as Hollis, the main line was clear, and there were no delays. Once you were on the Valley Stream division, though, drifts began to short the electric power, and at every stop and start, fire flared from the third rail and dyed the snow blue. You stared out at a winter world framed, at bare trees that looked like nervous-systems drawn on the sky, at downed wires trailing on roads of rutted ice, but all the while you were thinking of your father, alongside your sister in the seat across the aisle.

He was the only man you'd ever known whom you admired without envy; you held him to be so far your better in nature, judgment, and clarity of mind that you were able to relish his ascendancy, as if you were proud to be his inferior. You thought of the unfriendly faces he was soon to see, his brother-in-law Harry's and his sister-in-law Rae's, and you wondered how he'd act, what he'd say—and then you left off wondering, because, as you knew that you'd be harsh, you knew that he'd be mild.

The train reached Woodmere long too late for the services at the synagogue, but the funeral procession had awaited your arrival, and when you joined it there, the cars set out for Bayside Cemetery six miles away. They were an hour on the road. In the gathering at the Nevins mausoleum, only one was unrelated to your grandma, her Catholic friend, Sligo Ellen Lang—but in spirit, were they not consanguine too, as truly as mother and daughter? How they loved each other! you thought, and you remembered Ellen rapping your knuckles when you used a *fleischich* fork and a *milschich* dish, and you remembered your grandma helping Ellen dress on Sunday and sending her off to church. Without schooling, they were also without hate, and here one was come to see the other go. As the plain pine coffin passed her, you turned from her face to your father's, and like her but not like you, he wept.

SCENE 62

A LETTER FROM UNCLE DAVE (March 1934)

Barcelona 6 de Marzo de 1934

Dear Julian

Your letter received and as soon as I read it, I told the Boss that I was leaving for the day and told him the reason.

Filled with sorrow and remorse I wandered down to the Park and strolled thru the Zoo. Misery wanting company I suppose. Caged animals always appear to be miserable especially the big carnivorae.

It is four years since I saw my mother and now I'll never see her. Come to think of it, I was a rotten son, wasn't I.

Thanks for telling me all about it.

With love, your
Uncle Dave

SCENE 63

FROM WANDERING ON A FOREIGN STRAND (Early 1934)

After the longest absence of his life, your Uncle Dave returned to New York at the end of April, and within days of his arrival, he paid you a visit at your father's office, now on 42nd Street. You saw at once that four years had aged him more than four, that at fifty or so he seemed to be nearer sixty. Some of his spleen was gone, and his black beasts Charley and Gordon, though thieves still, were now only thieves among their kind in this den of a world. As ever, he had curses for the plutes, but they sounded in weariness, as if he knew that a century hence, they'd be no less bloated. He shook a match more slowly, he sat with more sag, his eyes were more palely blue.

"The Depression hasn't touched you," he said. "You look as well-fed as ever."

"I have a rich uncle," you said. "I've been feeding off him." You took a typewritten slip from your desk. "To the tune of $456."

"I told you to help yourself, but I didn't mean with both hands."

"I have a champagne taste, you wrote."

"And a beer pocketbook. On $456, I could go to the Pole and come halfway back. What did you manage to do with it?"

"Money goes," you said. "A little here, a little there."

"The money that went was mine," he said. "How do you expect to pay it back?"

"My only income is from the Estate. Unless you count the small change I lift from my father every morning."

"Didn't your book earn you anything?"

"I lost on it. The publisher stuck me for postage and the printing of the brochure."

"I thought these jackass Americans would read anything," he said. "Well, that's the second profession you've failed at."

You laughed, saying, "Maybe I should've gone in for medicine."

194

"You'd've failed there too. You're like me, I'm afraid—you can spend money, but you can't make it."

"Do you really think we're alike?"

"Your grandpa would've said so. He respected success."

"He gave Harry a gold fountain-pen. My father got a silver."

"I got none at all," he said, and as if agitated by the memory of his father, he rose and went to the window, where the only view was of other windows. "My mother was different. She liked the poor."

Taking a sheet of briefing-paper from a drawer of your desk, you said, "Here's something I drew up yesterday:

> For value received, I do hereby sell, assign, transfer and set over unto David W. Nevins, fifty percent (50%) of all income which may accrue to me out of the Estate of Abraham Nevins, deceased, as said income is received; until the sum of Four Hundred and Fifty-six Dollars ($456.00) shall have been paid unto the said David W. Nevins and I hereby authorize and empower the Trustees of the Estate of the said Abraham Nevins, deceased, to pay over to the said David W. Nevins such sums in the manner specified, up to $456.00 as I may be entitled to receive out of such income. This assignment is irrevocable. Signed: Julian L. Shapiro."

"If that's a sample of your legal style," he said, "you did well to give up the law. Why didn't you write a letter to Bernstein and say, 'Pay my bum of an uncle four hundred and fifty-six simoleons and charge it to me'?"

You studied the paper and then said, "It is kind of stilted, at that. It's also poorly punctuated."

He reached for it, saying, "I'll take it all the same."

SCENE 64

BEING OF SOUND MIND AND MEMORY (May 1934)

Under the will of your Grandpa Nevins, a trust had been set up for the benefit of his wife, Leah Nevins, during her lifetime. At the testator's direction, the fund was to be invested in bonds issued by the United States government, and the income derived was to be paid to the beneficiary in quarterly instalments. Upon the lapsing of your grandma's life tenancy, the trust was to be divided, and certain shares in it were to pass to you and your Uncle Dave, to be enjoyed in like manner for the duration of your lives.

Some weeks after your grandma's death, you received a notice from the Trustees that they were about to apply to the Surrogate of New York County for approval of the share they had alloted to you; accompanying the notification was a schedule of the holdings that constituted the corpus of the Leah Nevins trust. You found your father in his room, still a smoke-layered space though he'd put out his morning cigar. You handed him your papers and sat down to wait while he read them.

When he finished, he said, "Have you heard from Uncle Dave?"

"Not yet," you said. "But it won't be long."

"My guess is that he'll be furious."

"I'm furious right now." You indicated the schedule. "That's garbage they're offering me."

"I was under the impression that the Trustees were obliged to invest your grandma's fund in government bonds."

"This is their idea of a government bond," you said, and you read aloud from the schedule. " 'Premises north side of Windsor Road, 482 feet east of Manor Road, Borough of Richmond.' "

"I'm sorry to say it," your father said, "but that's one of the better ones. The White Street mortgage is on vacant land, the taxes are in arrears, and so is the interest. To made bad worse, the parcel is in foreclosure."

"This time, Uncle Dave just might fire that little pistol."

Your father looked away, waving slowly at the smoke as if it obscured thought as well as vision. "I don't recall the exact terms of the will," he said, "but if they called for a certain kind of investment, the Trustees were bound to comply."

"A provision like that wouldn't trouble Trustee Perlman," you said.

"Maybe not," your father said, "but Bernstein is also a Trustee, and as a lawyer, he knows better than to ignore the terms of a will. What got into him? I wonder." He touched the schedule lying before him. "How could he have consented to investments like these?"

You too waved at the smoke, but only to watch it surge. "Maybe he never did consent," you said.

"What do you mean, kid?"

"Well, you say Bernstein knows better, and I agree. If it'd been up to him, he'd've carried out the provisions of the will and put grandma's money in government bonds. But suppose he never had the money in his possession. Suppose at the time grandpa died, *Harry* had the money. Maybe it'd been loaned to him, and instead of paying it into the Estate, he simply gave grandma the interest on it."

"That's quite a scheme you've thought up," your father said.

"And now, when he has to produce the government bonds for me and Uncle Dave, all he can come up with is this junk." You put the flat of your

196

hand on the schedule, as if to keep it from blowing away. "Where it came from, Christ only knows—probably from his own speculative investments."

"Let me have one of your cigarettes," your father said, and after you'd lit it for him, he gazed at you for a moment through a blue-gray haze. "You're smart, Julian," he said, "or, to be more precise, you're sharp. I don't admire that kind of mind."

"You wouldn't want me to be simple, would you?"

"Not all your life, no. But you're too young to have those ideas."

"Are they wrong?" you said. "Is there nothing to them?"

"Unfortunately, they may be right," he said. "But I wish I'd had them instead of you."

SCENE 65

STUBBORN AND REBELLIOUS SONS (May 1934)

Your Uncle Dave came to the office on the following day. In his hand as he entered your room were the notice and schedule sent to him by the Trustees. He stopped before your desk, brandishing the sheaf as if it held all the world's evil.

"If that swindler Harry thinks he can unload this on me," he said, "he doesn't know this *muchacho*!"

"I got the same offer," you said.

"The God-damned beady-eyed son-of-a-bitch! He's robbed me at every turn. We never meet but what I don't come away poorer. This time, though, it's going to be another story."

"What do you think we ought to do?"

"Take the gonnif to court—that's what! Sue his crooked ass off!"

When the two of you went in to consult your father, he was asked by your uncle to represent him in an action for an accounting.

"I can't do it, Dave," your father said.

"Why not? Here's your chance to get revenge on Perlman."

"I'm not out for revenge," your father said. "I lived under the Nevins roof for six years. If I had a hand in a lawsuit against the family, it would be said that I was an ingrate—and it would be true."

"That's foolish, Phil. There'll be no lawsuit against the family, only against that rat Harry Perlman."

"Bernstein would have to be involved, and so would your sister Ida. They're Trustees too."

"Ida would never be in it. She doesn't know a thing about the Estate.

She just signs any paper the others stick under her nose."

"If one Trustee is responsible, they're all responsible," your father said. "I'm sorry, Dave, but what you ask is out of the question."

"There'll be a lawsuit whether you represent me or not. Someone else will take the case."

"That's as may be, Dave, although I strongly advise against it." There your father turned to you, saying, "As for you, Julian, I don't want you to get involved in a dispute over money. Dave may do as he pleases, of course, but as your father, I have the right to ask that you let the matter rest."

"Seven years ago," you said, "Uncle Dave and I got a good screwing from those people. I don't like to refuse you, but they're not going to screw us twice."

"I'll overlook your language," he said, "but what happened seven years ago was your grandpa's doing, not the Trustees'. The will they administered was his, and if your share was diminished in the process, I want you to turn away and forget it."

"After the reading of grandpa's will, I complained to Uncle Harry. He told me that if I persisted, he'd make trouble for me with the Character Committee—he'd tell them I'd been in jail in Florida. The bastard! This time, *I'm* going to make trouble for *him*."

§

After leaving your father, you returned to your room, and from there you called your one-time law partner Herb Ortman, then employed by a Wall Street attorney named John Lockwood.

"Herb," you said, "my Uncle Dave and I may have to go up against the Trustees of the Nevins Estate. Does Lockwood handle matters in the Surrogate's Court?"

"He does," Herb said, "and he's pretty damn good at it."

"Is there any chance of seeing him today?"

A consultation with Lockwood was arranged for that afternoon. As soon as you entered his office, you recognized what your father called "a gentile law practice." Reserve and formality were in the very air, and there too you sensed the suggestion that no client was quite the equal of his lawyer: one, you gathered, tore the fences down, and rather loftily the other mended them. Absent altogether were the laughter, the conflict of voices, the excitement of offer and counter-offer; here no door was left ajar, here no lounger came with an hour to kill and dropped ashes on the floor. When you handed Lockwood the papers, he withdrew from the room to examine them in quiet.

198

"You picked a fancy goy," your uncle said, and he glanced about at goyische order, at goyische restraint in color, at silver-framed schicksas on the desk. "But I'm glad you did. When Harry sees this Wall Street address, he'll shit himself."

When Lockwood returned to his desk, he placed the papers before him and then regarded them for a moment as though to weigh his interpretation for correctness.

Satisfied, finally, that he was on good ground, he said, "Mr. Nevins, Mr. Shapiro, as I read the will, the Trustees were given no discretion whatever in the matter of placing the funds. They were bound to invest in bonds of government issue, and in some cases they were specifically directed to bonds of the Home Owners' Loan Corporation, or the HOLC. From the documents before me, it is quite clear that the trust established for the benefit of Leah Nevins was based on private loans, contrary to the plain wishes of the testator."

You said, "Would you say, then, that they can be held accountable for such action?"

"In saying this, Mr. Shapiro, I'm sure I only confirm what you yourself know: a Trustee is chargeable with any violation of the terms of a trust that results in loss to a beneficiary. In view of what these people offer you and Mr. Nevins, shares in distressed mortgages, they evidently took their responsibilities lightly."

"Do I understand you to say that the Court would compel them to make good any losses to us?"

"It would unquestionably do so."

"Would you undertake the case?"

"If you wish."

"We both wish," your Uncle Dave said.

SCENE 66

A GOSHEN FAR FROM EGYPT (June 1934)

This one was some sixty miles northwest of Manhattan in Orange County, far, far from the land promised by Joseph to his brethren. Here, true, there were deep pastures and fruitful vales, but these ran toward the Shawangunk Mountains and not the hills of Palestine. Here, far, far from Pharaoh, there was a place where charioteers drove for gain and glory, and that place was known as the Good Time track, but alas, it was far, far from where Benjamin wept on the neck of brother Joseph.

While at breakfast one morning, you were called to the telephone and invited by your Aunt Ida's husband to be his guest for a day of racing at Goshen, the one from which the Kittatinny range could be seen above silks and sulkies, above the mannered gaits of steeds in harness.

When you returned to the table, you said, "That was Uncle Martin. He's taking me to Goshen to watch Single G. and Dan Patch."

"They're both dead," your father said. "You know what's on Martin's mind, don't you?"

"Of course. The lawsuit."

He looked at you and then past you, as at a wall in his memory. "I've never had much regard for Martin," he said, "not since he neglected to attend your mother's funeral. But I do like your Aunt Ida, and that's why I ask you again not to be so inflexible about pressing this claim. I want you to listen to what Martin has to say before you decide that what you're doing is right."

"You sound as if you knew he was going to call."

"I did know," he said. "He spoke to me yesterday."

The road to Goshen was unfamiliar to you beyond Suffern and Monroe, and it was there, while you were taking in countryside you'd never seen, that your uncle left off his dissertations on trotting and pacing that he interspersed with song (*A wandering minstrel I*) and began to speak of the legacy of discord that your grandpa had bequeathed to the family.

"This action that you and Dave are bringing," he said. "It's made a wreck of your Aunt Ida."

"If that's so, I regret it," you said. "We mean her no harm."

"But you've done her harm, Julian. You've named her as one of the defendants."

"We had to name her. She's a Trustee along with Bernstein and Harry. But I'll tell you this: if there was any breach of trust, it wasn't committed by her, and if we're called on, that's how Dave and I will testify. It was Harry Perlman who caused all this. He's the one you have to thank."

"The demand you and Dave are making for an accounting is going to break up the family."

"It was broken a long way back, when the Perlmans prejudiced grandpa against my father. That was the beginning, not this."

"You and Dave are still sore about not being able to touch your inheritance, but why be sore at the Trustees? This is the way your grandpa wanted it."

"It's the way Perlman wanted it."

"Perlman, always Perlman—but in going after him, you're hurting Ida."

"No Surrogate would charge Aunt Ida with Harry's doings. Dave and I

200

will look after her, even though no one looked after us seven years ago. Nobody took the en-jine off our necks."

The racing card had begun by the time you reached the track, and when your uncle left you in the stands, you watched him make his way toward a group of drivers, two of whom waved at his approach. It suited you to stay where you were, sitting in the sun and gazing out across the crowd at the distant hills of Palestine. Your eyes came back to your uncle, standing amid slashes of color near the rail, and you remembered back through twenty years to his wedding-eve at the Martinique, and you recalled too your mother, and her gown, and her pallor, and you saw what only she had seen then, that she was due to die within the year.

A field of pacers was entering the stretch, rocking with the left-side right-side rhythm of their gait, and even over the cries of the crowd, you heard the repeated *ha!* of the drivers and the pound of striding feet—and then the heat was over, and the sulkies turned back toward the sheds. But still before you as they passed was that night in 1913, and now as then you saw your Aunt Ida, dressed in gray for travel and hurrying for the door, hurrying away with this Martin, who wore white felt hats and tailor-made clothes and often sang of *rags and patches*. You saw hills in the distance, but they were not those of Palestine.

SCENE 67

THE QUALITY OF MERCY (June 1934)

You've always remembered that day. You were in your room, that semi-subterranean space at the rear of the apartment, and your view, had you looked up from the pages before you, would've been of the legs and feet of passersby, the wheels of traffic, ashcans, and whatever had been cast away or fallen from heaven—an orange-rind, a bird, a matchbox, dust. But you did not look up. You were writing of another day, the one when Little Sam had reached the end of the world off Montauk Point.

Your father spoke from the doorway at your back. "When you're finished with what you're doing," he said, "I want you to meet me at the office."
You turned, saying, "Will early afternoon be all right?"
"Yes."

"Anything special?"
But he was gone.

At the outset, the book about Sam had seemed to go well. You'd opened it with his awakening at the start of a typical day, and the task you'd imposed on yourself was an objective description of his bizarre conduct. No analysis of his actions was wanted beyond what might be implicit in their selection: once set down, they were expected to interpret themselves. But you knew even then at the beginning that description would not serve when you put Sam among people, when you took him away from the sound, color, and motion of his room: then you'd be compelled to enter his mind with your own and explain why hell had made it crook'd.

When you joined your father that afternoon, he nodded at the door, and you closed it. "Sit down, kid," he said, and he waved at a chair.
"What am I in for?" you said.
"That depends on you. I had a visit yesterday from J. Sidney Bernstein."
"I'll be damned! First Uncle Martin and now Bernstein. I think we have them on the run."
"We, meaning you and Dave, I hope. I'm not in this, and I never was."
But you were thinking of flight and pursuit. *On the run,* you thought, and you said, "Next it's Harry Perlman's turn. He's the one I'm really after."

You treated yourself to a vision. You saw silk-shirt Harry before you, his moiré tie dinged with ash from a chewed cigar, and his hat was in his hand.

"Bernstein came here to plead with me to call you off," your father said. "Apparently he was under the impression that you and Dave were acting on my advice and with my encouragement. I assured him that he was wrong, that so far from abetting you, I'd actually tried several times to dissuade you."
"I hope you added that several times you'd failed."
"I did, Julian—and so help me God, the man began to cry."
You stared at him for a moment, and then you laughed. "I wish I'd been here to see that."
"Do you?" your father said. "Are you that hard?"

And now you saw Bernstein, a few thin strands of hair drawn across his baldness, and but for two streamlets from behind his glaring pince-nez, he'd've seemed to have no eyes.

You said, "It's been seven years since Bernstein read that will to the family, and ever since he's run the Estate as if he were dispensing favors. There he'd sit behind that tin box doling out our skinny little portions with a damned reluctant hand. Every time I had to see him, he'd go out of his way to make me feel like some pissy-ass schnorrer, and I'd get a stare and a sneer and a

No. And now here he comes staring and sneering no more, but crying for the soft heart he never showed me. To hell with him!"

"I wish you could hear yourself, Julian."

You heard yourself, but oddly enough for the particular moment, you seemed also to hear Little Sam. No more than his roommate had done could you distinguish the words he spoke, but you somehow knew that he was speaking to someone who wasn't there, to someone dead, perhaps, or far away. You wondered why Sam had intervened. Why had you thought of him? What had he to do with legacies . . . and then you remembered *the dice of drowned men's bones.*

"And to hell with Harry!" you said. "I've never forgotten what he told me the day that grandpa died: 'You'll never have to worry about money as long as you live,' he said. Up to then, I hadn't given a thought to money. I certainly wasn't waiting for grandpa to die and make me rich. But once Harry'd put the idea in my mind, I couldn't get it out; it grew and grew till God knows what I expected to find in the will. As it turned out, it came to about ten bucks a week, with the principal in trust so that I couldn't ever touch it. It was Harry who got grandpa to do that to me. I can still see him making his way down the street with me, almost running for joy: grandpa's money was in his hands at last. And now he's stumbled, the son-of-a-bitch! He's down, and I'm going to kick him where he lies!"

Hart Crane in the Gulf Stream, you thought, and Little Sam in the cold deep of Hudson Canyon—a year apart, their leaps from the rail. You tried to apprehend their final moments in the dark, when only a barrier of holystoned oak stood between life and death, and you couldn't understand why they'd chosen nothing over all.

Your father said, "You're in such a passion about Harry that you can't think straight. In your excitement over the chance to—even the score, I suppose you'd call it—you've forgotten one vital fact: Harry's personal use of grandma's trust fund was wrongful, but it wasn't criminal. Do I make myself clear? He can be reprimanded, he can even be removed as a trustee, but he can't be put in jail. The most the Surrogate would do is compel him to make good any loss—and the same is true for Aunt Ida."

He saw that your attention had unravelled. You were with Little Sam on the deck of the *American Trader,* and you were also with Crane on the *Orizaba,* and it seemed to you that you knew what they were about to do—and you watched them do it.

Your father slapped his desk to bring you back. "Listen to me, Julian," he said. "Harry and Ida won't suffer, but Bernstein will. Do you hear me?

He's a lawyer, an officer of the Court, and a far higher degree of fidelity is required of him than of a layman. True, Harry may have profited by lending grandma's money to himself instead of to the government as your grandpa directed. But Bernstein gained nothing through Harry's finagling. He had no part in it; he merely stood by while Harry did as he pleased. A small offense, Julian, but do you know what it'll cost him if the facts come out?"

"I don't care a pinch of shit what it costs him!"

"Possible disbarment," your father said, "but surely a year's suspension of the right to practice law. Either penalty would be fatal. It would be his finish as a member of the Bar."

Disbarred, you thought, and you remembered the lawyer your father had stopped to greet in City Hall Park; you remembered the frayed suit, the bravely-worn but shiny hat, the faraway look that saw nothing. Your mind put Bernstein's face under the hat, Bernstein's body in the suit, Bernstein's look in faraway eyes.

"Be reasonable, Julian," your father said. "By the terms of your grandpa's will, you were entitled to get ten thousand dollars from him and five thousand more when grandma died. Bernstein says that Harry has been able to raise between thirteen and fourteen thousand in cash. I say that's close enough. I say that for a miserable thousand dollars — I mean the *interest* on it — you can't drive a man from his profession."

"He must've cried in a steady stream," you said.

He studied you for a moment without expression, and then he said, "That's a heartless remark."

"What does he deserve?"

"Mercy, damn it!"

The gentle rain, you thought, but it did not fall on you. The hat, you thought, the suit, the boundless stare.

"If nothing has touched you so far," your father said, "maybe this will. Bernstein is in line for an appointment to the Bench — the Supreme Court of New York County."

At first, the information stunned you, but when you comprehended the extent of your power, you couldn't avoid a smile. The gentle rain, you thought, the Gulf Stream, the black waters off Paumanok — but still you produced a smile.

You said, "You want me to stand mute while a guy like that puts on a robe?"

"It's the ambition of his life."

"A guy that can't execute a simple trust? He isn't fit for the Supreme Court Bench. Where does he come off to sit in judgment?"

Once again your father took time to study you, and then he said, "Where do you? Are you so pure? Does all virtue reside in you?"

"I'm not going to look the other way and let him do to others what he did to me."

"What are you, Julian—a hangman?"

"He'd hang me," you said.

Your father rose now, and looking down at you, he said, "I don't give a good God damn what he'd do to you or anyone else! I'm concerned with what you'd do to him for the interest on a thousand dollars! You're the one I care about. You're my son, and you're out to ruin a man for a two-bit error. I won't have that, do you understand? I won't have it!"

"Do you mean I'd no longer be your son?"

"You'll be my son till I die or you do," he said. "But you won't be the one I wanted or the one I thought I had. You'll fall, Julian, and you'll never rise again. That's all I have to say."

You thought of the pain of relinquishment. You thought of Little Sam and of the lyrics lost off the *Orizaba*. And you thought of a shabby yearning lawyer whom your father could not pass.

"I'll do as you wish," you said.

SCENE 68

OF ONE WHO WROTE TO EUGENE DEBS (June 1934)

Your Uncle Dave was staying at the Sloan Y.M.C.A. on 34th Street, and when you called him from the lobby, he told you to come to his room. It was on the third floor rear, its single window facing the blank wall of an alley. At first, you'd thought it an airshaft, but standing close to the jamb, you could see far to one side a trapezium of sunlight poised upon a roof.

On his visit to your office, you'd thought your uncle had aged faster than time had passed, but there in that dismal cube of space for young Christians, he seemed to have weathered even more, and he looked too old for the room. Looking about at the factory furniture, useful and unimpassioned, you wondered whether it was the indiscriminate bed that had grayed his ash-blond hair and speeded up his years. How many such had he known, how many four-wall nights had he spent, he who'd written to Gene in jail, sent him cigars from Cuba, hats from Panama, what were his honors for having God-damned the rich and lived against the grain?

"Uncle Dave," you said, "I came here to tell you that I'm withdrawing from the lawsuit."

He was seated partly in light that fell from a standing lamp. He'd been reading when you called, and the book was still in his hands (a life of Altgeld, was it, or something by Brann the Iconoclast?), and when you spoke, Blue Boar smoke from his straight-stemmed pipe could not be seen to waver.

"Why?" he said.

"My father wants me to."

"I didn't know you were the obedient son."

"Usually I'm not, but I am in this."

"What persuaded you?"

"None of his arguments, really. They didn't move me at all, nor could Bernstein and Perlman on bended knee. I was moved by my father himself. By the fact that he's my father."

"My father moved me too," your uncle said. "All the way to Peru."

"It's odd. After all these years, he still feels bound to grandpa. He married into the family, and in his mind he's still there."

"It's odd, all right, because I feel like an outsider."

"He's afraid I'm becoming money-hungry. It reflects on him, he thinks. It makes him look that way too—and he isn't."

Above your uncle's chair, his pipe-smoke had filled the lampshade, and in some inversion of spilling, it was now pouring upward outside the satin cone.

"I won't ask you to go against your father," your uncle said. "You'd only wind up where I did—here."

He glanced at the bed, the bureau, the walls and fixtures, and then at the darkening alley. Ill-lit at best, it was losing what light it had to the lengthening afternoon. Opposite the window, the bond was fading from the bricks to make a blood-red end to the view.

"If you want to pull out, pull out," your uncle said. "Hell, I'll probably do the same."

"I hope it won't be because of me."

He shook his head. "It's because of me," he said. "I cared for my father, and he for me, but he couldn't show it, and neither could I. We each wanted our own way, and we each got it, and now he's in the grave, and I'm in the Y.M.C.A."

SCENE 69

HARRIS FRIEDMAN (1933-34)

You remember, because of his quiet intensity, how your father had once appraised him. Always averse to superlatives, he'd nevertheless said, "I've known many a fine man, Julian, but he's the finest of all." He was referring to his brother-in-law, the husband of his elder sister Sarah, and in his presence thereafter, you'd now and then remind yourself of your father's phrase, *the finest of all,* and you'd study him for signs that illustrated the estimate.

In your mind, fineness derived from refinement. Of this, you found none in his lifelong immigrant accent, nor did you find it in his not at all courtly manner, nor yet in ill-fit clothes off the rack. You'd listen in vain for the mythical allusion (to Briseis, say, and how Agamemnon took her away from Achilles), and void of couplets were his words on mechanics' liens and chattels real; he made no *mots,* that finest of men, and he played no note of music. Wherein, then, you wondered, lay the fineness spoken of by your father? It didn't occur to you that you weren't fine enough to know.

You were writing at home that winter, and at the end of each morning's work, you'd take to the open air, walking for hours in all weathers, walking, really, to break away from words. Your wanderings one day wound up at the entrance to the Cornell Medical Center, a hospital on the far east side of midtown Manhattan, and only then did you realize that you'd been impelled there or drawn: in a room somewhere above you, your Uncle Harris lay. He'd undergone a complicated two-stage operation, and his stay in that room was expected to be long. You stood near the steps, thinking of how in his company you'd always felt excluded. At a gathering of the family, he'd regarded you hardly at all; he'd suffered you, in fact, as a guest uninvited. You'd sat at his board, you'd listened and laughed and talked, but you'd always felt that to him you were a presence that filled a chair. *The finest of all,* you thought, and further drawn or impelled, you entered the building and went upstairs.

"Julan?" your uncle said when he saw you, but the word seemed other than interrogatory; however weakly, it expressed surprise.

Julan, you thought, never Julian, and you said, "How are you feeling, Uncle Harris?"

"Not bad," he said, and he touched a tube dripping saffron urine into a bottle suspended from his bed. "And not good."

"My father said he'd seen you. He thinks you're looking better."

Your uncle's face was marred by a twitch that might've been a smile. "You want advice, Julan?" he said. "Don't get old."

Wondering what to say, you said, "How long will you have to stay in the hospital?"

"They don't tell me, but I can tell them," he said, "a long time," and he looked away at the errorless white of the ceiling.

"Does it tire you to talk?"

"I'm only tired laying here. I don't do nothing, but I'm tired. That's what it means being old."

Old, you thought, and it was a moment you might've brightened with a gesture, a beguiling remark; instead, there came to you only a memory of Faustus pleading with Helen to make him immortal with a kiss.

And then your uncle said, "We don't got the same blood, your father and me, but he's more better by me than my three brothers."

A nurse brought in a tray covered by a cloth. "I'm going to change Mr. Friedman's dressings," she said. "I'll have to ask you to leave now."

"I'll be back another day," you said to your uncle.

"Yes," he said. "Goodbye, Julan."

And you did come back, twice more that week and soon thereafter daily: you couldn't stay away. At the beginning, your visits were brief, lasting a quarter of an hour at most, but before long you perceived that your uncle had begun to look forward to your coming, and then your calls lengthened to an hour and sometimes to an afternoon. He carried the talk now, and you attended, for he was telling you what you'd never known—the story of his life. He told it piece by piece in so natural a way of speaking that you made no memoranda of its flavorsome turns, its unusual hues; you were confident of your ability to reproduce it at will. It was the most egregious literary mistake you ever made, for when the time came for you to write of your uncle, you found that all you'd come away with was facts that lacked his salt, scenes gone gray in default of his eye: his awkward, lulling, lovely way of speaking had been lost, and what you made him say, alas, was yours.

It would be forty years before you tried to tell, as he'd told it, of his coming to America,* and only the reason would remain, not the seasoning he'd given it in those days at the hospital. The basis for his emigration from Lithuania had been the possession of a Gladstone bag—no more than that—a Gladstone bag pressed upon him by way of payment by an employer short of cash. For

---

*In "Origin of an American," *A More Goodly Country*, 1975.

some service he'd performed, expecting pay in money, he'd been requited with an article so useless to him that he'd been ashamed to carry it home past the staring eyes of neighbors in the roads. To hide his chagrin, he'd contrived the only explanation that truly explained: he was leaving Lithuania, he said, he was traveling to the American States. Once told, the tale could never be called back: the Gladstone bag had become imperative, and the way it pointed lay westward across the Baltic and then the open sea. All because of a thing of leather made—a cowhide Gladstone bag.

That was the first of his stories. Others were still to come.

SCENE 70

ENCOUNTER IN A HOSPITAL HALLWAY (Spring of 1934)

On a livingroom wall in your uncle's home hung a portrait in oil of his daughter Harriet, the work of the artist Nicol Schattenstein. Something of a rage at the time, he was a painter of no little skill, and apparently persuaded by Sargent, his tendency was to idealize his sitters, to relieve the plain of their plainness and to add to the fairness of the already fair. With your lily-cousin Harriet, there'd been no need for gilding, but she'd been enhanced all the same, and seen within her acanthine frame, she simply wondered the eye. She was a beauty on her own, and rarely did you consult her heightened likeness if she herself was there.

At the hospital, you'd met her in the corridors and in your uncle's room, and since neither of you had forgotten the quarrel of years before, your meetings were lukewarm at best, and only when you addressed each other in her father's presence did you try to conceal the estrangement. That spring, she was several months gone with her second child, and over the course of the weeks, she grew before your eyes—grew in looks, you thought, as well as size. She moved more slowly now, and having longer to watch her approach, you'd sometimes find that you were thinking of her portrait, as if the real and the image were one at last.

On a day when you were having that fancy, she surprised you by pausing as she reached you and offering you her hand.

Without releasing you, she said, "I don't know why you come here so often, Julian, but whatever the reason, you're doing my father good. To tell the truth, he seems to enjoy your visits; he even looks forward to them. You give him a chance to talk, and while he's talking, his mind is off his illness."

"He calls me Julan," you said.

THE COLOR OF THE AIR, X

GEORGE CATLIN — 1872

PAINTER OF THE PAINTED INDIAN

Oh how I love a people who don't live for the love of money.
                                                            —George Catlin

When he was born there, they were still talking about the Wyoming Valley massacre. They were still plowing up powderhorns and now and then a mildewed moccasin, still finding buckles and bits of faded cloth, and the swamp where the womenfolk fled still yielded the odd set of bones. It was only a dozen years back to the day the British and the Mohawks attacked from the north, to the stand that was made at Forty Fort, and the night of killing after the fight was lost. He must've heard the story young and often: they were still telling it to each other, those that survived, as if once they stopped, they'd stop being alive.

Dwelling on how prisoners were cooked on coals, fried in their own fat, he could've grown to hate the Indians more each time the tale was told. It would've been easy to say hell was too cold for the kind who pleasured in their victims' pain, who were quick to madden and slow to be satisfied, who were two-faced, malign in the mind, stiff with pride, and born with a craze to kill. You'd've sworn he'd hold, as so many did, that no Indian was any good, not even a dead one.

He never believed that, though. To him, the whites were the thieves and murderers, the whites were the perjurers, the cheats, the makers of war and in war the savages, it was the whites who had jails, poorhouses, locks and keys, and law. He said *Nothing short of the loss of my life shall prevent me from visiting their country and becoming their historian,* and he did visit them, Sauk and Mandan, Assiniboin and Cree, and on his little canvas reservations he kept the red man green. And he never really lost his life: he gave it away to a people who died without Jesus but lived without greed.

SCENE 71

A LONG LAST SEASON AT THE SHORE (Summer of 1934)

By your own choice, your quarters were in the carriage-house at the rear of the Friedman grounds, far from the main building and further from the road. It was used as a garage now, but always on the rise from the planking was the redolence of hay and harness, and in your room on the upper floor, sometimes you'd imagine sound to go with it, stamping damped by straw, a long slow sigh, a kick against a stall. You'd lie there in the dark, looking up through a cedar or a poplar at the sky, and you'd wonder yet again why the region seemed to you home. It was neither your domicile nor your place of birth, but nowhere else did you feel native to your surroundings, to the beach, the vegetation, the kind and color of the earth.

At the invitation of the Friedman family, you were there now. It was their belief that your uncle's recovery had been due in part to you, and they were unwilling to abandon the process by which it had been achieved: the stories, the *megillahs*, must continue to be told, and you must be there to hear them. Accordingly, they'd sent for you as soon as they opened their summer home at West End, and with your typewriter case and a satchelful of clothes, you arrived on a day in early June. It was thought odd that you elected to work and sleep above a stable, but that was what you wanted, and with an unspoken *meshugeh*, they let you have your way.

For a long time after his release from the hospital, your uncle was restricted to the second floor of the house. His bedroom opened onto a small balcony rather like the bridge of a yacht, and there, in the afternoons, he'd sit in the sun and relate the day's instalment of an accidental life, a life determined by a payment in kind instead of cash. Far back now was the Gladstone bag, lost or stolen somewhere between Grodno and the lower East Side, and at times you'd wonder whether it had ruled another life, whether the thief or finder had been made to cross water without real desire, to *go* merely because he possessed an adjunct of travel — a Gladstone bag.

In the days at the beginning of the summer, your uncle's narrative had reached its new-world chapters: he was no longer the worry-free journeyman of *guberniya* roads, nor even the quanderied possessor of what the neighbors called his leather hold-all — a stylish box. Nay, by then, he'd come to these heedless shores, and like myriads of his kind, he'd found the way to Chatham

Square, to Delancey, Stanton, Orchard, Henry—to the point or place of beginning.

Thereafter, being alone in a nation of sixty millions and with neither a family nor friends to fall back on, he had to guard against falling at all. He came a cropper, though, in his very first employment. Hiring himself out as a house-painter's helper, he agreed to accept shelter under his employer's roof as the larger part of his wage. The roof, however, covered only a two-room flat in a cold-water tenement, and your uncle's place of rest was a pair of chairs in the kitchen. As he described the man to you, the painter was a Polish *momser*, drunk half the day, half-drunk the other half, and a Jew-hater all day long. He had a wife, whom he beat often, sometimes even while copulating, and a sickly child not quite twelve months old. It slept in a cradle alongside your uncle's bed of chairs, and it was his duty to rock it whenever it awoke and cried in the night. His own slumbers being thus interfered with, he somehow developed the ability to hear the puling in that other world, and, without himself waking up, to rock the cradle in this one. But a day dawned, he said, when for all his rocking, a dead child stared up at the light.

Your uncle's laughter, fifty years after that death at night, was still his only way of voicing hysteria—still, so long later, he was seeing that stiff little bundle of Polish waste. There, on a balcony looking out upon a mottled sycamore, he wept still over his slum and searing past.

§

After breakfast each morning, you returned to your room above the disused stalls and hayracks of the carriage-house, and there all summer you tried to think your way into the mind and history of the forty-eighth passenger on the *American Trader*—Little Sam Ohrstein. Much of what you'd thus far written was a series of scenes introducing him as a character and putting him on display during a typical day at home and at school. You'd shown him in his own particular surroundings, in neighborhood encounters, and among his pupils in the classroom, and having established, as you thought, some of his peculiarities and obsessions, you'd reached the point where it was necessary to provide him with a background that would account for his present confessory mania.

To explain the redemptive role he'd been playing at the end of his life, you created for him a hatred of evil in existence at the beginning, and the evil you'd chosen to suppose was his mother's adultery, committed almost in his presence while he was still a child. His special torture, as you conceived it, would be that he was never to know whether his suspicion was founded. Persistently would his mother deny what he thought he'd seen and heard, and with equal persistence his doubt would remain. The showing you made involved a child's interpretation of sound as meaning, a child's understanding of language, and a child's pronouncement of guilt, all of it connected with what might or might not have occurred one night in an adjoining room. He was not to learn whether he was right or wrong, but one or the other was to make crook'd his mind.

You were a long way beyond your depth. You knew nothing of the nature of evil, and you were limited further by your elementary readings in the science of the mind. You could *state* the antagonism between the mother and the son, but you could neither explore it nor explain it—and what stopped you time and again was your own life, so far removed from the one you were trying to present. You lacked the experience that might've fitted you to comprehend.

But what distressed you was less your lack of knowledge than the failure of your imagination. You'd believed once that what you did not know you'd be able to invent, and it dismayed you to find that you were wrong. Day after day in that mews beneath the trees, you saw yourself outside a wall you could not scale, a world you could not enter—the involuted workings of Little Sam's mind. All summer long you worked to force them, but when fall came and leaves lay grasping at the browning grass, you had to turn away from a forty-eighth passenger still as vague as the other forty-seven.

§

That day was yet a long way off when, one morning, your Cousin Harriet sought you in your room. The quarrel between you, a doused fire, would always smoke. You knew that, and so did she, but both of you, to provide a front, tried to pretend it was out. As she entered, misshapen and ungainly, you were taken once more by a beauty that nothing seemed to reduce.

"Just by being here," she said, "you're doing the family a favor. I wonder whether you'd be willing to do us another."
"If I can," you said.
"I'm due in August, as you may know. That's nearly two months away, and my Danny is already too much for me to handle. He's a wild one, and he needs looking after that I can't give him. Would you, in your spare time, take charge of a five-year-old boy?"
"Yes," you said.

Ah, how he could eat in those days! your uncle would say. Anything, everything, *kosher, terephah,* all day and well into the night—what an appetite he had, and what a capacity, and what a lean purse with which to pay! He'd haunt the saloons for the free lunches that went with a nickel glass of lager—sandwiches, pickles, cheese, sauerkraut, beans—and he'd stuff and stuff till the barman threw him out. Food! It was his constant and insatiable need, and he'd fare far to fill it, but as in a frustration dream, the more he tried to fill it, the more bottomless it seemed. Hearing of great plenty in a place called Virginia—where, it was said, a worker was virtually force-fed—he straightway went to that place and rolled cigarettes in return for wages that consisted largely of victuals. For those heaping platters, he said, he hand-rolled three thousand cigarettes a day—three hundred an hour, five a minute, one every twelve seconds. Every twelve seconds, it was paper, pinch, paste, and roll, but always before him were those steaming heaps, and he was happy.

And then, alas, came the machines, creatures that rolled in a single day thirty thousand in return not for bread and meat and fruits of the tree and vine, nay, for only a squirt of oil.

Gott im Himmel! how he could eat in those days! But they were gone, Julan—his pancreas functioned poorly, and there was sugar in his blood, and he ate gluten instead of fine white flour, and his carbohydrates were the things of dream.

At table one day, he said, "You know what is the best thing, Julan? The best in the world?"
And you said, "What?"
"On your plate—the mashed potatoes."

Danny, your first cousin once removed, was the son of the family's beloved Harriet and regarded by all with hope and favor. Because of your estrangement from his mother, you'd seen and heard little of him until that summer, and, now, unexpectedly, you found him in your care, a round little boy with wide brown eyes. It struck you that you might've been construing your own photo as a child: at thirty, you thought, you'd become the guardian of yourself at five.

It was a good summer. With your smaller self for company, you walked the dirt roads, the scrub pine woods, the cornfields, the empty beaches; you took him to see the severe white lady of Freehold, the Tennent Church, and to Asbury Park, where the *Morro Castle* still smoldered on the sand; and at the end, you learned that he wasn't you at five, wasn't you at all.

§

Returning from the tobacco factories of Virginia, your uncle became a house-painter in his own right—what a *shikker* Polack could do, he said, he could do, and in no long time, he was doing it well enough to court and marry your father's sister Sarah, a woman with *goldene* hands, adept in the art of wig-making and hardly less so at the stove, as well she had to be, for her husband's appetite had in no wise diminished as his ability to pay increased. O God of Israel, how he now could eat!

But on a certain night, he said, while his Sarah was sorting hair, a knock was heard on the outer door, and who should be there but a stranger, a cer-tain Jacob Mendelson bearing a letter of introduction from the *mischpocha* in Grodno. The hour was late, but as no one was ever turned away—it was a sin and a shame to turn callers away—the man was invited in, seated, suffered to talk as only the lonely can talk, and finally fed.

And then, *Shema, Yisroel!* then and only then did your Uncle Harris behold someone who could eat more than he. . . !*

§

It was a good summer. It lasted well into November.

SCENE 72

THE SAME PILGRIM, THE SAME PLYMOUTH ROCK (Fall of 1934)

> *pilgrim*—one who travels, usually far and often to strange lands, to visit some holy place or shrine as a devotee

From the train to Boston that weekend, you watched New England transfer its image to your windowpane, a long decalcomania of streams, towns, bare

---

*Told in *To Feed Their Hopes,* University of Illinois Press, 1980.

trees, and leaning poles. On the seat beside you lay a book you'd brought along, a magazine, a newspaper, but if you read from one or another, you remembered nothing: all the way, it seemed, you were staring as if at passing things, but seeing only those already past. It was seven years, you thought, since she'd been brought to your room, and now, seven years later, you were recalling that beginning from this end. Between you, the old division, the old insuperable wall—but you knew at last that the wall was you.

That evening—where did she live now, Vernon, Brimmer, Bowdoin, Joy?—that evening, you sat with her in her rooms, but not in the dark as before. You wanted to watch, as for a print that might appear, a message written in sympathetic ink. A lamp was on, and her chair stood full in a downfall of light.

"I didn't want to call on you that night," she said, "but he insisted. As soon as I saw you, though. . . ."
"And as soon as I saw you."

Were those the first words spoken, or were they among the last?

"It should've come to more than it did, Jule."
"Do you know why it didn't?" you said.
"I only know what you've told me. That you couldn't get over the way we met. That you could never jump the ditch."
"I believed that for a long time. Or I thought I believed it."
"What do you believe now?"
"People meet in all kinds of ways, some common and some strange. Our way was neither. You were simply on display. . . ."

A summer afternoon at the shore, you thought, white-dressed women rocking slowly in the shade, a man with a suitcase staggering toward the porch—a suitcase that you knew was filled with fragrant linens embroidered in milk-blue silk. An offering of linens, you thought.

"He was displaying you," you said.

You remembered how a tablecloth was flirted open to fall across a skirt, its eyelets and edging faintly blue against the white.

"He didn't come to sell you, though. He came to give you away."
"You've always carried on about that, Jule, and you've always been wrong."
"You never told me whether the two of you were lovers, and I never asked. But I knew."
"How could you know?"
"If you believe something, you know it, even if it isn't true."
"That sounds deep, but it's really stupid."

"Would I have taken your word about it? Could you have convinced me that you two were merely friends?"

"My relationship with him—why did it matter so much, and why does it still? Not every girl is—what's the word?—pure, you know. Some of us made the mistake of losing our virtue while waiting for you."

"It wasn't that, Lou. It wasn't that at all."

"What, then?"

Could you really bring yourself to express it? After seven years, were you about to say what you'd made yourself suppress. You could almost watch the workings of your mind.

"Things would've been different," you said, "if I'd met you without meeting him."

"If you'd picked me up in the street, you mean?"

"I never cared what my number was—I could've been your first or your fortieth. But I didn't want to know any names."

"Excuse me for being crude, but what you're saying is that it would've been all right if I'd screwed for the milkman."

"I didn't want to compete against someone I knew."

"How do things change if the man is a stranger?" she said. "*I* know—and that's where the competition is."

"The competition is in *my* mind, not yours. I'm the one who does the measuring."

"Measuring, for God's sake! Is that what you've been doing?"

"For seven years, I tried to tell myself it was something else—but it wasn't. I was always comparing."

And now you were saying, and she was hearing, what you'd come so far and taken so long to say.

"We'd known each other since our Lafayette days," you said. "I didn't particularly cotton to him then, but neither was I particularly put off. I'd never associated with anyone so tall, so broad, so thick through the middle. Arms, hands, fingers, feet—all of him was huge. I thought of him more as a curiosity than a person, but at the time I wasn't feazed by his size. In fact, it seemed to feaze him: walking, sitting, standing, he was always trying to shrink."

You thought of Little Sam, and for all you knew or would ever know, his size had doomed him. Yours, as you'd come to realize, had done the same to you.

"When he put you on my doorstep that night, he didn't vanish. He moved into my mind."

"You've never believed that he moved out of mine."

"A guy brings a girl (*his* girl?) to my room and says, 'Here, this is for you.' Does that make her forget where she came from? I don't think so. She knows she's a gift, and she remembers who gave her away. A God damn giant! And from then on, he's the standard."

Walking one day in the Place Vendôme, you'd stopped before a bar of steel embedded in a wall—the standard meter, it was, the meter by which to measure all meters.

"From then on," you said, "no matter how brightly I spoke to you, it was always comparative. No matter how gallantly I behaved, it was always a criterion of gallantry. No matter what I said or did, it was always *against*, always in competition. Jule was in a race, and the giant was winning! Was Jule as poetic as the very model of a poet? Did Jule inspire the dewier dream, the faster heartbeat, the more copious flow from the inguen? Or was Jule a gun of smaller caliber, and did he sometimes go off half-cocked?"

"You fool," she said. "You faint-hearted fool."

§

You were to see her once more, four years later, and by then, of course, it would not matter.

SCENE 73

POOR MAN'S PARTY (End of 1934)

The year-end shivaree was drawing near, and one evening while you and your sister were rueing the absence of invitations, a suggestion came from the far end of the room, where your father was reading a newspaper.

"Why don't *you* give a party?" he said.

You and your sister looked at each other, your faces still disconsolate, and then slowly shadows of hope began to show through the gloom.

"What kind of party?" you said.

Your father said, "All your friends are in the same fix as you. You're broke, and they're broke, and none of you is going to ring the New Year in at the Ritz. Why don't you ring it in here?"

"How? Ruthie and I could hardly scare up ten bucks between us."

"One from him and nine from me," Ruth said.

Your father said, "Didn't you ever hear of a poor man's party?"

"Not on Riverside Drive."

"Too swell a neighborhood—is that what you mean?"

"I suppose."

"Kid, when your father can't pay the rent, you stop being swell."

Ruth said, "What's a poor man's party?"

"The host provides the place. The guests bring the food and drink."

"Wouldn't we be interfering with you and Aunt Jo?" you said.

"We've got richer friends than you. We're going to an all-night shindig at Judge Stackell's."

"Let's make out a guest-list," your sister said, and she went to your room for a pad and pencil.

"Not so long ago," your father said, "I'd've peeled off some bills and sent you to Boston."

"Would you? To see my gentile friend?"

"But these days, kid, I couldn't send you to Brooklyn."

Seven years spun by, and you said, "She's a crackajack girl, that one."

"What would you do if you had the means? Would you marry her?"

You thought of Charles Street, you thought of Blossom Garden and Louisburg Square, and you said, "I thought of it once."

And then your sister returned to the room.

§

You made a list of eight friends, all of whom you had reason to believe would be as idle as you on New Year's Eve. To each, you addressed the same brief note:

Their prospects being dim for December 31st, Ruth and Julian Shapiro invite you to join them at their home for a dim little celebration beginning at 10 p.m. Bring refreshments and a friend—or two, if you have that many.

On the day of the party, you set to work early on the only ingesta you could afford to furnish—a tray of canapés. These, each about the size of a domino, were made not with caviar, not with pâté de foie gras, nor even with saumon fumé—nay, they were constructed of cream cheese and slices of olive, of rosetted radishes and little tickets of ham. It took you several hours to prepare some two hundred of those one-bite *bonnes bouches*, and when you'd covered them with a damp cloth and stowed them in the refrigerator, alas, your work was done: the house of Shapiro could offer no more save light and warmth against the dark last night of 1934.

And at ten, the doorbell began to ring.

§

Within an hour, you learned that the eight you'd invited indeed had friends — and that these too had friends. By eleven o'clock, the six-room flat held many dozens, almost all of them unknown to you or your sister, and before midnight came, the crowd had grown so dense that the outer door was left open, and the party spread to the hall. For a while, you'd kept count of the arrivals, fifty, there were, and seventy, and eighty-five, but when you reached one hundred and forty, you couldn't recall why you'd begun. Strangers were everywhere, and from their mouths came torn strips of words. In a wadding of smoke, glassware touched and glassware broke, and you heard laughter, you heard one song played on the piano and another being sung, you heard the telephone ring ten times before ringing off. Friends and the friends of friends, you thought, and you fought your way through them in order to get to the door.

In the street, wearing someone's coat in the cold, you stood looking back through a window at unfamiliar integers, close but always separate, and among them you sought a face, two faces, that you knew you wouldn't find.

§

At nine in the morning, after the last guest had gone, you and your sister surveyed the scene of the recent engagement. The dead were all around you, and they contained little blood: you found a score or more of bottles, each holding a stain of drying liquid.

Later in the month, when the telephone bill arrived, it listed a forty-dollar toll-call. A friend, or a friend of a friend, or no friend at all, had spoken for fifty-nine minutes to someone in Toronto.

A poor man's party.

SCENE 74

GONE TO SIT AT THE FEET OF MARY (Early 1935)

What were you doing in the days of Ellen's dying, what high mission, what duty kept you away? In some room a few miles off, a short walk from where you were, a streetcar-ride, she lay morphined against the claws of cancer. Facing the Christ-on-the-Cross you knew so well, her little ever-bleeding figurine, she need not have prayed for her sins' forgiveness: she had none, unless her love for your grandma, a Jew, was cardinal, venial, or in between the two.

What did she think of in those final days—the glory just going or the one on the way? Did she dwell on mounds of food and laundry or on masses and missals and screened-off priests? Did she tell her beads or remember tea with Grandma Nevins on a winter's evening? Did she behold the beatitude of Mary or that on the face of an olderly lady? Did she see the Moy and the Niemen flow across the world to join in a Harlem kitchen? And did she recall the lummocky boy who blocked the doorway. . . ?

You weren't with her when she died, you weren't there to wash her feet, as she was washing Mary's. You were somewhere else when she called for you, a short walk, a streetcar-ride away.

And *your* priest cannot relieve you.

SCENE 75

THE PAINTED WOMAN GOES (Early 1935)

As the years passed, your resentment of her dwindled, and you were able at last to see what your father had seen and your Aunt Rae belied—the *un*-painted woman, the woman as she was. She wore no rouge at the breakfast table, where each morning you studied her longer, knew her better, and in time you came to realize that she had no need of art to hide time's harm: her true coloring was pastel-milk, as delicate as Limoges. It would've been gall to your aunt that all age had brought her was a sadness that merely lighted the beauty—would the glow never dim? you'd wonder, would the bloom never go?

You were beginning to esteem her, to respond, even, to her lifelong desire for admiration. A remark on her complexion, on the luster of her hair, there was always some feature worthy of praise, and you were growing to enjoy her enjoyment—she was a girl, you thought, a girl of fifty-five!—when you saw that your father's attention lay somewhere else. Her fascination had spent itself, her sparkle had become a memory of fire. There were no quarrels in your presence, there was no sign of spite, meanness, anger: there was only a sense that what had begun twenty years before had come to an end. You were not the cause this time—they themselves were—and when you came home one day, you knew that someone long present now belonged to the past. Josephine, Josie, Aunt Jo, the painted woman—she was gone.

SCENE 76

WHO WAS THAT LADY . . . ? (Early 1935)

Your father was a kidder, meaning that he liked to josh, to quiz, to rag, and most especially his pleasure was the act of kidding you. He'd done that since your childhood—often he'd even call you *kid* instead of *Julian*—and he did so still, when you were over thirty. There were plays on words (*I deny the allegation,* he'd say, *and I defy the alligator*), and he had kidding ways of spelling and pronunciation (*sir,* he'd say, *c-u-r, sir,* and *justice* became *just-us*), and if you accused him of giving you a dirty look, he'd say you had it before. Oh, he was a kidder, all right, always laughing when he turned the proverb around and said *It's a wise son that knows his own father.* You learned early to kid him back, and late you kidded too, saying *I call my father Necessity; he knows no law.* Ah, you were a great pair of kidders!

At breakfast one morning, for no reason at all you said, "Counselor, who was that lady I seen you with last night?"
And too quickly he said, "Where?"
You looked up and saw a sign of fluster, and making a stab, you said, "In the Hotel Astor lobby."
His unconcern became so studied that he gave himself away by trying to butter a roll without using butter. "I was nowhere near the Astor," he said.
Your sister joined the game, saying, "I was with him, pop."
"I'll describe her," you said. "She was a blonde."
He glanced at Ruth and then at you, and he said, "What were you two doing at the Astor?"
You laughed, saying, "We weren't there."
"But you were, pop," Ruth said. "Who was she?"

SCENE 77

AUNT RAE (Early 1935)

At no time had your sister been estranged from her; she'd never shared the bitterness felt by you and your Uncle Dave; indeed, more than once she'd tried to unite the family, and on the instant occasion, she was trying again.

"It isn't right, Julian," she said. "You ought to go and see her."

"So you've told me."

"She's just out of the hospital. How long are you going to carry on the feud?"

"There's no feud," you said. "There's also no feeling."

"How can you say that about your mother's sister?"

"It's all gone. I'd be calling on a stranger."

"I don't turn away from my own blood."

"It's been eight years," you said. "What does she look like these days?"

"Call on her and find out. It's the right thing to do."

Not that day, though, nor the next, but another, when you were on a crosstown walk through a midtown street, you passed beneath the porte-cochère of a residential hotel. You were slow to apprehend the name painted on a band of glass overhead—*Knickerbocker,* it said—and only when you turned and read it again did you remember that somewhere above you your Aunt Rae lived. You stood there for a moment, wondering why you didn't turn again and walk away, but at a blurred memory of a size-2 shoe, you moved instead toward a revolving door.

The moment you saw her you knew that forever lost was the way you remembered her. Presto! and your memory, her picture, aged. Her face seemed to have collapsed, like that on a shrunken balloon, fallen in on itself, sagged into a crisscross of crimps and rimples. Her hair, dark brown once, was threaded with gray, and her pale blue eyes seemed paler still. It pained you to look further, and you looked away, sought the salve of the size-2 shoe of another day—but, sad to say, they were 2 no more, and it was with sadness at last that you met her gaze.

"You look like your mother, Julian," she said. "I never realized. . . ."

Behind her, your Uncle Harry entered another room and closed the door.

THE COLOR OF THE AIR, XI

THE KING RANCH—1885
THE RUNNING *W*

> *Be it remembered that Richard King deposited his Brand and Ear*
> *Marks for Horses & Cattle in Book B for Registry of Brands.*
> —County records, Texas

For all anybody ever knew about him, his life began at the age of
eleven in the hold of the *Desdemona,* a sailing-ship a few days out
of New York for Mobile. He was a stowaway, and when found,
he gave a maybe name and mightbe date of birth, and then he quit
talking as if there were nothing more to say. It came to be a paying
habit, that one, keeping his eyes wide open and his mouth nearly
shut, and in the sixty years he lived he hardly missed a trick. He
hardly missed a hectare, either, or a cow, or a hog, or a mustang
mare, and by staying mum, he departed rich, this Richard King that
Cristo knew where he came from, and *Dios* knew where he went.

He was well-nigh half a century between the Nueces and the Rio
Grande, and next to the fief he put together there, the surest thing
about him is that he wore out lawyers in spans of two and teams
of four. In fact, he demoted them to notaries, and it was their lifework
to attest the rights, the *derechos,* he bought up from the Eusebios
and Faustinos who still held a share in a Spanish grant, a *poco* thirty-
second or a *poquito* sixty-fourth. What parchment they must've con-
sumed, those *abogados,* what seals and tape, what ink! What palms
they must've crossed to quiet titles, what gifts made to scribe and
appraiser, to *jefe* and registrar, what compliments paid to *niños,* in-
laws, the crucifix, and Bolivar!

It's all but lost now, the cost to King of a Texas league, seven
square miles of hock-high grass. The numbers are under lock and
key, they're in sequestered libers and impounded minds, and there
are deaf ears and blind stares, and questions fly with no dry land to
light on. But someone slipped once—King, was it, or King's
counsel?—and the truth is on file in the County of Starr, a far cry
from the first parcel the man took in fee simple. It's in the Mendiola
grant, and for one time, by a few words only, too much is said.
For *three hundred dollars, the receipt of which is hereby acknowledged,* it
conveys to King forever and a day all that part of the earth known

as the Rincon de Santa Gertrudis—fifteen thousand acres for the *gringo,* two cents apiece for the Mex!

Cancer of the stomach killed him, but before he died, the *patron* of the Running *W* owned more ground than fast mounts could ride him around in a week. A million acres were his, together with all their trees and game and grain, all the water that rose, all the rain that fell and ran. All the space between heaven and hell were his, all the flies and ticks and flowers and dust, all the wild horses and the half-wild spics. And, as his title-deeds pray, much good, much good, much good may it do him!

SCENE 78

AN AFFAIR OF THE HEART (From Early 1935)

They were called kiosks, those glass and wrought-iron entrances to the subway, and some were still in use on older parts of the line. Covering the stairways, they slanted up from the sidewalk and bloomed into translucent domes that were always dinged with dust and grime. As a child, you'd likened them to the heads of snakes, their mouths agape to swallow their prey—passengers—but what of the ones who emerged and walked away?

You and your father had left his office and boarded an uptown local at Times Square. He'd bought his evening paper, the *Sun,* and while he scanned it, you recited in your mind the slogans that insisted from the concave cornice of the car—*You can teach a parrot to say* and *Time to Retire* and *The Road of Anthracite.* The train stopped, and you looked out at white tile with a colored legend—*50th Street 50th*—and then the station (or you) began to move, and all you could see was the dark gray wall of the tunnel. And then there were halts at *Columbus Circle* and at stations with numbers for names—*66th, 72nd, 79th, 86th, 91st*—and at last you came to 96th, where you and your father left the train. From the platform, you remember, it was twenty-four steps to the street.

Halfway up, in a downdraft of winter air, your father paused, letting his folded paper fall. He turned from the remaining steps, saying, "I can't make it, Julian."

You made him sit on one of the treads, and alarmed by his pallor and the chill of his skin, you felt for his pulse and found it fast and irregular. Holding his hands, you tried to chafe them warm, all the while thinking of his butcher-boy days, when he'd carried fifty pounds of meat up six flights of stairs (*on Fridays, I carried more*).

"The pain is going," he said.

He started to rise, but you forced him to stay where he was for several moments more before letting him try the rest of the steps. He climbed them like a child, one riser at a time, and when he reached the street-level, you took him home in a cab.

"The pain is gone," he said on the way.

§

After making him lie down, you and your sister went to your room, where, after closing the door, she said, "What do you think it was?"

"I don't know," you said, "but it didn't look good."

"I hope to God it wasn't his heart."

"That's just what I'm afraid of—and before today, I never gave it a thought. He always seemed so strong."

"He won't go to a doctor. He doesn't think much of doctors."

"All the same, we ought to call one."

"Who?" she said. "We don't go to doctors ourselves—not that kind, anyway."

"I play handball at the Y. with a Dr. Nelson. He lives upstairs."

"Go get him."

At one time, you'd played squash on the four-wall courts of the Y., but when you could no longer afford to have your racquets restrung, you switched to handball, at which your only expense was five cents a day, the price of a towel. Among your usual opponents was Dr. Nelson, a man who often beat you though he was nearly your father's age.

After making his examination, he took you and Ruth into another room and said, "I'm no cardiologist, but from what Mr. Shapiro tells me and what I hear with the stethoscope, I think he ought to consult one."

"What exactly did you find?" you said.

"That's just the point—it wasn't exact. Only a thorough check can show what caused the spasm. In my mind, though, there's no doubt that it was angina—or angina pectoris. All that means is pain in the chest. What we have to know is the reason."

"Could it be a serious reason?"

"Yes, it could."

"He has no very high regard for doctors."

"So he informed me," Nelson said, and he went to the door, where he glanced back to say, "Don't delay."

§

Through your Aunt Sarah, you made an appointment for the following day with a heart-specialist named Bernard Robbins. You escorted your father to the office, and after he'd been shown into an examination-room, you sat for an hour with racked magazines that you had no desire to read. *Angina,* you were thinking, and the definition you'd found ran in a streamer through your mind: *a peculiarly painful disease, so named from a sense of suffocating contraction within the chest. It is usually associated with organic change in the heart or aorta.* What else, you wonder through the haze of fifty years, what else did you think of while waiting to learn whether your father was going to die? Did you rerun his life, replay him, hear him a second time, see him again through Havana smoke, and did you feel as before that he was studying you for—what? what had he hoped to find? Were you thinking of his presence, with you even when he was not, of cold hands that would not warm, of year-old you riding on his arm, of how the world would drain and dry if your father were to die?

When summoned to the consulting-room, you sat next to your father, both of you facing the doctor across his desk. "I've examined you as thoroughly as I can in the office," Robbins said. "For an accurate diagnosis, though, Mr. Shapiro, further investigation is required."

"What does that mean?" your father said.

"I want to put you in the hospital."

"You must have some idea of what the trouble is."

"That's true," Robbins said. "What I want to know is whether the idea is right or wrong."

"What do you suspect, then?"

"I'd rather wait until I have something definite to say."

"I've never been in a hospital."

"They're not all like Bellevue, Mr. Shapiro. Certainly not the one I'd send you to."

"What one is that?"

"The Doctors' Hospital. It's on East 86th Street opposite Carl Schurz Park."

"I'll think it over."

"I'd advise against that."

You spoke for the first time, saying, "We'll do as you say, Dr. Robbins. I'll take my father home for his things."

"When you leave this office," Robbins said, "you will go directly to the hospital. You will not go home for anything."

§

On reaching the hospital, only a mile or so away, you found that Robbins had telephoned to authorize your father's admission, and he was taken at once to his room. By the time he was installed, the afternoon was ending, and sitting between his bedside and the window, you watched blueing sky close upward over the Sound, the river, and Hell Gate.

"Why don't you go home, Julian?" your father said. "Ruthie is alone."
"And when I go," you said, "you'll be alone."

§

On your return to the hospital in the morning, you were not permitted to see your father. An orderly stood beside the door, on which a sign in a slot read *No Admittance,* and when you identified yourself, he summoned Dr. Robbins from the room.

Walking with you along the corridor, he said, "I've been here since midnight. In his sleep, your father suffered a thrombosis of the left coronary artery. A thrombosis is a blockage, generally by reason of a clot, that shuts off the supply of blood to the tissues of the heart. In your father's case, it was very nearly fatal at once. If he hadn't been in the hospital when it happened—if he'd been in his office or in the street or even at home—he'd've died then and there."

You remembered what your father had said the day before—*I'll think it over*—and you said, "You were afraid of this, weren't you?"

"I didn't want to alarm him more than I had to, but when I looked him over yesterday, I found every indication that an accident was on the way."

"When may I see him?

"Not for a couple of days. The pain is severe, and I've got him doped up."

"What are his chances?"

"Do you want the truth?"

"Yes."

"The blood in that closed artery—broken, really—must find another route to the heart. If it doesn't, he could die at any moment. If it does, he may live."

"May?"

"The outlook is very poor. With the best of luck and the best of care, he just might last for two or three years."

Two or three years, you thought—and then *you* would be alone.

§

It was always a city to be walked in, but you rarely set out with a particular aim. You'd make your way as whim willed you, along a river, through a park, or up or down or across a street. It'd seem to make no difference whither you wended; there was ever something to see, or see anew, no matter where you went. But on that day, doing as you'd done on other days, you were aware of nothing you could ever remember. There must've been sights and scenes that you passed, there must've been vistas, colors, smoke, and commotion, but, as good as blind, you missed them all. *Two or three years,* you were thinking as you stood before some display, *two or three years,* near someone's statue or underneath a tree.

You tried to see beyond the numbers, but it was as if what lay there was a void, and then, amid cars and people in the dusted sunlight, you sought to imagine emptiness, and what you conjured was the world without your father. The brightness, the clarity, the sight of things separate from other things—all of it reminded you of the day of your mother's funeral. Then too there'd been brilliance, distinct objects, the vacant room of the world. *Two or three years,* you thought.

§

"I can't understand why papa didn't tell us," your sister said.

And you said, "He may not have known it was coming."

"There must've been a sign. A thing so serious gives you warning."

"Maybe there was a warning, and we paid no attention: the Depression. That's what started all this. It made nothing out of a lifetime of work—for Pop and everyone else. At fifty-odd, he was broke again, and it was once too often. He never spoke much about it, but if we were looking for a sign, we'd've found it in a down-and-out clientele and a practice gone to hell. Some people shot themselves or jumped out of windows; Pop did neither, but he's dying all the same."

"Don't use that word, Julian."

"Robbins used it," you said, and then a memory made you smile. "Remember what Pop used to say about the man who invented whisky? 'He should never have died.' If Pop dies, I'll say the same about him."

"Julian," your sister said, and she glanced around at familiar forms—a bookcase that had belonged to your mother, a rosewood piano, cut-glass, silver, standing lamps. "Julian, what will we do?"

§

Three more days passed before you were allowed to see your father, and what you found was a man who seemed smaller than you remembered him, as if he were already dead and had begun to shrivel. His eyes were closed, and his face, under a four-day growth of hair, was peculiarly blue. Taking up his hand, you smoothed it until he became aware of your presence. He lacked the power to raise his eyelids, and when he spoke, it was as if through drawn blinds.

"Julian," he said, but you soon knew that he was in another place and another time. "Your mother says you got off a good one today. 'I drink milk and it goes to my head.' "
"That *was* a good one," you said.
"My little blond kid," he said, and then he fell asleep.

You waited for Robbins near the floor-desk, and when he came, he refused to talk to you until he'd read the charts and scanned the latest electrocardiogram.

"How do you think he's doing?" you said.
"To be frank," he said, "I didn't think he'd live this long."
"Has he got a better chance than he did the other day?"
"A better *chance,* yes. I don't deal in sure things."
You'd hoped for reassurance, and you were cast down at being given little.
"My father died instantly," he said. "I didn't get any progress reports."

§

On your next visit, Robbins was in the room, and your father, more wakeful now, was watching him as he examined one of his hands.

"You look at my nails every time you come here," your father said. "Why do you do that?"
"To see if you need a manicure," Robbins said.
When he left the room, you followed him into the hallway, saying, "Why *do* you look at his nails?"
"For signs of cyanosis. That's a morbid condition due to insufficient aeration of the blood. From *kyano-* meaning blue. The nails are particularly susceptible."
"Are my father's blue?"
"Less than they were."
"That ought to mean something," you said.
"All it means is that they were bluer once."

230

"You're not very encouraging. You seem to be preparing me for his death."

"A doctor's trick. If he lives, I'll get credit for a miracle. But the real miracle will lie with you."

"With me?" you said. "How so?"

"What you say is true—I'm *not* very hopeful. Your father has had one of the worst coronaries I've ever seen, and if he survives it, he'll last only so long as he turns away from the grind that put him here. Under the same stresses, he could die in a month."

"How can I prevent that?"

"As I said—with a miracle."

After Robbins had gone, you returned to your father's room to find him rubbing his beard, now nearly a week old and blue-black against his pallor.

"How'd you like me to give you a shave?" you said.

And he looked at you, saying, "Would you do that?"

§

The next morning, you brought his shaving gear along. He'd had breakfast by the time you arrived, and you set to work at once. After softening the growth of hair with hot towels, you built a thick barbe of lather, and then, using a fresh blade, you began to shave him—for once, you thought, you were shaving a face other than your own. You couldn't know, therefore, whether the razor was pulling or when you were going against the grain: you could only wield it lightly—*molliter,* as the lawbooks had it, gently and with a gentle hand—and trust that you were doing well. At the end, while you were pressing a last hot towel to your father's face, you glanced at his hands. In the hospital library, you'd read that cyanosis was caused by an incomplete saturation of the haemoglobin with oxygen, as at high altitudes. The same condition had been produced by the arterial rupture: under each fingernail, the color of the matrix had changed. You thought of your mother, remembering how she too at the last had seemed to you blue.

§

Thereafter, you shaved him every morning, and though he never said so, you knew that he enjoyed the service. *Why* did he never say so? you wondered, but you did not wonder long. You were far from being the wise son of Proverbs, he that maketh a glad father, but you were sensible enough to understand that, while asking for nothing, he rejoiced greatly in whatever he received.

231

You could recall no demands that he'd made on you, no duties imposed. Instead, he'd ruled you with his power to charge the air, and in those days at the hospital, as you patted him with witch hazel and combed and brushed his hair, it seemed to be charged with pleasure.

§

After leaving him one day, you went to his office for the first time since his illness. He had only a single room now, part of a suite rented in joint tenancy with three other lawyers. They employed but one stenographer, and she answered the switchboard and typed for all. Gone were the flush times on Nassau Street and across from City Hall; there were no concourses in the rooms and corridors, no tongues and smoke on the air; there was only a sense of passing hours as dust drifted through funnels of sunlight.

On your father's desk, a few bills lay on the greensward of his blotter, from the corners of which curled the calling-cards of one-time builders and brokers, kept, you supposed, as reminders, souvenirs of the throngs and excitement of other days. Idly you opened the shallow middle drawer, and idly you gazed at a tray of pencils, pen-holders, and rubber-bands (*gummelappen*, you thought), and you opened the drawer wider on a disarray of paper—correspondence, bank statements, cancelled checks, old bills still sealed in their envelopes. Again you were reminded of an empty house, this time littered, flaked over with thrownaway paper, the mute embassies of the years. Why did such discards affect you? you wondered, why your regret over words that had done their work, run from Marathon and in Athens died? What did it matter now? you thought—but you knew that matter it did, and you were saddened by the residue of a career three decades old and just ended.

Knowing that you'd grieve only the more, still you could not turn away from the desk: it had somehow come to stand for your father, to hold in its several compartments an abstract of his life. Once again you opened a drawer, the deep catchall to the left of the kneehole. What you saw resembled a stuffed waste-basket. It was filled with vouchers, deposit-slips, rent-receipts, carbon copies of dead originals, memoranda of names and numbers that would never be used, a soiled shirt, a frayed tie—a confusion that you felt forced to subdue, to reduce to order.

You sorted the furling check-stubs, booklets that looked like rosettes, and you stacked the business-cards and the stockbroker confirmations of long-ago trades through Schmidt & Deery, and you threw away the shirt and the tie. At the bottom of the pile, you uncovered treasure—ten letters from your father to your mother and three from her to him.* Save for a few others found in a trunk at your Grandma Nevins', you were seeing the only surviving correspondence between your parents.

Some of it was fragmentary, with only a page remaining of several, and some, lacking an envelope, revealed neither the place nor date of mailing, but as well as you were enabled by the content, you arranged the thirteen letters in calendrical order. From the first, you learned that they'd be hard to read. They began with a letter written by your father in 1903, while your mother was carrying you, and they ended with another in 1914, four months before her death. They embraced, therefore, the entire relationship; they contained all you would ever know of its nature; they suggested occurrences behind closed doors, bated words, glances exchanged above your head. You were prying, you thought, you were spying out secrets you had no right to share. Still, knowing that you were eavesdropping, you read on from *this little letter to my dear little wife* to *enclosed you will find check for $25 as you requested* — and when you were done, had you been any other, you'd've wept.

You remained in the office for the rest of the morning and much of the afternoon. There were no phone-calls, and no clients came. When you left, you took the letters with you.

§

You were at the hospital before noon every day, sometimes with your sister and sometimes alone, and often the two of you would board a crosstown bus after supper and visit your father again in the evening.

After the third week, Dr. Robbins took both of you aside and said, "His electrocardiograms are showing progressively greater regularity of the heart action. That signifies an increasing supply of blood, which could only occur if it had made a shunt."

"I don't understand," Ruth said.

"His blood has found a new route to the heart. Unless there's a further accident, your father may make it."

"Still only may," you said.

"We're dealing with life. That's always a may."

Beyond Robbins and halfway along the corridor, you noted a dark-dressed woman of about forty. She was unknown to you, but you'd seen her before, and now, when she became aware of your gaze, she turned away.

"Tomorrow," Robbins said, "I'm going to let him sit up."

---

*Given in full in *The Color of the Air*, Vol. 1.

It would be the first time. Until then, you hadn't realized that for three weeks, he'd never left the bed.

§

"Did you see her?" Ruth said.
"The woman with the veil?"
"She's been there twice this week that I know of, and I saw her last week too."
"Maybe she's visiting someone."
"She is, and the someone is P. D. S."
"How do you know that?"
"She's always in the hall. She's never coming out of a room or going in. She's never doing anything—she's just waiting."
"For what?"
"Julian, you're dense. She's waiting for us to leave. Remember how we were joking about a woman in the lobby of the Astor?"
"You think this is the one?"
"This is the one," Ruth said.

§

As the weather grew milder, there were evenings when you'd sit before an open window of the apartment, watching the sunset colors deepen over Jersey. They were all giving way to blue, you'd think—the cyanotic sky, you'd think—and you'd watch too as cigarette-smoke drifted into the draft and dispersed in the outer air.

"It was hard to talk about things," Ruth said, "when I thought he was going to—"
"Die," you said.
"But now that he's going to live—*unbeschreien,* as grandma used to say. . . . What does that mean, exactly?"
"*Schreien* is screaming, so it means without screaming. I suppose the idea is avoiding a jinx. Hemingway calls it *mouthing yourself.*"
"I started to say there are changes coming. Everything is going to change, Julian."
"I've known that, too, I guess, but like you, I couldn't get past the idea of Pop dying. I never really knew what a presence he is. To think of him gone is to be one of Columbus' sailors: I'm at the edge of the earth."
"There are going to be changes for us all," she said.

§

Early one day, your Aunt Sarah telephoned to say that she wished to see you. The request, quietly made and deferential, was nonetheless a summons to appear at the time and place named, and that afternoon, your visit to the hospital over, you presented yourself at her door. In your father's view, his sister was an altogether faultless woman, and though none too sure of her regard for you, you were an admirer too. You knew that your mother's sister Rae had always referred to her as *a Shapiro,* an outsider's summary embracing all the characteristics of your father's blood, few of them favorable. Within the family, though, its import was otherwise. There, to be *a Shapiro* was regarded as a virtue, not a brand of lower nature, and none was held to be more virtuous than the queen of them all—your father's revered elder sister.

It was because of your father that she had asked for the meeting.

"Julian," she said, "I have prayed for my brother Philip night and day, and, God be praised, Dr. Robbins says he will live and be well. What I think of your father, Julian, is no secret in this family. To me, he is an angel on earth. He is honest, he is generous, he is good, and I would give all I own to buy for him even only one more day of life. You hear what I am saying to you, Julian?"

"You're telling me how much you love my father," you said. "But that isn't why you sent for me."

"No, it isn't. You're here so as I can find out how much *you* love him."

"Well, I don't follow his advice very often, and sometimes I don't even hear it—which means, I suppose, that I'm not much of a son. But I hope no one in the family thinks I dishonor him."

"Honor is one thing," she said, "and love is another. Honor, you feel. Love, you show."

"I never thought of them as separate. They go together."

"I'm not a deep thinker, like you, Julian—a regular *Philosoph.* But from my experience in a hard world, I say that if you love a person, all that counts is what you do about it."

"There's a saying," you said. " 'Among the Jews, it is the old men who are beautiful.' You make me think it's the women."

"Like your father—a *Schmeichler.*"

"Isn't it time, my dear Aunt Sarah, that you said what's on your mind?"

"Yes," she said. "You must give up this writing business, Julian."

For the first time, the conversation summoned up images. *This writing business,* she'd said, and you saw, as in some emporium, bins and boxes of merchandise, all containing words; there were counters, shelves, and stacks, all displaying words. *This writing business,* you thought, and you saw words being weighed, sacked, sold, and bought, and money being paid.

"And do what?" you said.

"Step into your father's shoes and practice law."

"There's no practice left to practice on."

"You're young yet," your aunt said. "Apply yourself, and a practice will come."

"I've been applying myself to the writing business."

"You're making a living at it? It pays well?"

"So far, no."

"How long would it take to throw off something you could depend on?"

"It's hard to say. Some writers make a fortune overnight. Others work all their lives and can't pay the rent."

"Which ones are there more of?"

"The failures—fifty to one."

"So if you keep on writing, you have a good chance of being a failure."

"In the sense of not getting rich at it, yes. But there are other things."

"What other things?"

"There are good books that don't sell."

"Like *Water Wheel,* maybe?"

"It's a better book than people think."

"Books I don't know from, but I can tell you about shoes. If nobody buys them, you got to go out of the shoes business."

"The shoe business, the writing business," you said. "I'm not in business at all, Aunt Sarah."

"You're supposed to be a smart boy, Julian, so answer me a *Frage.* If not with business, how would you support your father?"

Like a stone in a well, the question took a long time to fall, and you found yourself listening, as if for the sound of a splash. What you heard, though, was a repetition of the words: *how would you support your father?* Until that moment, only a vague notion had flown through your mind, a thought like the shadow of a bird, but now you saw the bird itself, its shape sharp and its colors vivid: how would your father be supported by *you?*

"It's something that never occurred to me," you said.

"Now it occurs. Your father is a sick man, and he can't provide for you like ever since you were born. He can't even provide for himself. With him helpless, things are turned around: the providing falls on you."

"The most I ever earned was four dollars a week as a law clerk. What would that provide?"

"Four dollars more than your writing," she said. "But you're not a law clerk now. You're a lawyer. In time, you could make a decent living and take care of your father. He can't do it himself any more."

"I'm a writer, Aunt Sarah. I gave up the law."

"I'm starting in to think you're maybe not as smart as people say. *Somebody* has got to look out for your father. Who should it be but you? Honor, you feel. Love, you show, Julian."

What had your concept been before? you wondered—or had you had none at all? In your thirty-year life, had you ever thought of how your wants had been supplied, had you ever inquired where the wherewithal came from, or had you simply extended your empty hand and drawn it back filled? What had you supposed, that some magic was at work, or had you supposed nothing and spent the handful as you willed?

"You could write at night," your Aunt Sarah said. "You could write on Sunday."

"It can't be done that way," you said. "Nothing can. Could I practice law on Sunday?"

"Then give up writing for a year, two years. Just till you get established."

"To do that would be to give it up forever."

"For such a father as yours, a son should be willing to sacrifice anything. There is no limit."

"Have you discussed this with others in the family?"

"With those I respect, yes."

"And what do they say?"

"One and all, Julian, they say you should give up this *narrischkeit,* this foolishness, and go back to the law."

"Isn't it odd, Aunt Sarah, that my father has never asked me to do that?"

"Ah," she said, "if a father has to ask!"

As uttered, the words expressed all the bitterness, all the rue of age. You were the focus, as if the shortfall of youth were chargeable only to you, and her gaze was sorrowful, less like the hunter's now and more like the prey's.

"I can't do it, Aunt Sarah."

It took her a moment to comprehend that you'd refused her, and then quietly she said, "You can't do it. He fed you and clothed you and sent you to college, and he loved you all your life, and you can't do it. You disregarded him over and over, you squandered his money, you stayed away from his home for ten years—and you can't help him now when help is what he needs. A sick man, and you can't help him because he didn't ask."

At no point had she raised her voice; it was almost as if she'd spoken within her mind, rehearsed a speech that she meant to make. But whether you heard or merely apprehended her, you knew that she was right—worse, that she'd still be right in times to come. No matter how you fared at *the writing business,* you'd never be able to defend the choice you were making now—the word over the blood. You loved and honored your father, you told yourself, but you were going to do what only he would ever forgive. You'd be scorned by all, and all included you.

"I can't do it, Aunt Sarah," you said.

§

The regimen prescribed by Dr. Robbins was gradual even for the medical way of the time: only after several weeks was your father permitted to leave his bed, and then but to sit for an hour in a chair. There, near the window, you'd shave him and comb his hair, and then the two of you would talk until he tired and turned away to stare at the red-brick and brownstone facades across the street, at glassed-in people who sometimes stared at him.

What he'd speak of was not yet the future, as if he were still unsure that a future was in store, and therefore he'd dwell each day on the day before, on how things had gone at the office and at home and on the state of the world at large. You made no mention of your Aunt Sarah's request and your refusal—you knew that you couldn't justify what you'd done and were doing, and you knew too that you wouldn't change. It'd be thought, and you'd be one of those to think it, that you were putting yourself before your father, and sadly you'd say *How true!*—but you knew you would not change.

One day, more certain of calendars, of pages not yet reached, your father said, "When I leave here, my sister Sarah wants me to go straight to West End. In fact, she insists on it."

Had she reported your talk? you wondered, had she told him of his son, a very prince of a boy?

"I'm to stay for the summer, she said. There's a special room on the second floor. It was added on for Melvin."

Melvin, you thought, prayed for as dead on his marriage to a gentile—dead Melvin.

"Do you ever see him?"

"Mel?" you said. "I saw him yesterday."

"What is he doing nowadays?"

"Same thing—selling print for Haddon Craftsmen."

"The family hates Jesse for giving him a job—but, hell, they hated him long before."

"Why?"

"For making Dora have a second child. He wanted a son, and Dora had a rheumatic heart. Aunt Sarah begged him to let her alone, but he wanted a son, and it killed her."

You said nothing. You thought nothing.

"Your mother had a rheumatic heart too," he said. "But I never knew it."

238

What went through the mind of Yonkel Layv? What did Chai Esther's son say, the one she idolized as Julian?

"But I'm far afield," your father said. "I was talking about West End. If I go there—and this worries me—what will happen to you and Ruth?"

Love, you show, you thought.

"It'd mean giving up the apartment," he said. "When *I* fail to pay the rent, at least the landlord has a claim. But he has no claim against *you,* and you'd be out in the street."

"Go to West End," you said. "Ruth and I can look out for ourselves."

"Where would you stay?"

"With friends," you said. "With relatives." But what friends, you thought, what relatives? "Go to West End and get well there."

He gazed at you for a moment, and then he smiled. "You know what I'm curious about? Where you get your two bits a day. My change-pocket isn't there."

"I steal from Ruth," you said. "She's careless with her purse, leaves it lying around, and when she's out of the room. . . ."

§

The Camden printing-plant of Haddon Craftsmen was owned by Jesse Satenstein, a son-in-law of your Aunt Sarah and therefore a brother-in-law of Mel's. When no one would aid the outcast—who could help a dead man?—he'd flouted the family by putting him to work, and, lo, dust and ashes lived!

Attached to the New York offices of the company, he solicited orders for printing and binding, and as he made his rounds, he came to know nearly every publisher and editor in the trade. For months, he'd been carrying the manuscript of your second novel from house to house, hoping to strike fire with it and failing everywhere; he gave you no reports, and when you inquired, all he'd say was that the book was being read.

While you were shaving your father one morning, the telephone rang. Leaving him half-barbered, you answered the call and heard Melvin say, "Big news, Julian! *The Trampled Vineyard** has been accepted!"

"Great!" you said. "By whom?"

"A. & C. Boni."

"That's great, Mel, just great! By God, Book Number Two!"

"Wait," he said. "Part of the news isn't so good. Boni will only advance you a hundred."

"A hundred!" you said. "Christ, I spent more than that on paper!"

"The important thing is to get the book out."

---

*An early title for *The Old Man's Place.*

"Can't you work them for more?"

"I'll try, but they're tight. My advice is, don't kill this for a few extra bucks. The book has been rejected a dozen times."

"Hell," you said, "take the hundred."

When you hung up, your father said, "What book were you talking about?"

"The one about the Adirondacks. Mel placed it with A. & C. Boni."

"Congratulations! Come here, and I'll give you a kiss."

"I'm only getting a hundred bucks in advance."

"That's all right, kid. I don't kiss for money."

§

A. & C. Boni were in a building on the west side of Fifth Avenue between 12th and 13th Streets. You knew the neighborhood well, and when you left the bus and stopped on the sidewalk, recall seemed to take on substance, and almost real again was the Playhouse where Mel had met his usherette, and nearby too were the book-filled windows of Dauber and Pine, the dim doorway, the counters you'd culled for *Virginibus Puerisque* and the stories of that germanesque Russian, Tchekhoff. Had you been alone when you bought these things, or had you tried to impress someone named Lou? And at the called-up face, you turned to peer down the avenue, as if you and she might emerge from the hotel and come walking past the spot on which you stood. But it was eight years too late for that; you were there, and she was not.

You were meeting Albert Boni that day for the first time, and of course you shook his hand; the connection was brief, however, and broken by you, less for a reason you knew than for one you sensed but couldn't explain. You judged him to be a man of about fifty, small in size and dark-hued, and, given to fixing his eyes on whatever he found before him, he put you in mind of some minor creature, a mink, say, or a marten, a fera staring from a limb or the mouth of a burrow. And in an instant of clarity, you understood why you'd withdrawn from the handshake: he'd offered you a paw.

He touched a sheaf of papers lying before him on his desk, saying, "This agreement we're about to sign—it calls for the publication of a novel known as *The Trampled Vineyard.* Tell me, Shapiro, what the title is supposed to signify."

"The wrath of the Lord," you said. " 'He is trampling out the vineyard—' "

"Vintage," he said. "The actual word is vintage."

"Is it? I never knew that."

"It makes no difference. The title would be poor with either word."

"Vintage makes less sense than vineyard. Grapes of wrath aren't stored in a vintage—or a vineyard, either. In fact, grapes aren't stored."

"We aren't dealing with wine," he said. "We're dealing with a blood-soaked book."

"Then maybe you'll like the title I discarded: *The Great Grey Drayhorse.*"

"From the Hopkins poem?"

"*Felix Randal.*"

"What have we to do with a Catholic poet and a dead blacksmith?"

"I was thinking of the bright and battering sandal of one of the characters— Martin Flood."

"We have several characters. Our title ought to suggest them all."

"There used to be a magazine called *Contact,*" you said. "I pulled a story once because they wanted a change of title."

"You pulled a story from Bill Williams?" he said. "That took more nerve than brains."

"He thought so too, but for some reason or other, we stayed friendly."

"Are you always this hostile, Shapiro?"

"Only when somebody wants a book *and* a title-change for a hundred bucks."

"Your cousin said you'd take a hundred."

"I need more."

"Do you mean to revise the manuscript?"

"Of course."

"I'll pay you a hundred now and a hundred more when you deliver it."

"Is that the best you'll do?"

"Yes."

You signed the agreement, but when the time came for a parting handshake, you managed to be holding a match to a cigarette.

§

You and Ruth watched as the storage-men swiftly dismantled the home you'd known for more than five years. In the course of a morning, all the rugs and furniture had been removed, and only a pair of suitcases remained, standing side by side near the door. The emptied rooms resounded as you took a last look around at where a family had many times gathered, at where a table had been placed, a piano, a couch, a chair, and on the wallpaper you noted the slightly darker square where a picture once had hung. The first home you'd had since the death of your mother twenty years before—and now, in two hours, it had been reduced to spaces and divisions, used, worn a little, and lightly sifted with dust.

"We had some good times here," Ruth said.

The times came back in a rush of stills, as if you'd flipped through an album; all you caught was a glimpse of passing pages, and only now and then did an image stay. One of these was of an evening with friends, some of whom, having gone to Harvard, sat or lay on the floor. Lou was there, paying you scant attention, but knowing that you were watching her from a chair. And then that page too seemed to pass.

"Yes, we did," you said.

§

By earlier arrangement, Ruth was to be put up by a cousin who lived nearby, and after seeing her off in a taxi, you returned to the apartment for your luggage. As you stooped to take it up, you stopped, straightened by a memory. In an alcove before you, there had stood an armchair so fat and ungainly that you rarely sat in it. Soft-sprung, it would engulf you, you thought, it would embrace you, draw you down, drown you in wadding. Even so, there'd been a time when you ran its risks, and on the occasion, as if to sound it, you'd thrust your hand into the crevice at your side. Wrist-deep, you found no bottom, and only on probing to the elbow did you touch a solid. Bringing it forth, you stared at a leather-bound pocket dictionary—French-English and English-French. *Why, that's mine!* Ruth had said. *It's been missing for years!* That was your final thought on leaving the apartment. It meant nothing, of course, and you soon forgot it.

One of your Harvard friends, a bright young man who discoursed with equal ease on Max Planck and Dada, had offered you the use of a room while his family was absent for the summer. He'd given you a key, and when you closed the door behind you, you headed for your latest furnished room.

§

A few days later, after a stay of eight weeks, your father was released from the hospital. You called for him early one morning, shaved him as usual, held his clothes, and then gave him your arm as he quitted the room.

At the doorway, he paused to say, "You're a good kid, Julian."
And you said, "Not so very."

Using your Aunt Sarah's car, you started for West End. You drove to the 42nd Street ferry, and while it crossed toward Jersey, you sat staring through its dark innards at a small bright sky ahead.

"Not so very, pop," you said.

242

SCENE 79

LABOR DAY WEEKEND (Late Summer 1935)

On the Saturday morning, your father was permitted to go downstairs for the first time since his arrival at West End three months earlier. You helped him to dress and then took his arm as he descended, step and stop and step again, to the ground-floor landing. There, at the foot of the flight, the entire family waited to embrace him, and afterward he was escorted to a table set for one in the sunlight on the porch. Drawing up chairs, they ringed about to keep him company, and when Rosie the cook brought his breakfast, she managed to kiss his hand. You stood back from the group, watching the way they were watching him, and in your mind you heard the phrase *two or three years. Two or three years,* you thought, and then there'd be an end to *You're a good kid, Julian.* There'd be none to say it, none to think it, not even you, for you knew, and no one better, that you weren't a good kid at all. You'd chosen, just as Olga had done, and after that, whatever your regret, the *goldene Kind,* in some alchemical disaster, was forever brass.

Later, when you and your father were alone, he asked how far along you were with the revision.

"It's finished," you said. "I delivered the manuscript yesterday. On my way to the boat."

"When will there be a decision on it?"

"There's none to make. The changes were done on my own."

"Do you think the book will do well?"

"Boni thinks so. That's more to the point."

There was quiet for a moment, the quiet of small sound, water running, dishes colliding, the whirl of mower-blades, sound so usual it was scarcely heard.

Into it you spoke, saying, "There's something I have to tell you."

"What's that, kid?"

"The book will be published under a different name."

"Not *The Old Man's Place?*

"A different name for *me.*"

He said nothing. He merely looked away at the view, at the lawn, the driveway among the trees, the hedges, the almost hidden house across the road.

"I hope I haven't hurt your feelings," you said.

"You'd better worry about your own."

"My own? How so?"

"I know you pretty well, kid," he said, "and not because I'm so wise. What you have in your mind is always on your face. You're no greasy sneak, like your Uncle Harry. You do wrong only too damn often, but you never pretend it's right. You suffer for it, and Harry doesn't, and that's what makes him a piece of cheese."

"Well, I'm going to suffer as John B. Sanford," you said, and unfolding a dust-jacket that you'd been given by your publisher, you displayed it for your father from the far side of the table.

It was a lithograph in black and green on white, with the title spread across the top and the author's name at the foot of the sheet. In between, stark against a sky of india ink, stood your three ex-soldiers, a simple-looking Trubee, a gigantic and lowering Flood, and a pimple-face Pilgrim, all of them looking down at a ploughed field and the shanty farmhouse of Walter Pell.

" 'John B. Sanford,' " your father read. "The hero of *The Water Wheel.*"

"Behold, I have become my own fictitious character," you said. "Listen to what it says on the front flap:

> *The Old Man's Place* is the first novel that we have accepted for publication in three years. Readers of the manuscript have been aroused to a unanimous enthusiasm that has not been equalled in this office since we first received the manuscript of Thornton Wilder's *The Bridge of San Luis Rey. . . .*"

"Who wrote that?" your father said.

"Not I," you said, and you read on:

> "Unlike that novel, however, *The Old Man's Place* is American both in treatment and episode, and Mr. Sanford's expert handling of its theme entitles him to a place in the narrative tradition so ably sustained by Edith Wharton in her *Ethan Frome.*"

"Sounds to me as if Boni likes it," your father said.

"He goes too far. *Ethan Frome* is a very fine novel. I wish I could write one as good."

"Maybe you will some day."

"Maybe," you said, and as you rose, you took a check from your pocket and put it before him. "The other hundred that Boni promised me."

He didn't touch the check. Instead, he touched your sleeve, saying, "Keep half, kid. You need a new suit."

He was always right: you *did* suffer.

SCENE 80

A BAR OR TWO OF MUSIC FROM AFAR (Summer of 1935)

The only surviving version of *The Old Man's Place* is the one that was sent to the printer. It is an original manuscript, typed on the blue-margined paper known in every legal office as testimony bond,* and its 236 pages contain some 50,000 words. It shows only a scattering of corrections, leading you to suppose that your revisions were extensive enough to require a retyping of much of the book. Here and there a strike-out appears, a respelling, an interlineation, but except for a few such changes, the copy is unusually clean.

All through a hot city-summer, you'd worked daily at a desk in your Harvard friend's room. In the rest of the flat, the awnings were down and the green shades drawn, and what light these left was a warehouse gloom. At times, you'd walk the floors, hoping your mind would respond to your body's motion, but the air too was that of a warehouse, drained and unrenewed, and it bore the ghosts of a strange cuisine, of stale upholstery, of clothes and camphor. In the evenings, when the streets began to cool, the brick, the iron, the glass, you'd go outdoors and drift toward the Drive to gaze at the broken rays of light still lying on the river.

The home of your Harvard friend was only a few steps from West End Avenue and its facing rows of apartment blocks. Breaking this order and enclosed by a spiked wrought-iron fence, was the anomaly of a huge private pile, the imitation chateau of a squandering tycoon, his Amboise for the Valley of the Hudson. Between the bars of the black array, you'd stare at street-lamp shadows on the walls, at windows that stared back in surprise, at angle towers and the steeps of the slated roof, and smoke from your cigarette would flow away like mist.

"Julian?"

You turned to a girl who'd stopped after passing by. Thinking slowly back to your Harlem days, you remembered someone's younger sister, a mere occupant of space, an object usually caught in the act of disappearing through a doorway or behind a chair or skirt, a staring presence living on a level far below you, never spoken to and seldom wholly seen, a plain little thing—but she was little no longer and not quite as plain as you'd thought.

"You *are* Julian," she said.

---

*Used thereafter for every manuscript.

"And I know who you are now," you said, and then you laughed. "I also know where I got a figure of speech I use: something watching me from the mouth of a burrow. You'd look at me like that."

"My sister and yours were best friends. You lived in the flat right above us, and they were always sending secret messages to each other up and down the dumbwaiter."

"I never saw one," you said. "I never knew the secrets."

"Do you live around here now?"

"A friend is letting me stay in his apartment for the summer. I'm getting a book ready for the press."

She nodded, saying, "I'd heard you were writing."

"From whom?"

"My brother-in-law. He'd read a book of yours—*The Wheel,* was it? He didn't like it."

"You wouldn't, either."

"Why do you say that?"

"Because you didn't read it yourself. You accepted his opinion."

"I asked him to lend it to me, but he'd thrown it away."

"My publisher still has two thousand copies. If your brother-in-law buys them, he can throw those away too."

"He said it wasn't fit to read."

"Maybe he isn't fit to be a reader."

She began to walk now, and you walked with her until she paused before a building across the street from the turreted fortress. On the wall behind her, a brass plaque shone: *Esplanade.*

"I live here," she said.

"What does esplanade mean?"

"I don't know."

"Before we meet again, you must ask your brother-in-law."

"*Are* we going to meet again?" she said.

§

On Friday afternoons, you'd leave off work on *The Old Man's Place* and catch the last Jersey Central boat for the shore, the *Monmouth* at times and at times the *Sandy Hook.* In all respects but their name, they were identical twin-screw steamers, built in the same yards and capable of the same number of knots—twenty-two, as you recall it—but the *Monmouth* had always been your favorite. You could not have told why, but it seemed to conjure more than a field of battle (*Poltroon!* Washington had said there of Charles Lee, *Scoundrel!*), and besides, you liked its soft sound, like that of an exhalation.

Your father's room was at the rear of your Aunt Sarah's summer home, overlooking a curve of gravel driveway leading back to the carriage-house among the trees. Once or twice a day, he'd pace slowly in the upper hallway, but most of his hours were spent in a chair near the window, where he could watch other things in motion, a car coming or going, a gardener mowing the lawn, or merely leaves flipped by the wind. He was not yet allowed to use the stairs. On your weekend visits, you'd sit and talk with him for hours, and though always in your mind was that phrase of Dr. Robbins'—*two or three years*—you could never see beyond the measure of time he'd named: nothing was there.

"Ruthie wrote to me from Sandusky," your father said.
"I heard from her too."
"She asked me whether I wanted her to stay on with Hortie or come home for Labor Day. Answer her for me, will you?"
"Saying what?"
"Find out what she means by home."

§

It was a warm evening, you remember, and the coverings on the furniture gave off the scent of flax, slightly sweet, like that of privet, and it made you quit the flat. Even outdoors, it remained for a while in your mind, recalling nighttime walks at the shore past hedges that lined the way.

At the Esplanade, you called the girl from a telephone near the desk, saying, "Which word would you use—effluvium or emanation?"
"Neither. I'd say smell."
"Come on down, and we'll take a bus-ride through the smells of the city."

At 72nd Street, you boarded a coach headed for Washington Square. Only a few passengers were on the upper deck, none of them at the rear on your favorite bench, and there you sat through the darkness and the street-corner intermissions of light.

"While waiting," you said, "what do you do with yourself?"
"I'm in my senior year at Barnard," she said. "Waiting for what?"
"Marriage."
"I didn't know I was doing that."
"You're not being candid."

After a stop at Broadway, the bus joined the traffic moving downtown toward Columbus Circle. Smoked air flowed back over the deck, and the street-lights seemed to wear it, like an aura.

"You're right," she said. "I'm not."

"And what will you settle for?"

"You have a way of making me name things. Security."

"Is that what you're studying at Barnard—insurance?"

"Security isn't something you have to study. You grow up knowing it. You know you're going to marry some day."

"What you're studying, then, is whom."

She glanced away across the railing at dark shops and bright displays, silverware against velvet, a vase on a pedestal, mannequins in dotted swiss.

"You don't know his name yet, of course, but you must've learned something about him."

"He has to be someone whose eyes are open," she said. "But he has to do more than see—he has to know what he's looking at."

"You're describing my dentist."

She went on, hardly having heard. "He can't sit inside himself and make himself the world. He's got to see it steadily—is that Walter Pater?—and see it whole."

And then there were two spired cathedrals, one at either hand, opposing faiths vying for the passerby. "He can't be like you," she said.

"What do you know about me?"

"What you wrote about you. I read your book."

"In spite of your brother-in-law?" you said. "By the way, is he a dentist?"

At the Square, you left the bus and walked for a while through the park and the surrounding streets, and finally you found yourselves on the cobblestones of Washington Court, a mews that ran from the Avenue to University Place.

Somewhere in its darkness, you said, "I'd stand you to a cup of coffee, but all I hve left is the fare."

§

There were other walks, on summer evenings and summer days. One of them was for an afternoon at the Museum of Art. You'd mentioned the Havemeyer bequest of Degas and what a friend had said of Courbet: *His still-lifes are like a novel by Zola.*

"What friend?" she said.

"A friend no longer, I'm afraid."

"What happened?"

"I put his sister in *The Water Wheel*."

"Was she your girl?"

"I went with her for a time, yes."

"Do you put all your girls in your books?"

"Well, that one I did, and my friend resented it."

"Do you think he was right?"

"She was part of my experience," you said, "like my mother's death when I was ten, or a teacher that I'd known." And after a pause, you said. "Teacher. Everybody is a teacher, and they all belong in a book." And then you walked on for a way before saying, "What do you think of that remark about Courbet?"

"Wait till I see the picture."

At the Museum, you climbed the steps to the entrance, and there you were confronted by a sign on the inner side of the glass door: *Admission—25¢.*

"Courbet is only for the rich," you said.

And she said, "Let me pay."

"No," you said, and you led her away.

"Pride?"

"Chagrin. I thought it was a free day."

"You have no money," she said, "but you seem to get along without it. How?"

"It has a way of turning up when I need it. In small amounts, of course."

"You don't think much about it, then?"

"I thought *too* much once, and I didn't like myself."

"Most people would say you have no ambition."

"What would *you* say?"

You were back in the park, behind the Museum and passing the base of Cleopatra's Needle. "We began the afternoon with a walk," the girl said. "Let's finish it with a walk."

Statues of marble and statues bronze, the Boat Pond, children running after dogs. "What would *you* say?"

"We have different patterns. You have no respect for mine: you'd call it selfish, unintelligent. But I couldn't live according to yours, never. I know what I want. I know what I must have."

"Describe it," you said. "Maybe it only costs 25¢ apiece."

§

And still another walk brought up near the canopy of an apartment house on Central Park West. Your gaze ascended its perforate face, some of it filled with light and some of it void.

"Did we stop here for a reason?" you said.

"My brother-in-law lives here," she said.

"The dentist! The man whose eyes are always open!"

"He isn't a dentist."

From a window on the fourth floor, you looked down at the spot where, only a moment before, you'd stood looking upward, and for some reason, the distance seemed to have increased, as if you were watching a point in the past.

"What're you working on now, Julian?" the brother-in-law said.

Which brother-in-law, you thought—the one sitting behind you or the one in the glass? "Something called *The Old Man's Place.* Another novel."

His wife said, "What's it about?"

"It isn't easy to say what a book's about. I heard a story once, but I hope the book turns out to be more than what I heard."

"I read a review of the other one," the brother-in-law said. "The heading was 'An Unpleasant Egotist.' Did that mean you or the character Sanford?"

"I like to think it meant me. I'm unpleasant."

"I haven't seen Ruth for a year or more," the wife said.

"Right now, she's out in Ohio. She's visiting a friend she met in college."

Sandusky, you thought, and Sullins College, and for all you knew, the words might've been spoken aloud by someone else; your attention was elsewhere, on the girl, seated partly in shadow and partly in a lampshade of light.

"How many copies did they sell of *The Water Wheel*?" the brother-in-law said.

"Oh, six-seven hundred, maybe."

"At how much to you a copy?"

"Two-bits."

"So give or take, you made a hundred and a half on the book."

"I didn't make anything. I lost."

"Lost? How's that?"

"I got no advance, I got no royalties, and I was never paid back for expenses—postage, stationery, and the like. I figure the book actually *cost* me three hundred."

"If you keep on writing," he said, "you're apt to lose quite a bit of money."

"It's certainly a gamble."

"Don't you care about money?"

"I care about writing."

"That's no answer."

"I'm sorry," you said. "I thought it was."

You glanced at a grand piano draped in an embroidered shawl, at a wedding photo in a frame inlaid with jade, at two runners made on the steppes

of central Asia—and at discretion, you thought, at tokens of security, at the
order of the day.

"After all those questions," you said, "how about a few from me?"
"Ask," he said.
"What do *you* do for a living?"
"I buy and sell real estate."
"And you do well at it?"
"Look around you."
"I've looked," you said. "By 'well,' I meant you buy low and sell high.
Is that right?"
"That's the system."
"The system, then, is to buy something for less than its value."
" 'In all labor, there is profit.' Proverbs."
"Scripture or no scripture, I don't like your system. Excuse me for saying so."
"I will, but the system won't. It'll reward you poorly. Remember *The
Water Wheel*."
"I'm not looking for much in the way of reward," you said. "If I knew
I could go on writing, I'd settle for fifty bucks a week for life."

He looked first at you and then at his wife, and from her he turned to
his sister-in-law, still sitting quietly, still crosscut by light and shade.

He shook his head, saying almost as if to his own astonished mind, "Fifty
bucks a week!"
His wife said, "Julian doesn't mean that."
And you said, "Julian does."

Later, you walked the girl back to the Esplanade. Traffic was sparse in the
roadways, and there were few pedestrians on the streets.

"I wonder what you'd've done," she said, "if you knew the kind of real
estate he deals in."
"And what kind is that?"
"He calls it distressed."
"I've heard that one before. A euphemism for 'under foreclosure.' Like 'passed
away' for 'died.' "
"When taxes on property are in arrears," she said, "the city files a lien against
it. If it isn't paid off—satisfied, they say—the property is sold at auction."
"And that's where your brother-in-law buys?"
She nodded, saying, "The tax-lien business, it's called. Well, what *would*
you have done?"
"Pissed on his shoes."

§

And then there was an evening when you did not walk, when you sat with her before a window, and talk was soft in the dark. You did not touch her; you spoke to the open window, and she listened as if to a voice outside. When you left, you found an all-night telegraph office and sent her the longest message you were able to pay for: *I love you,* it read, and you signed it *Julian.*

§

On the following day, you received a letter from her that you would write about only after forty-five years:*

A NINE-PAGE LETTER

I know absolutely what is best for me, and I am completely selfish about it.

Dear Julian, she began, and ink flowed in phalanges, phrase on phrase it strode without a falter across the page. *You can't realize how I feel about the sudden change in our relationship,* she said, and her lines dressed left and dressed right, and in her white and private spacing, words never mingled, letters never met. *Somehow you came to believe in a possibility that does not exist,* she said, and now, like some hostile force, a grammar of cases, genders, tenses, moods seemed to be advancing against you in open order. *Knowledge of myself made me long ago invent a pattern for my life,* she said, and her words were then upon you, trampling, and in their tread was your doom. *Your way of living could bring me only very great misfortune.*

The letter might well have ended there, at the foot of the second page. Whatever it had to tell *Dear Julian* had been told by then, and more would overfill the already full and merely spill away. But more there was for seven pages, and you wondered (you wonder still) what made her waver so, what turned her corps of clauses to a crowd. The writing sagged and climbed now, lagged behind, ran ahead, floundered, fell, and, fallen, died. There were crossed-out dead on every page, corpses hastily buried, as by an army in retreat. There were swarms between the margins, a last stand of words, it seemed, a Thermopylae. . . .

---

*In *To Feed Their Hopes,* University of Illinois, 1980.

You never replied, you never called again—but is that what she wished, is that what the seven pages were meant to do? *I know absolutely what is best for me,* she said, but was she trying to persuade herself in the pages sent to you?

THE COLOR OF THE AIR, XII

ALBERT EINSTEIN—1905
A WANDERING JEW

It is strange to be known so universally, and yet to be so lonely.
— Albert Einstein

In the legend, he was one of those who lined the way walked by Christ behind the Cross, and they say he taunted the Son and urged Him faster, crying *Go on! Go on!* and thus, they say, did the Savior answer: *I go, but thou shalt stay and no wise taste of death till my return.* So runs the tale, and many are they who claim they saw him, the mocker, *der Ewige Jude,* snapper at the heels of the Lord.

If ever onesuch was, this creased, this slack and often shoeless, this mild and wild-haired little Jew could not have been he, for despite the high hand holding him, he'd be gone before the Second Coming: he'd be dead, he'd die in his sleep in another fifty years; he'd sigh a last few words in German, his aorta would explode, and he'd die, never having known where Calvary was nor stood beside the road.

All the same, there'd be some who'd vow that he was the Jew the ages knew at Leipsig, at Ypres, at Altbach and Astrakhan—he'd died, they'd allow, but in doing so defied the Will, set aside his sentence, and gone before the appointed hour, and seeking the secret of his power, they'd relieve him of his brain, together with the meninges that invested it, and burn the rest and strew the ash on a running stream.

The brain they'd test in other fires. They'd observe it first, each fissure, each convolution, and then they'd wield their calipers, weigh it, palp it, and describe its color, texture, conformation; to inure it, they'd steep it in brine, arsenic, alcohol, formaldehyde, whatever would firm it while staving off decay; and then it would be dissected, stained, and microscoped, it would be pulverized, it would be titrated and centrifuged; and always it would grow smaller, their prize, it would be spoiled in part and partly mislaid, it would be left in trains, stolen, played with, flushed down drains, it would be shelved between semesters and regimes, it would be forgotten during illnesses, vacations, wars, hurricanes, and there'd be demises and retirements, there'd be new Christs or none and rumors of an old vag haunting the streets of Brussels, Prague, Valladolid.

And so seven years would pass, and though still there'd be some of that Jew's taciturn brain and someone still to twist the screws, it would not speak, it would not confirm, and no agony would ever break it, no shame. It would occur to no scientific team to try eating it, to accept, as savages would've done, that they'd thus absorb its properties, its arts and inclinations, and therefore when the kilo of matter was down to a gram, they'd tire of the minikin lump, and they'd throw it away, let it go as the body had gone, wandering down a running stream.

SCENE 81

ALONG A LIFFEY OF YOUR OWN (Summer of 1935)

At your Harvard friend's home, you were still within sight of the Hudson and the hills of Jersey, and in the late afternoons, done for the day with *The Old Man's Place*, you'd walk to the Drive and watch the lights come on to bead the Palisades. The lines they laid down upon the water seemed to converge in reverse and meet in you, as if you were the vanishing point, and you'd see too, if a train were running in the shade of the cliffs, a rise of painted steam fade against the sky.

How you'd've liked the river of 1609, how you'd've longed from the *Half Moon* for its shores! There'd've been clear shallows where shad and barbel swam, and there'd've been cold black channels through the reeds. But that river no longer ran here; in its place another, sewage-brown and dense, and instead of perch and salmon, there'd be schools of rubber fish; gone these days the trees, the little silver falls that fed the stream. Had you gone bad? you wondered, had it been you, not time, that spoiled the view? *Ah, if a father has to ask!* you thought, and then you turned your thoughts away.

§

The first version of *The Old Man's Place* was written at the Hotel Sutton, after you and Nat West had returned from your summer in the Adirondacks. Based on a story told to you by Harry Reoux, owner of the Viele Pond property, it made use of events that had occurred in the district a dozen years earlier, soon after the end of the war. An ex-soldier, whose father worked a meagre backwoods farm along a branch of the upper Hudson, had brought home with him from France two of his army companions. The trio, freed from military restraint and having little or none of their own, had soon begun to run wild over the countryside, and, hardly less than marauders, they had committed a series of acts ever increasing in outrage until they came to a close in murder.

There'd been no more than that to the story. As related, there were no names, no details of time and locale, and no aftermath. It had been offered as fill for a few moments while you stood on the little dock or sat on the cabin porch, a mere episode in local history, a narrative acted out by pronouns (*he, they, it*) and verbs predicative of their evildoing (*smashed, burned, stole, shot*). Anonymous, faceless, undefined, like danger in a dream, the tale drifted on the come-and-go of your mind. It was always there, half-awash and half-submerged until one day, as if finally cast up and stranded, it lay in the clear. In thought, you saw sequences of motion start, and you heard voices speak from forming faces, and there were colors, places, fire, food, and rain, and a story based on a story began to grow inside your mind.

You bestowed names on the three ex-soldiers—Martin Flood, perceived as an outsize brute from the Middle West, James Pilgrim, a ruled-off jockey, and Trubee, a victim of his well-meaning father, Walter Pell—and once they possessed identities, the novel soon evolved. For some reason, you chose to write the first draft in the open air, and you did so sitting in the sun on the hotel roof. In a style so unadorned that it might've been used in speech, you began the book with terse recitals of three lives as lived before the opening page, three sketches that accounted for the presence of the soldiers at a certain time and a certain place.

You were too much the novice then to realize that with those little summaries, you'd put a limit on the novel's range: what they showed quite clearly was that the war hadn't ruined your three soldiers; it was the soldiers, being already flawed, who'd brought ruin on themselves. In presenting the three soldiers as formed before war ever found them, you were dismissing the effect of war on character, leaving yourself with only a Flood, a Pilgrim, and a Pell who, peace or war, would've come to grief. During their spree at the farm, with war disregarded as a causative factor, you could account for

255

one enormity only by another, greater in degree and more depraved, as if violence were its own explanation. The book, then, could never become significant; it could only be a measure of your ability to tell a story.

In the writing, you made, as you thought, a change of position, turning from the inward focus of *The Water Wheel* to the external view of the non-participant. Striving for a cinematic effect, you reported only what you "saw" and "heard" from where you stood; in fact, however, what you saw and heard were the sights and sounds in your head. In doing your bidding and saying what you wanted said, the soldiers became your agents (what was the law-school maxim? — *Qui facit per alium facit per se*), and what you wrought through them you wrought yourself. The blows, the shots, the flows of blood, all were ascribable to you.

§

Sitting there in your Harvard friend's room, you'd look up from the pages at times, and through the window you were facing, you'd see between two buildings a wedge of river flowing by. A river risen three hundred miles away, you'd think, clear there, cold, soft as mist — and here it was an outfall, fit only for the sump of the sea.

SCENE 82

THE OLD MAN'S PLACE (Fall of 1935)

After the Labor Day weekend, your father began to spend the greater part of each day downstairs with the family, and he was even permitted to walk about the grounds. On the lawns and driveway, maple leaves lay brown and half-clenched, dry little hands that held nothing, and the grass grew more slowly now, and always sweepings somewhere smoldered, and their smoke was on the air. Smoke, you'd think, wondering how much he missed those forbidden cigars. You'd watch him toy with a cigarette, but it was plain that he didn't care for their feel and flavor, nor did he like the way they burned. Still, he'd light one and forget he held it, and a signal you couldn't read would waver up from his hand.

"I'll be going back to the city in a few weeks," he said one day, "and we'll need a place to live."

"What have you got in mind?" you said.

"There's a residential hotel on 75th Street, or maybe 76th, I forget which. It's between Broadway and West End—the Milburn, it's called. Nothing grand, kid, not your speed at all."

"If you think the Sutton was grand, counselor, guess again. It was a twelve-story whorehouse."

"Well, you have a taste for good things. Even when you were five years old, it was the Astor House for you, and the Savarin, and Shanley's, but never the Exchange Buffet."

"Where did I get that taste, I wonder?"

"From your mother, may she rest in peace. How she loved the good things! Which I almost never could provide. You weren't aware of it—to you, clothes were just clothes—but she dressed you and Ruthie in the best. You had linen suits with embroidered collars, lisle socks, patent leather shoes, Leghorn hats."

"I remember something about that mahogany table we have and the matching bookcase. I don't know how old I was—six, seven, maybe—but something was going on over my head, and I heard it. They cost three hundred dollars, as I recall."

"Three hundred that I couldn't afford," he said. "In the end, though, I gave in."

"It was a sore point, and it stayed sore for a long time. Am I right about that too?"

"She loved good things," he said. "Next week, take a look at the Milburn. See if you can find a two-room suite."

"For how much?"

"I'd go a hundred and a half. That's not your speed, but it'll have to do."

"Did I really wear patent leather shoes?" you said.

§

At the Milburn, you were shown a suite of rooms that overlooked a row of private houses and the courtyards at their rear. Above them, the top floor and the cornice of the Esplanade were visible. Esplanade, you thought, and you recited its definition in your mind: French, from the Italian *spionata,* a clear level space or stretch of ground. An odd name, you thought, for the mass that nullified the clear space, the level stretch of ground, and then you thought that somewhere in that mass, on the fourth story, the fifth, the seventh, a telegram signed *Julian* might be lying in a drawer, a box, a pigeonhole, still saying in capital letters *I love you.* And then, forgetting the girl, the telegram, the *spionata,* you went downstairs and engaged the suite.

It consisted of a sitting-room, with a studio couch for your sister, and a bedroom for your father and you; opening off a short passage between the two were a bath and a small kitchen. Home, you thought, and to the list that began with the Hotel Cecil in 1910, you added another name, the Milburn. You moved in with your belongings, and on the following day, you borrowed a car and made a round-trip to West End, bringing back your father.

When you showed him into the suite, he looked about and said, "A hundred and a half doesn't buy much these days."

"We've lived in worse," you said.

"I have, but when did you?"

"At Stein's, on 124th Street."

"How can you remember Stein's? You were what—eight years old?"

"It was a warehouse before they made a hotel out of it. On the Seventh Avenue side, it was next to a beer-garden."

"You've got a good memory, kid. It *was* next to a beer-garden."

"Mother took me there one afternoon, and we watched people dance the Turkey Trot. She shocked me by ordering a drink—grenadine."

"Grenadine wasn't alcoholic. It was a syrup, and it was served with seltzer. She liked the taste."

While you unpacked his clothes, he sat gazing through a window at walls of brick and brownstone, at light and shade, at clouds, at nothing that he saw outside.

"I never thought I'd hear you say a thing like that," he said.

"Like what?"

" 'We've lived in worse.' "

"What would you have expected?"

" 'We've lived in better.' "

§

Because your father could not be left alone, you arranged with your sister to take turns at keeping him company. When free in the evenings, she'd go to the theatre, use her subscription to concerts at the Hall, or pass the time with friends, and on her return, usually before midnight, you'd take an airing that always ended at the 72nd Street entrance to the subway. There, in string-tied bundles still warm from the press, the morning papers would be tossed from the trucks, and in their warmth a review, perhaps, of *The Old Man's Place*.

The only reviews that mattered, Albert Boni had told you, were those in the Sunday and daily editions of the *Times* and, to a lesser degree, the similar pair in the *Herald-Tribune*. Journals such as the *Nation* and the *Saturday Review*, he said, could neither make nor break a book. That power resided in the *Times* and the *Tribune* and nowhere else, and therefore when you opened one or the other each night, you knew full well that you might come upon your own obituary and learn that you were dead (*SHAPIRO, Julian, also known as John Sanford, son of Philip D. and Harriet Nevins Shapiro, aged 31, suddenly*). And when you found that you still had at least another day of life, you folded the paper and walked away.

In that suspended state, not yet done for but awaiting judgment, you'd sometimes wonder how you yourself appraised the book. You knew what you'd set out to do — to see outward, to become a witness instead of a performing party, to hear and observe without interfering while a series of violent acts were in the course of commission, these to be noted and described free of comment, as if they were in the usual round of an ordinary day. It was in this last that your misgivings lay: having turned your eyes outward, had you seen into others, or, as you feared, had you merely seen their outer side?

§

After an examination by Dr. Robbins, your father was given leave to resume his practice, beginning with no more than a few hours a day. You accompanied him on his first visit to the office, and it pleased him that he was greeted so well and warmly by the three other lawyers who shared the quarters. Then, opening his door, you watched him cross the room and seat himself in his swivel-chair.

"Counselor," you said, "I'm glad you're back."

He rocked the chair once or twice as if to test its springs, and he said, "It feels natural."

"When I think of some people, I see them on their feet, running, walking, standing still. But you, you're always sitting down and usually at your desk."

"It's where I've lived for thirty years."

"In the early days in Nassau Street, you had a chair upholstered in black leather, I remember. It was too high for me, but when you were out of the room, I'd climb up and make believe I was you. I'd dictate to an imaginary stenographer, using phrases I'd heard from you — *beginning at a point 200 feet from the southerly corner of Hunts Point Avenue,* I'd say, and *Know all men by these presents.* What were presents, by the way?"

"The writing itself, the deed, the lease — *per has literas praesentes.*"

"I never knew that," you said.

He smiled, saying nothing, but you seemed to hear him all the same: *My dear son, there's a lot you never knew.* Then, shaking his head, he said, "What isn't so natural is the quiet. Where have all my clients gone?"

"The snows of yesteryear," you said. "More will come along."

"Not for me, kid; I'm out of it. Others will go where I suppose mine went—to other lawyers or the grave. Wattenberg is buried in Palestine, and he was by far my best. Your Grandpa Nevins brought him in, and he's dead too. Rubin sent for his papers, and so did the Klebans—and they're my cousins—and Morris White has left me for someone with a daily gardenia stuck in his lapel. Your old man is out of it, kid, and to tell the truth, I don't much care. I made a lot of money—your mother *zelig* didn't live to see it—and now that I've lost it, I'm going to enjoy being poor. I don't want to make it and lose it again. . . . I had some good times, though."

As you watched him relive them, you felt that his pleasure now equalled his pleasure then: it seemed to have made no difference that the good times had passed, for in his mind they still were here. And it went even further, you thought: the good times need not have been high on the hog; he'd worn the same expression for a cigar, a streetcar ride, a dish of coffee ice cream, a long Seder service where, as the prayers rolled on, he'd suddenly intone in another language—"O God of Israel, on what page do we start to eat?"

"Morris White," he said, "the only client who drove to my office in a Rolls-Royce. Did I ever tell you about a hotel he bought? It was a complicated deal involving three parties, and it took me a week to work the thing out. At the title closing, he put a blank check in front of me and told me to fill in my fee. He was a good client, so I went easy on him and put myself down for a thousand. You know what he did? He tore the check up and wrote out another."

"A cheapskate in a Rolls-Royce!" you said.

And your father said, "The second check was for five thousand," and he savored the memory as he had the moment.

"You enjoy yourself, don't you?" you said. "You live all day long."

"Why not?" he said. "What can be so bad after twelve days in the steerage?"

§

The Old Man's Place was a poorly-made book, an *Ethan Frome* on the cheap. The dust-jacket, a chromo then, has not improved with age, and the stamping on the spine seems crude to you yet. For the printing, a crown octavo sheet was used, and when folded, it gave eight leaves of 5 x 7½, a small-sized page. For you, what redeemed the book was the typography, the work of your cousin Mel Friedman at Haddon Craftsmen. He lent added force to the text with a 12-point Caslon Old Face, a clear type with a distinctive italic, and he designed a title-page in red and black that you still regard as fine. And on that page, the colophon of a piping Pan, and thus, as with the dragon, you were following the lead of Dr. Williams.

§

Reviews* began to appear late in October, and they continued through the end of the year. Sixteen clippings have survived the fingering and folding of time, and, browned with age, they lie one to a page in an album before you. Some are from journals long dead, and they speak without menace from the grave, but others, fifty years old now, still hold the doom of living thunder. Here under your eye, the findings of the minds of strangers, the prejudices and preferences, the perception and "the ever-during dark"—the judgments that were made on your second novel.

The notice of William Soskin, literary columnist for the New York *American,* a Hearst publication, was captioned *A Horrid, Horrid Book About Horrible Men* and followed by several paragraphs expressive of the reviewer's revulsion; in his turning away, however, he misread your name, and his scolding fell on one John B. Hanford. In the Cleveland *Plain Dealer,* Ted Robinson, though scarcely more restrained, nevertheless commented on the quality of the writing:

> As for fiction, the most striking example I have run across is *The Old Man's Place*, by John B. Sanford. In an era of brutal fiction, *The Old Man's Place* will take a prize for brutality. If there be tenderness among the sons of men, if there be mercy, if there by any pity or forbearance, or even a shuddering away from the more obscenely ruthless acts of gratuitous savagery, such effeminate weakness has no place between the covers of this sadistic novel. But . . . this John B. Sanford writes well. He has a talent for it: he is vivid, realistic, skillful, dramatic.

You had never believed that violence long-continued lost its power. You judged it by its effect on yourself, and just as successive acts successively affected you, so you supposed they worked on others. It gratified you, therefore, that the violence in your book had shaken such readers as Soskin and Robinson, but after a few more reviews in a like vein, you began to wonder whether they'd been shaken too much, whether in their disquiet, they'd overlooked what redemption the violence might bring. Your original aim had been to tell

---

*Because of your change of name, an occasional reviewer supposed the book to be a first novel.

a story, but in the telling, the story seemed to pursue an aim of its own—through its very violence to salvage Trubee Pell. The *American Mercury*, literate though it was, failed to see that far:

> This first novel is a fine example of the narrative story, written without psychological implications or the much-belabored "stream of consciousness" motif. Out of a simple and forthright melodrama, Sanford has brought splendid material, spun with skill and force. It is the story of three men . . . and the tide of violence mounts to a swift crisis. By employing the correct pace, by utilizing action instead of reader implication, Sanford gains his end, which is, primarily, to tell a story. In this field, it is safe to assume that he can hold his own with any of his contemporaries of high rank.

§

On those evenings when your sister was not at home, you'd sit for hours with your father while he talked of times that were gone, times flush with things you'd never heard of. He spoke of family customs, of the follies and foibles of this uncle or that in-law, of hardships, marvels, wise sayings, and, above all, of his mother's cuisine, still relished after half a century. She made a dish, he said, that no one could spell—*chullent,* it sounded like, a stew of *flanken* buried in potatoes, carrots, onions, and herbs, all of it simmered through a day and a night in a great shallow pan that covered half of the wood-range. Ah, the perfume that filled the rooms! he said.

Often too, of course, he spoke of the reviews, a few of which lay beside him on a table. "Violence," he said. "All they talk of is the violence."

"I hate to admit it," you said, "but when I began the book, I was out to write just that—a story of violent men. I had half a notion to blame the war for the violence, but it didn't hold water, and what I had was simply three men going from one outrage to another without a reason and without an end. Somewhere alone the line, though, the story took the lead, and it went on to an end of its own—Trubee's atonement."

"But nobody sees that," he said

"Not yet," you said.

§

In Canada, the savagery of your ex-soldiers was savagely condemned. A notice in the Montreal *Star* denounced both the book and you in a slashing paragraph:

Another convert to the Faulkner-Caldwell cesspool of imaginative filth . . . a horrible story of three human beasts . . . devoid of a single gleam of decency . . . a mass of repulsive abomination.

The Memphis *Commercial Appeal* followed suit, flaying writer and writing with equal vigor:

It is the tale of three extremely unpleasant young men, who retire to the New York farm of the father of one of them, and there engage in practices as despicable as they are brutal, until a climax is reached and the rottenest of the three is shot. In another and more horrendous climax this rottenest one so surpasses himself that we are in a mood to accept the author's implied belief that the other two are more to be pitied than scorned—nay, that the son of the farmer is, after all, a regular and nice kid and by way of being a hero.

On the table near the clippings lay a presentation-copy of *The Old Man's Place*. Reaching for it, you turned to the dedication-page.

" 'This book is for The Governor,' " you read. "Governor, I apologize."
"What for?"
"For tying you to a book like this."
"Don't worry about that," he said, and then he laughed. "Nobody knows me as Philip D. Sanford."
You laughed too, and then you stopped, saying, "Did I hurt your feelings when I used another name?"
"Did Pep hurt Max?"
"I never asked," you said.

§

In many of the smaller cities, the dailies, having no book editors of their own, would print syndicated reviews, and it was common, therefore, to receive duplicates from your clipping service. Readers in Wichita, Richmond, and Sacramento, all were served the same hack work, and all of it came back to you with the same Romeike label, black print on pink paper. Independent reviews were rare, and what you took to be one such was handed to you by Albert Boni when you entered his office on a day in November. You read it while you stood beside his desk.

And in the evening, you read it again, that time for your father:

Charles Boni woke up one morning and accepted a manuscript entitled *The Old Man's Place* by John B. Sanford. . . .

"Charles?" your father said. "I thought it was Albert."
"It *was* Albert," you said:

> . . . which nearly ever publisher in town had rejected. Naturally it is almost a masterpiece—certainly one of the most important novels of the year. . . .

"Not bad," your father said.
"It gets better," you said:

> . . . We give warning that it will horrify the stupidly conventional, for both the language and the story are severe; but those who have an appreciation for literature will be struck by this young author's power of description and characterization and his unique ability to express himself with the uttermost brevity. Would to God that he might teach 1,001 other writers how to condense. . . !

"Well, well," your father said.
And you read on:

> . . . In 263 pages he tells the story of how Trubee Pell's life is ruined by a weakness in character which drives him to several disastrous and brutal attempts at self-assertion. He marries at the outbreak of the war. His friends criticize him for entering this contract for the sole purpose of dodging the draft and to regain their approval he turns against his wife, abandons her and goes to war. In the army he makes friends with two gangsters. . . .

"Gangsters?" your father said.
"It says gangsters," you said:

> . . . gangsters. He eventually returns to his father's farm with these two men and again endeavors to assert himself by dominating his father. The rest of the book is concerned with the crimes these three young men commit at the farm. One of them, Pilgrim, through a Sweetheart Club, persuades a young girl to come to the farm on the pretext of marriage. The high moments involve rape and murder. A mediocre writer would certainly make a melodramatic mess of this material, but Sanford has reached the heights of drama. As an example of the style and vigor of description we quote the following passage. . . .

"And then," you said, "the fellow goes on for fifteen lines, a long paragraph from the book—the part where Walter Pell kills Flood—and he winds up with this:

The whole scene is described in one page."

"That's a damn fine review," your father said. "Where did it appear?"

"The New York Sunday *Enquirer*."

"I hope Mr. Boni was impressed."

"He said, 'Julian, do you read the *Enquirer*?' I said, 'No.' He said, 'Do you know anyone who reads the *Enquirer*?' I said, 'No.' He said, 'What the hell *is* the *Enquirer*?' And I said, 'To tell the truth, Albert, I never heard of it.' "

"Well, it has to be a newspaper," your father said.

"Oh, it's a newspaper, all right—the kind they stick in mailboxes. Your fine son is now a wrapper for the garbage."

"Don't feel bad, kid," your father said.

§

In the Columbus *Dispatch*, as so often elsewhere, readers were warned of the book's brutality:

A melodramatic but interesting story, a robust tale of violence, lust, treachery, and murder.

And in Pittsburgh, the fastidious were put on guard by the *Post-Gazette*:

Erskine Caldwell, Ernest Hemingway, James M. Cain, and John O'Hara have all chalked up records for the amount of stark brutality they have been able to pack into a single work of fiction. As far as brutality goes, these gentlemen are now out of the running, for John Sanford has bowed himself on the literary scene, and Mr. Sanford is a supreme master at squeezing the last drop of terror and excitement out of a sordid, savage situation. Until the bitter end, the story sweeps along with an ugly force that will send sensitive souls in search of the smelling salts.

The reviewing assignment for the *Nation* had gone to a woman named Eva Goldbeck, who found the book a social as well as an emotional affront:

The masses have become fashionable; like the middle-western farmers of fifteen years ago, the disinherited are now being invited to publishers' teas. And just listen to the dirty language of the Great Unwashed! It is hard for a guileless reader to differentiate between a proletarian subject and a proletarian point of view. Irresponsible books like this warn the revolutionary writers to be morally and stylistically more careful than ever.

What the passage meant you did not know at the time, nor do you know yet. Was it written in cipher, you wonder, in a code you'd never break?

§

The three reviews that Albert Boni had been waiting for appeared during the same week, and each was the comment of a a critic well thought of by writer and publisher alike. They were John Chamberlain, book editor of the daily New York *Times*; Fred Marsh, fiction editor of the Sunday *Times*; and, in the New York *Herald-Tribune,* Vincent McHugh, an able novelist and a member of the editorial staff at the publishing house of Simon & Schuster. They were lucid writers all, they were unbiased and therefore perceptive, and they were read with respect wherever books were thought to be important. Had the three, or any of them, condemned *The Old Man's Place,* all hope would've ended abruptly; as it was, with only their qualified approval, hope died a lingering death.

Chamberlain's review was unusually long, filling both columns of his everyday box called *Books of the Times*—160 double-width lines of print:

> John B. Sanford gets excited about America, not for any ascertainable philosophical reasons, but simply because he loves its patterns and its contours. He is to the novel what the school of Thomas Benton or Grant Wood is to painting—a "nativist" who takes a purely esthetic delight in the salt and savor, even in the occasional flaring brutality, of the American character. His *The Old Man's Place* is a first attempt to catch this character on the wing, and his ambition is to make his next novel as American as Brady's pictures. He gets excited about this Brady—Mathew Brady—who was the national photographer of the Civil War. . . .

You hadn't realized how much of your inclincation the book revealed; you'd not yet consciously written of your predilection for the visible America, for the natural place, the populace, the ruin that one had wrought upon the other. All that, you thought, had been reserved for later books—and yet here it was, a personal and pervasive flavor.

What followed Chamberlain's opening was an almost point-by-point abstract of the story interwoven with analyses of its three main characters, and there you were surprised by the finding that the war *had* shaped them all, that the war had forged their violence and brought on their violent end. It was an opinion you were unable to share. The brief biographies with which the book had opened showed only too clearly three natures formed before the war had begun—and yet here was a reviewer, and one of the best, who would not credit what you knew to be true. The war, he said, the war had done it all:

> If there is any sermon in *The Old Man's Place*, which is pre-eminently a novel to read for the "story," it is a sermon about the World War. For France brutalized Trubee, smothering the character in him, and throwing him "on the town." It also brutalized Martin Flood, the giant from Nebraska. Pilgrim would have been a bad egg, war or no war. But not Trubee, and possibly not Martin.

You thought of a story you'd heard about a composer who'd conducted a performance of his own composition, only to read in a review that he hadn't understood the music. Had you misunderstood your book? you wondered. Could others read what you didn't know was there? Chamberlain concluded with this long paragraph:

> In its frank brutality, *The Old Man's Place* reminds one of Ramon Guthrie's post-war *Parachute*. And the brutality is possibly true to life. War either shatters or brutalizes the troops; we have the word of men as far apart in character and time as Walter Duranty and President James Garfield for that. Having seen the practice of international gangsterism at close range, why should Trubee, why should Martin Flood worry particularly about giving an Italian fruit vendor a light tap on the head? Mr. Sanford does no moralizing himself; he would probably look at you with horror if you were to draw social implications from his novel in his presence. Nevertheless, the implications are there.

§

As you recall it, Fred Marsh's review in the *Times* and Vincent McHugh's in the *Herald-Tribune* appeared on the same Sunday, and each, though less than you'd hoped for, was quite possibly more than the book deserved. Marsh began with this:

> Here is a first-rate piece of swift-moving and dramatic story-telling in restrained and effective modern American prose. Most men and some women will get a thrill of recognition and the catharsis of vicarious experience out of it. Plenty of both will declare that there is no point in reading about three toughs, a moronic girl and a dull-witted old man, even if they are true to life. But so long as American society throws up such people as these . . . just so long will novelists and painters and poets and playwrights use them to their purpose;

and just so long will people of heart and mind want to know more . . .

Anybody who has been around a little bit, who has not shut himself in . . . has run into James Pilgrim, Martin Flood and Trubee Pell. Sanford's portraits are executed in broad, quick and sure strokes with a wry though never awry touch of caricature. They are instantly recognizable, but they are also revealing. His story reminded us of Conrad's *Victory* for some not quite explicable reason. . . .

Then, after finding in your three soldiers, the monolithic Flood, the stunted Pilgrim, and Trubee the farm-boy gone bad, a resemblance to Conrad's girl, gambler, and henchman — in short, after raising you high, he let you fall with this:

> But there is no Heyst here and consequently no ultimate meaning that relates the ugliness and tragedy of human wreckage to the scheme of things entire. That is why this novel is a good story and a sound piece of representation (not without its significance) but nothing more. . . .

You can still remember your throe of disappointment on reading that pronouncement. You'd long been uneasy with what you'd written, but until then there'd been the chance that you'd written better than you knew. Once *The Old Man's Place* had been measured against *Victory,* that chance ceased to exist. At the time, though, it was hard to accept Marsh's finding that your book had no larger meaning than the meaning on the page, nor was pain allayed by the favorable way in which he concluded his review:

> Sanford is not writing rough tough stuff for its own sake. Indeed, a kind of gentle melancholy runs through the prose. But he writes the story as he has figured it out . . . and you'll spot James Pilgrim, the scrawny little chap who grew up in an orphan asylum, Martin Flood the farm-grown bully, and Trubee Pell, the good lad gone wrong. Call them Aramis, Porthos and Athos, and they still, in a way, stand up on an uglier, more realistic and more sordid plane. The girl and the old man stand up too . . . The story gets going at the shabby old homestead. It doesn't stop until the last page. We shall not outline the story; you must read it for yourself. If you start it, you'll likely finish it whether you enjoy it or are willing to admit you enjoy it or not.

§

Vincent McHugh, in the opening line of his review, addressed a different element:

268

Mr. Sanford's first novel is an able melodrama of character,

and in much of what he went on to say, he treated the story as a study in relationships. After describing the three principals and their origins, he wrote:

> The material is hardly more bulky than that suitable to a novelette . . . But Mr. Sanford has a living story to tell, and he gets it off with a good deal of clean skill. His handling of pattern is good, his judgment of pace and relief prevents any effect of merely mechanical violence. In some measure he has even succeeded in converting the form of psychological melodrama patented by Dashiell Hammett — a form in which the reader's curiosity as to what is going on in the minds of the characters can be relieved only by action — into a legitimate dramatic device for the transfer of emotion.

Here McHugh evidenced his acquaintance with the two publications of the Dragon Press:

> More than anything else, the quality and tone of *The Old Man's Place* recall William Carlos Williams's stories in *The Knife of the Times.* Mr. Sanford's style — an easy colloquial American idiom showing remarkably few lapses into color-writing — runs more smoothly than Williams, though it operates in a much narrower range of implication. There is in both writers a strong and warm sense of place as distinguished from local color. Mr. Sanford's work picks out the Lake George region clearly, but in such a way that one is conscious of its relation to New England, the farmsteads of Pennsylvania, even the outposts of the Mid-West.

And then again, in the final paragraph, he spoke of character:

> Engaged with a theme not unlike one of Erskine Caldwell's, the author's attack is savage enough to disconcert anyone liable to visceral flutters. But he has turned his emphasis away from Caldwell's relatively dehumanized comic satire toward a field of more emotional gravity. The small twisted ex-jockey, for example, who painted himself for his wife-to-be as a six-footer "standing a hard day's work like a real man and never tired out from it," is at once cynical, deeply conscious of his wrecked life, and hopeful as a sparrow in the morning. *The Old Man's Place* is a minor novel, often deliberately low-toned, but a work of very genuine skill and feeling.

§

"Well, the big stuff is in," Boni said, "and it's not enough."

§

Nor would a good letter from William Carlos Williams be enough, nor would anything be changed by what Clifton Fadiman said in the *New Yorker* toward the end of the year:

> THE OLD MAN'S PLACE by John B. Sanford: John Chamberlain's review in the *Times* convinced me, too late, that this novel was more than a mere tough tale.

A few more reviews were to come, but they too would be late, and then all mention of the book would stop.

The only royalty statement you ever received from A. & C. Boni reported sales of 1,055 copies.

§

"How do you feel about it, kid?" your father said.
"Roughed up," you said.
"And how does Boni feel?"
"When I turn up now, he's usually busy."
"That's the way it goes."
"You know what I'm going to do?" you said. "God damn it, I'm going to write another book!"
"Nobody can say you've got a glass jaw," he said.

THE COLOR OF THE AIR, XIII

JOHN REED — 1914
A LAND TO LOVE

It was a desolate land, without trees. You expected minarets.
—John Reed

He saw it for the first time from the roof of an adobe on the Texas side of the river. A mile or so away, across sand, scrub, and a russet stream, it began in the town of Ojinaga. By day, vines of smoke climbed the air, and the sun broke on gun-metal, and pigmy figures

270

crawled, men in white cotton, women in black, and dogs, and when the last light bloodied the sky, toy sentries rode in toward the fires.

A land to love, he called it, and it drew him as the pickets were drawn to warmth. Its colors stunned him like a disembowelment — the yellow water and the tangerine clouds, the red and lilac mountains, the stove-blue membrane all around and overhead. The heat stunned him too: a fanatical sun seemed more to rear than rise, and from ninety-three million miles off, it so enraged the earth that it shook, as if about to explode.

A land to love, it was, and he went there, and in its squares he found strewn straw, and in its streets women wended with water-jars among the droppings of burro, dog, and man. The stink of piss made a new element, thick in the sun and lank in the shade, and saddles stank of sweat top and bottom, and somewhere a game was seen, one that was played with a ball, and somewhere else a nameless grief was sung, and from under vast sombreros, small lives spat at death.

It was a land to love, but the minarets would be in another part of the world, and he would go there too, and die, and lie at last at their feet.

SCENE 83

ANOTHER BOOK (January 1936)

God damn it, I'm going to write another book!

In his quarterly magazine *Pagany,* editor Richard Johns had printed a story of yours called "I Let Him Die."* It was one of several that you'd written during your stay at the Hotel Sutton, and it dealt with an upper New York state farmer, who, having found a cold and hungry tramp lying in his barn on a winter morning, had ordered him off the property, an act resulting in the man's freezing to death in the snow.

And it snowed too on a later day, not a fictional fall, but a fall in fact, and you walked in the great meringue that lay on the city and the things of the city, the streets, the steps, the hydrants, and the smallest twigs of trees,

---

*Vol. II, No. 2, Spring 1932.

and so soon did it fill a footprint that you seemed to be going where none had gone before. *Another book,* you thought, and conjured by the snow, you suppose, the Adirondack story rose through your mind.

It stayed there for days, suggesting nothing beyond itself, an idea exhausted in a single use, and still, though empty of promise, it would not go away. Its constancy prompted you to look for a reason, and on taking up a copy of the issue in which the story had appeared, you dislodged a note made long before in a class at law school. *See Wharton's Criminal Law, Sections 455/6,* it said; on those two sections, you remembered, "I Let Him Die" had been based. Their wording had become vague, but the note was no longer a void name and vain numbers: it was an imperative. *See,* it demanded, and at the main branch of the Public Library, you saw—that Wharton was *WHARTON, Francis, 1820-89,* and that the full title of his work was *A Treatise on the Criminal Law of the United States.*

At Section 455, you read:

> We have already seen that an omission is not the basis of penal action unless it constitutes a defect in the discharge of a responsibility specially imposed. And the converse is true, that when a lawful duty is imposed upon a party, then an omission on his part in the discharge of such duty which affects injuriously the party to whom the duty is owed, is an indictable offense,

and at Section 456:

> As, in conformity with the definition just stated, the responsibility must be one specially imposed on the defendant, the omission to perform acts of mercy, even though death to another result from such omission, is not within the rule. One man, for instance, may see another starving, and may be able, without the least inconvenience to himself, to bring food to the sufferer, and thus save the latter's life; but the omission to do so is not indictable unless there be a special responsibility to this effect imposed upon the defendant,

and following that second section, citations were given from four jurisdictions:

> Burrell vs State: 18 Texas 713
> Connaughty vs State: 1 Wisc. 159
> Rex vs Smith: 1 Car. & P. 449
> People vs Smith: 56 Misc. 1.

Looking up from the tome, you took in the rows of oaken tables and their lamps with green-glass shades, the veneer of books on the balcony walls, the space beneath the ceiling where all sound seemed to go, and then you came back to readers rapt before the printed word. The word about what? you wondered. What point was being verified, what place or career explored? what minds were under scrutiny here? what theories were due to fall? And who, you wondered, who, full of the dictum of the great and small, who would perform an act of mercy *without the least inconvenience* and save another's life? Would he, that sat there facing you, would she across the aisle?

Turning again to the pages before you, once more you read the rule that had given rise to "I Let Him Die":

> *The responsibility must be one specially imposed.*

And if not so imposed, then he who faced you and she across the aisle might remain where they were, might continue with their readings in comparative religions, in the customs of primitive peoples, and in the history of the earth. Unconstrained by law and therefore blameless, they might watch, they might even gorge, while another starved to death.

And now you thought of your father (*two or three years,* the doctor had given him), and suddenly from the Wharton, a single word rose as if under magnification — *responsibilty* — and you knew then what your new book would be.

SCENE 84

170 WEST 73rd STREET, APT. 10b (February 1936)

The suite at the Milburn had become an expense that your father could no longer bear, and one morning, after a final breakfast there, he led you and your sister to the flat that he'd leased a short distance away. It was in an old block, ten stories of ruby-colored brick set off with granite sills and lintels and, at the corners, dentelles of the same gray stone. The five rooms of Apt. 10b were large and bright, and from their windows, though for once the Hudson was out of sight, the view lay northward across the water-tanks on lower roofs, the aerials and clothes-lines scrawled abstrusely on the sky. The rent was seventy-five dollars a month.

"With the seventy-five we save," your father said, "the Shapiros can have a housekeeper and eat their meals at home. The Sanfords too."

After he and your sister had gone downtown, one to his office and the other to her sales job at Lord & Taylor's, you remained behind to await the arrival of the storage-van. In your mind, as you walked about the rooms, you disposed the piano there, in that space beside the door, and you placed the dining-table here, in front of the mantel and beneath the chandelier. Your footsteps resounded on the bare parquet, as if there were nothing, no nine floors below you, only a column of air. And there, you thought, the mahogany pieces your mother had longed for, and there the deep and damask chair, and above your sister's couch, you saw her Cézanne print, a still life of fruit, and your *Mlle. Victorine as an Espada,* and you sorted books and shelved them, you thought, and they looked like a shiraz hung against the wall.

And then the doorbell rang, and someone in a leather apron said, "Where do we put this stuff?"

SCENE 85

QUEER STREET, APT. 10b (February 1936)

Q.: How do you get by?
A.: On the coins in my father's change-pocket.
Q.: How much do you take?
A.: Fifteen cents a day.
Q.: What do you spend it on?
A.: A dime for a small pack of Luckies, a nickel for a towel at the Y.M.C.A.
Q.: What would you do if nothing was there?
A.: There's never nothing.
Q.: Suppose your father forgot?
A.: He never forgets.
Q.: Why is that . . . ?

Having no money for fares, you walked to wherever you were going, and you walked all the way coming back, walked the city in every weather, in the sun and under snow and tufted by the rain. No more little gifts for the girls now, the two-bit bunch of violets, the candy-bar, the roasted chestnuts in the twisted sack. And there were no ferry-rides when the nights were fine, no side-by-sides in the dark where celluloid images spoke. And there were no excursions to Boston, and even on the free-days, you stayed away from the Museum. You pressed your own clothes, you darned your own socks, you turned the frayed collars of your shirts. You were Dolgoruky in *The Possessed*—or was it Stavrogin or someone else who put his feet down squarely to lessen the wear on his shoes?

Q.: Why is that, Julian?

Your only contribution to the household was the quarterly check from your grandpa's trust fund, a small enough share, less than the cost of your keep, but even so, when you reached into that change-pocket each morning, those coins were always there—a dime for a pack of cigarettes, a nickel for a towel at the Y.M.C.A.

Q.: Do you know why, Julian . . . ?

SCENE 86

EXERCISE ON AN EMPTY STOMACH (March 1936)

That winter, you played handball nearly every morning. You'd rise around six, and before the rest of the household was awake, you'd dress, help yourself to your fifteen cents, and set out for the Y. a dozen blocks away. Along your route, you'd pass coffee-shops, bakeries, soda-fountains, where outflows of breakfast flavors made fragrant zones in the air, and thinking of poppy-seed rolls, of hot biscuits, of the corn meal on a rye-loaf heel—always of bread!— you'd swallow salivation and continue down Broadway.

Doc Nelson was your doubles-partner, often against the team of Fred Allen and Don Novis. They'd usually manage to win the rubber game, but you gave them a little trouble with a high soft serve, and the Doc had a forecourt kill that stuck in the corners like a dollop of custard.

He'd laugh when he saw one die there, and he'd say, "I call that my Charlie Chaplin shot."

§

Your father, seated near a window, watched a straight-down fall of snow that seemed to give a woven texture to the air, and when he spoke, it was as if he were speaking through it to something beyond.

"There was a wind then," he said, "and it blew across the city for three days without a let-up, piling snow against the buildings as high as the second floor. I was only ten at the time, but I remember hearing that people died when they climbed out and tried to walk on it. That was in '88."

§

"The meat was delivered to the butcher-shop around three o'clock on Friday mornings," he said, "and somebody had to be on hand to pay for it in cash. Some weeks, the holiday weeks, the bill came to five hundred dollars, and those momsers on the truck wouldn't even bring in a chicken until they had their money. I was only fourteen years old, but being strong, I was elected to sleep on the counter and unlock the door. Five hundred dollars, I sometimes had, but no one ever tried to rob me."

"What would you have done?" you said.

"I've often wondered."

§

You remember a certain evening just before the spring of that year. You can still see your sister on the couch in the livingroom, and in the downpour of light from a standing lamp, she's reading your pocket edition of *The Prussian Officer*. Why does that stay, you wonder, when the stories do not? And your father, facing you in an armchair, is holding one of your cigarettes, and a blue-gray haze hangs above him, dimming the zouave colors of *The Fifer*, a poster sent to you from Paris by Mlle. Dykmann—*Musée de l'Orangerie*, reads the legend, and *Juin-Septembre 1932*, and *Tous les Jours*. And in the outside world, there's rain.

"Coming home from the Y. this morning," you say, "I ran into Uncle Jack. He blew me to breakfast."

"He likes company," your father says.

"He had company. A little guy named Murph."

"One of Jack's old-time pals from the Harlem days."

"He ordered kippers. I thought it was the English that ate kippers, not the Irish."

"Murph is a Jew. His name is Moe Silverman."

"I'd never met him before, but he seemed to know about me. He asked me how the practice was going, and when I told him I had no practice to speak of, he said I could have a damn good one if I liked."

Your father says, "What was Jack doing?"

"Eating kippers too."

"When this Murph said you could have a good law practice, what did Jack say?"

"Nothing. He just kept on eating."

"Well, then, what did you say?"

"I said I didn't understand, and Murph said he knew people who'd pay good money to have me appear for them. I had the gift of the gab, he said, I dressed conservative—not conservatively—and, best of all, I was clean. That's when Uncle Jack spoke up. He said, 'The kid takes a bath once a month, whether he needs to or not.' "

"That's *my* joke," your father says.

"I told Murph I couldn't see people hiring me just because I talked English and wore a Brooks suit. He said for all his people cared, I could talk Turkish and wear a fez—it was the clean thing they'd be glad to shell out for."

"You should've asked him why."

"I did, and he said they needed a respectable front. That was when Uncle Jack really took a hand. First he said, 'Drop it, Murph,' and then to me he said, 'His people are low-lives.' "

Over the top of her book, your sister says, "Somebody has to represent that kind."

And you said, "That's what I said, but Uncle Jack came back with this, 'To be a lawyer for that kind, you'd have to be in on their low-life secrets. Once that happens, you belong to them.' "

Your sister says, "That's only in the gangster movies."

"Murph is a gangster," your father says.

"What does he do—rub people out?" you say.

"Oddly enough, he's on the up-and-up. He has to be. He's what they call a bag-man, a go-between, and what they give him to deliver—a dollar or twenty thousand—he delivers to the penny. But make no mistake: he's a gangster all the same."

"Uncle Jack wouldn't go around with a gangster," your sister says.

"He doesn't go around with Murph," your father says. "He just eats kippers with him."

§

And there was a time when you said, "Did you ever want to be a judge?"
And your father said, "Yes."

"You'd've made a good one. What happened?"

"The Owasco Club, over on Lenox near 122nd Street, was the Democratic headquarters for my district. I played pinochle there occasionally, always in one of the smaller games—a quarter a hundred and sometimes even less. You couldn't get hurt that way—a bad run of cards, and you'd lose maybe twenty–thirty bucks. I was just finishing a hand one night when the steward came in and said that the Leader wanted to see me in his office. I joined him, a man named Flynn, Jimmy Flynn, and he told me to close the door and sit down, and when I did, he said, 'I like you, Philly, and so do the boys at the Hall.' He didn't mean Carnegie; he meant Tammany. I said, 'I'm glad to hear it, Jimmy.' He said, 'We think you'd look pretty good on the Bench. We've got the Magistrate's Court in mind for a couple of years and then General Sessions.' I said, 'What would I have to do to get there, Jimmy?' and he said, 'Whatever we tell you.' "

He stopped, and you said, "What did you say to that?"

"I said, 'Jimmy, I've got to get back to the game. I'm three dollars behind.' "

"Did he ever bring it up again?"

"No, and we were friends till he died."

§

Seated at your mother's mahogany table, you wrote the opening lines of *I Let Him Die** on a page of scratch. Only the typed manuscript remains, and it may be that those lines lasted, that what you'd said in longhand, you kept on saying in print:

> At five o'clock in the morning, Platt floated up to the surface of sleep—slowly, like a drowned man, sprawling—and then, awake. . . .

Lightly crayoned in the margins are directions for the linotype operator—*12-point Electra on 14, #1 ornament, 36-point Dwiggins initial flush left as in corrected sample.* When followed, they'd result in the book that lay beside the manuscript in a scarlet and lavender jacket. But then, at that glass-topped mahogany table, you had little more than this:

> . . . A last thin silt of flakes still tumbled in the quiet air. . . .

Putting aside the evening newspaper, you found your eye drawn to color, the red cover of *The Prussian Officer,* and taking up the little volume of stories, you opened it to an inscription on the flyleaf: *Julian L. Shapiro, Jan. 4th, '35.* 1935, you thought, a late day in your reading of Lawrence, and glancing at the bookcase, you scanned a shelf of his writings, all of it acquired at least half a dozen years earlier. Why, you wondered, had you bought the book you held in your hands? what had you thought to find that you hadn't mined before? You let a few pages run and turn, thinking, What's new here? what has not long since been said? And standing there beside the bookcase, you began to read paragraphs in the story of the title, and though you remembered

---

*Later *Seventy Times Seven,* A. A. Knopf, 1939.

nothing of the Captain and his orderly, somehow they struck you as familiar, as if you'd met them elsewhere under different designations. And it was so, you soon thought—you *had* met them, in the other places of all those other books. And wherever met, they'd been the same, save that the Captain had been carried to Mexico and the orderly to the land of the kangaroo. Coursing through them the same *dark forces,* the same slow thick stream, the same laval flow of passions, a magma that nothing could resist. These men and women, this Captain and his orderly (his woman!), they were simply borne along on their urges, but no longer were you borne with them, and you watched them go unmoved.

Your sister entered the room adjusting an earring. Noticing the book, she said, "Rereading Lawrence?"

"This is the first time I've ever read him a second time," you said, "And now I know why."

She put a finger on the glass door of the bookcase and counted off to eighteen. "And you're holding the nineteenth."

You pointed, saying, "What about the Verga? It's a Lawrence translation."

"Twenty, then. Why did you have to read so much to know what you were reading?"

"In my room at the Sutton once, Pep picked up a copy of *The Rainbow* and said, 'I sing the body electric.' He was right, but I didn't realize it. Too much flame. It's even in the flowers."

She said, "Joe's coming over."

"And that means Julian goes."

And you went, walking up Broadway on a cold night through the light under the street-lamps and the dark in between, without a destination, without silver for a seat before a silver screen.

SCENE 87

AND OTHER VALUABLE CONSIDERATIONS (May 1936)

Since the publication of *The Old Man's Place* during the previous fall, Albert Boni had moved his offices from lower Fifth Avenue to a private residence on West 56th Street. Above them were his personal quarters, beginning with a library that extended through the entire depth of the second story. From the bay window at the front end, the sidewalks could be seen as far as either corner, and while you stood there waiting for Boni to enter, you looked down on flows of people, a come-and-go of hats equipped with feet. Behind you, you heard a door being closed.

"I called you," Boni said, "because I wanted to show you this."

He handed you a legal document stapled within the cover of a lawyer named Howard Reinheimer; it was an agreement between the publisher and one Bartlett Cormack.

"Who's Bartlett Cormack?" you said.

"A playwright. He wants permission to dramatize *The Old Man's Place*. To try, at any rate."

"I never heard of him."

"A few years back, he had something on Broadway called *The Racket*. It had a pretty good run."

"Have I got a say about this? Or is it between you and him?"

"According to our contract," Boni said, "I can dispose of the dramatic rights. All I'm obliged to do is pay you your share. Of course, if you object, I'll tell Cormack it's no go."

"I'm not up on these things, but *The Racket* doesn't promise much in the way of quality. I'd like *The Great God Brown* a lot better."

"So would I, Julian, but I haven't heard from Eugene."

"This agreement," you said. "How much time does Cormack get?"

"A year to write. Another year to produce."

"What do you recommend?"

"If I could get $250 for my signature, I'd write it all day long."

He sent you to Cormack's agent, Leland Hayward, on Madison Avenue at 60th Street, and there, below a clause reading

> The terms and conditions of the above mentioned contract are
> hereby approved and accepted by the undersigned,

and over the typed identification *Novelist,* you wrote *John B. Sanford.*

Walking away from the building, you went toward the Grand Army Plaza. Ahead of you, forever at a prance, was the St. Gaudens statue of General Sherman, a gilded rider on a gilded charger. You pressed your arm against your jacket, making paper crackle in an inside pocket—a blue binder, was it, or a valuable consideration?

§

When you reached home, your father said, "What did Boni want to see you about?"

"Some guy thinks *The Old Man's Place* can be made into a play."

"What do you and Boni think?"

"We gave him a shot at it," you said, and you passed him the check you'd been given at the Hayward office. "Turn it over."

He did so and read, " 'Pay to the order of Philip D. . . .' How come, kid?"

"How come you've always got change in your change-pocket?"

SCENE 88

BY THE LIGHT OF THE DOG STAR (July 1936)

Your sister, with another spot on her lung, had been sent to West End to avoid the damp swelter of the summer. You'd remained at the apartment with your father, and save for early-morning handball at the Y., you were much of the day in his company and, when the weather prevented sleep, much of the night as well. Then, sitting with him in the dark, you'd face an open window and gaze toward Central Park over the roofs across the street. Sometimes a stir of heat would swirl in and brush you, and sometimes there'd be no motion at all, and smoke from your cigarette would stall and stay on the air.

"This reminds me of when you were little," your father said.

And you said, "How so?"

"If you cried, I'd get out of bed and walk you, and from a different window, I'd see a different park—Mt. Morris, opposite the Gainsboro."

"Did I do much of that? Crying?"

"You did your share."

"When I was little, you said. What did you think of me when I was little?"

He laughed, saying, "If I tell you that, I'll have to tell you what I think of you now."

"I withdraw the question," you said.

"I'll say this, though. Sometimes when I look at you, I don't see you at all. I see your mother."

"That ought to be in my favor."

"It is," he said.

When you were little—the words came back to you at times that summer, and often you wondered how little you were now. What went through the minds of others, what did they say at the mention of your name, did anyone defend you or were you low to all?—and in the end you knew that you'd never know. In those breathless nights, you could only guess what your father, your friends, your family may have thought, and even strangers who'd caught the way things stood—and on one such night, the room seemed to become murmurous with presences rehearsing for their turn to speak. And they spoke:

UNCLE HARRIS: Your best friend, Julan, is your father.
GRANDMA NEVINS: Run, Juno, and give to that olderly man this money.
AUNT SARAH: Ah, Julian, if a father has to ask!
PEP WEST: The dedication in *Miss Lonelyhearts* is "To Max." But, Scotty, I don't think I ever did another thing for him.
AUNT RAE: I should've been married to your father. I'd be different.
UNCLE HARRY: A dollar is a dollar, no matter how you get it.
A HARVARD FRIEND: Julian, the marmoreal scrivener!
GEORGE BROUNOFF: There comes a time, Julian, when you put away childish things.
HERB ORTMAN: If you give it up, Jules, you're crazy.
UNCLE DAVE: I wanted to go to Cornell, but my father wouldn't put up the money.
LOU G.: My father drank till my mother got tired of it and locked him out of the house. Locked him out of her life. How could she, Jule?
OLGA: My father quarreled away a career.
HERB ORTMAN (again): Don't ever give it up, Jules.
YOU: I won't, but some day there'll be no one to forgive me.

Off to the north, you saw lightning make a chart of the sky, and after a moment, the curtains bloomed with a first cool sigh of air.

"I'll take one of your cigarettes, kid," your father said.

SCENE 89

A MAN CALLED MORRIS (August 1936)

You never learned whether the Morris came first or last, whether he was Morris-something or something-Morris, and for all you knew, he might've been a man with one name—Morris-nothing. He had charge of the locker-room at the Y., and when you walked up to the wicket, he'd pull your basket from the racks behind him, hand you a fresh towel (with Y.M.C.A. in white on a red stripe), and drop your nickel into a till. He seldom spoke, or seldom to you, making you think he thought the *Shapiro* on the basket sorted with the *C.* on the towel. Or, as you'd now and then wonder, was Morris himself a Jew?

A morning came when you gave him no part of your mind. Your father had passed a poor night, with a pain in his chest that only a nitroglycerin pill had relieved, and at breakfast, you'd urged him to forego his usual trip to the office.

And he'd agreed, saying, "Nothing's waiting for me there, anyway—not these days. I can remember a time when I closed twelve titles between ten o'clock in the morning and midnight. Barney Chambers and Jack Freeman helped out, and sometimes there were a hundred people in the waitingroom and the hall outside—buyers, sellers, brokers, title-searchers, lawyers. I made ten thousand dollars that day, Jack and Barney got a thousand each, and three typists split another thousand."

And you said, "Where did a Yid get the name Chambers?"

"The same place you did. It used to be Scheinberg."

You'd offered to remain with him at the apartment and let the handball go, but he'd refused, persuading you that he could do without your company for an hour or two (*Strange as that may seem,* he'd said), and off you'd gone to the Y. There, you'd put on your gym-clothes, rank with sweat baked in the drier, and headed for the courts, clenching your stiffened gloves until they softened and gave. You found Doc Nelson warming up alone.

"Hello, Shappie," he said. "How's your pop?"

"He had to take a nitro pill last night."

"That'll happen. The main thing is not to let him scare. That'll speed up the heart action and make the pain worse."

"I guess it's hard to stay calm."

"I'd be scared too," he said. "Are you ready for a beating?"

You were halfway into a second game with him—and you *were* being beaten—when, just before a serve, Morris opened the door.

"Shapiro," he said, "call your home right away."

When you reached your locker, you were still wearing your handball gloves, soaked with sweat once more, and for a moment you stood there, staring at them as if they belonged where they were, a dark brown skin that you'd grown on your hands. When you did take them off, finally, you simply let them fall to the floor. All you could think of was a phrase—*two or three years,* you thought, *two or three years*—and it was still the only fix of your mind when you were standing at a pay-phone and scraping your pockets for money that wasn't there.

"You need a nickel?" someone said, and, turning, you saw Morris watching you through the wicket. "Catch."

You caught the coin he flipped and dropped it into the slot, and then, dialing your home number, you listened to the ring, and it rang three times before your father answered. "Papa," you said, "are you all right?"

"Did my call upset you?"

"Well, when a guy breaks up a game to tell me to call home. . . ."

"Who was the guy?"

"The locker-room attendant. Man named Morris."

"I didn't mean to alarm you, kid, but I wanted to get a message to you. Albert Boni says you're to go straight over to Leland Hayward's and see a Miriam Howell."

"What's it about?"

"Nothing much. Paramount Pictures is after you."

When you hung up, you looked at the attendant and said, "I owe you a jit, Morris."

And as you went down the stairs to the street, you thoght *Morris-what, or is it what-Morris?*

§

"Bart Cormack is a client of ours," Miss Howell said, "and I gather he's been talking about you on the Coast. Yesterday, Paramount called to offer you an assignment."

You heard what she was saying, but the effect of the words was checked. It was as if they'd been received in some anteroom of your brain and there directed to wait. In other chambers, there were warmer receptions, and you were aware of a desk with a surface of tooled leather, a breakfront bookcase, photos of the famous on the walls, the sounds of typing, bells, and traffic on the street.

"If you'd like us to represent you," she said, "sign this form, and we'll go over to the Paramount Building and do battle."

§

Sitting beside her in one of the Paramount offices, you stared at a glass prism on which, in letters of black and gold, *Wm. Auerbach, v.p.,* was painted.

"Bill," she was saying, "you can't be serious about offering one of our clients a mere two hundred a week and a three-month deal."

"We think it's a pretty fair offer, Miriam."

"Not for our kind of writer."

"A writer of two books, neither of which sold."

"Two *good* books, Bill. If they weren't, you wouldn't be talking to us."

284

"I don't question their quality."

"I'm glad to hear it," she said. "Because Leland has had his eye on this young man, and now that he's a client, we mean to bring him along with care."

"What would Leland consider taking?"

"The truth is, he has half a mind to keep Sanford in New York and fund him through the finish of his new book." She turned to you, saying, "What's the working title?"

"Of what?" you said.

"The book you spoke of."

"*I Let Him Die.* It's based on one of my short stories."

And then to Auerbach, she said, "But Leland says if I can get three-fifty for six months, he'll let the boy go. With that kind of money, he'll be able to finish the book."

"Three-fifty for six—that's kind of steep for an unknown."

"He won't be unknown long," she said. "Talk it over with the Coast, and if you can, let me know this afternoon. But it has to be three-fifty for six, or it's no go. Always good to see you, Bill."

You said nothing on the way downstairs, nothing in the gilt and marble lobby, nothing as you went out into the street. On the Broadway sidewalk, you stopped, a stone in the stream of foot-traffic.

"I'm glad Hayward likes my books," you said.

"He hasn't read them," Miss Howell said.

"Then why has he had his eye on me?"

"He's never even heard of you."

"Then that stuff about backing me was just bullshit."

"Without bullshit, Sanford, us agents would be out of work."

"Something tells me we just bought twenty-six hundred dollars worth."

"Go home and stop worrying."

"I will if you lend me the fare."

§

Late in the day, you and your father were in the livingroom, he reclining on your sister's couch and you seated in a nearby chair. The events of the morning, from the handball court to the meeting at Paramount, had been gone over by and large and then in detail, and now both of you were waiting in the hope that the phone-bell would ring.

"A bird in the hand," your father said. "Were you tempted to go back and take the offer?"

"Yes," you said. "But I couldn't stop wondering about the two in the bush."

"I'm not criticizing you, but that's called gambling."

"I know—and if I lose, everybody'll say, 'Well, that's Julian for you.' "

"Julian," he said, and it was as if he were pondering some object difficult to account for. He could describe you, in the sense that he knew your dimensions, but beyond those numbers, he seemed to find you strange. "Julian," he said again, and you saw that though he turned you and turned you in his mind, he could give you no more than a name. "Julian."

And then a bell in the hallway rang.

You were out of the room for only a few moments, returning with a page of notes—numerals, abbreviations, disunited words. Sitting down beside your father, you were impelled, before all else, to do what you'd so often done before—smooth his ash-gray hair.

And then you said, "Counselor, can you stand a little good news?"

"From you, kid," he said, "it's what I live for."

"Paramount agrees to three-fifty for six."

His response was one you'd not have looked for: his immediate pleasure derived not from you but others.

He said, "Now let them say, 'That's Julian for you.' "

"There's more," you said. "Paramount is asking for options on another four and a half years. Six more months at four hundred, then a year at five hundred, a year at seven-fifty, a year at a thousand, and finally a year at twelve-fifty. I haven't figured it out, but Miss Howell says it comes to over two hundred thousand."

"In options, Julian," your father said. "Do you know what an option is?"

"It gives Paramount the right to hold me for the next period in the contract."

"Exactly. It gives *them* the right."

"Why would I be trying to get out of it?"

"Julian, *they* might be trying to get out of it—and the option is theirs, not yours. They can hold you, but you can't hold them. Once you sign the contract, all you can be sure of is six months at three-fifty—ninety-one hundred bucks. So don't go around thinking you have a five-year contract."

"Well, whatever it amounts to, it's a lot better than stealing fifteen cents a day from you. Mr. Sapira, what do you say to a drink?"

"Well, I sure as hell don't need a nitro pill."

§

A morning or two before the Labor Day weekend, you caught the early boat for the Highlands (was it the *Monmouth,* your twin-screw yacht, or, for that last sail down-bay, was it the *Sandy Hook*?). After the short train-ride to West End, you walked the gravel country mile to your Aunt Sarah's home, passing houses trimmed with a lace of woodwork that made them seem to be peering through curtains as you went by in the road. You found the family, gathered for the coming holiday, at their noontime meal on the glassed-in part of the porch. There, from a long table seating twenty, all that could be seen outside was trees, sky, and shrubbery, a view that had often made you think of a luncheon on the grass.

"Julan," your Uncle Harris said when he saw you, "come and sit."

Your sister, downstairs that day, said, "What brings you here in the middle of the week?"

And your Aunt Sarah said, "*Er kommt* without a satchel. Something is wrong with my brother Phil?"

"Your brother Phil is all right," you said. "And considering the kind of son he has, he's in good spirits.

"*Gott sie dank.*"

"What *does* bring you?" your sister said.

Rosie came in from the kitchen and greeted you as *Mr. Julah.*

"Well, folks," you said, "Mr. Julah could hardly leave for California without coming to say goodbye."

Cups and cutlery hovered, voices died, some at a pronoun and some at a verb, and even out-of-doors sounds seemed to stop. An aunt and an uncle stared at you from their ends of the table, and there was staring from across and along the board, from first and second cousins and from cousins once and twice removed, and Rosie stared too—at Mr. Julah.

"California!" your sister said.

And others said, "California!"

And someone said, "But why? How?"

And you told them.

§

Upon the signing of the contract, Paramount provided you with a railroad ticket from New York on the Commodore Vanderbilt and from Chicago on the Chief. Two days before your departure, you recalled what your Aunt Sarah had said—"*Er kommt* without a satchel"—and you realized that you were still without luggage, this time for a far longer journey than a boat-ride to the shore. When the thought came to you, you were walking on Broadway with a girl named Selma, a friend of the one who, with her nine-page letter, had recently foregone you as a do-little with a future he valued at fifty dollars a week. In calling on Selma, your hidden reason had actually been your only reason: you knew that whatever you told her of your sudden good fortune would at once reach the ears of the one you had in mind. As you strolled through the warm evening, therefore, you spoke casually of large sums and long durations, of quids and quos, of John B. Sanford, the party of the second part, but never of those options that resided in Paramount Pictures, the party of the first—indeed, you'd almost come to believe that if you were bound to Paramount, it was no less bound to you. And as you walked with Selma, talking as you went, your eye fell on a shop-window where on display there were edifices constructed of leather—Gladstones, suitcases, valises, aye, even a satchel—and at the sight, the words *Er kommt* rose through your mind.

"Selma," you said, "how much money do you have in your purse?"
"About thirty dollars," she said. "Why?"
"Would you lend me enough to buy a satchel?"

§

At midafternoon, you and your father were in a taxicab on the way to Grand Central Station. You'd just entered the park at the 72nd Street gate, and before you, above the trees, reared a wall of tall buildings, blue in the shadow and bright where sunlight struck a sheer of windows. At four o'clock, you'd be leaving those buildings, these trees, and the man who rode beside you. Drawn by a New York Central electric, a train with you aboard would be passing the docks and coal-yards along the Harlem River, the scows, the mud-flats, the ball-parks, and then it would wind with Spuyten Duyvil to the Hudson, where once more you'd see Jersey and the Palisades, and now your mind would race ahead, past Tappan Zee and the falls at Troy, to Thurman Bridge where you and Pep had cast for bass among the reeds.

"Papa," you said, "I'll be sending you a check every week. Will fifty bucks do?"
"I'm afraid not," he said.
"How about seventy-five?"
"That'll be fine."
"Then seventy-five it is," you said, but you knew it would never be fine; you'd always regret the offer of fifty.
And then you were saying goodbye under the train-board. "Keep well," you said. "That's all I ask."

And he said, "You're a good kid, Julian."
But you shook your head, saying, "Not good enough."

And then you kissed each other, and you went out under the train-shed, and as the distance between you grew, you thought that if you were lonely now, what would you be in two years or three?

Printed April 1986 in Santa Barbara & Ann Arbor
for the Black Sparrow Press by Graham Mackintosh &
Edwards Brothers Inc. Design by Barbara Martin.
This edition is published in paper wrappers; there
are 300 cloth trade copies; 150 hardcover copies
have been numbered and signed by the author; & 26
copies handbound in boards by Earle Gray have been
lettered & signed by the author.

JOHN SANFORD is the name of the principal character in *The Water Wheel*, a first novel by Julian Shapiro published in 1933. Adopting it as a pseudonym, the writer has used it ever since. Born in the Harlem section of New York on 31 May 1904, he attended the public schools of that city, Lafayette College, and finally Fordham University, where he earned a degree in Law. He was admitted to the Bar in 1929, and at about the same time, influenced by his friend Nathanael West, he too began to write. Published at the outset in vanguard magazines of the period — *The New Review, Tambour, Pagany, Contact* — he soon abandoned the legal profession and produced through the years a series of eight novels. Concerned always with the course of American history, he interspersed his fiction with critical commentaries on the national life from the Left-Liberal point-of-view. As a result of such dissent, he was summoned before the House Committee on Un-American Activities, and for refusing to cooperate with it, he was blacklisted. In spite of difficulty in obtaining publication, he continued to write in his chosen vein, ultimately stripping his work down to its historical content only. During the last several years, he has written four books of creative interpretations of the Land of the Free: *A More Goodly Country, View from This Wilderness, To Feed Their Hopes,* and *The Winters of That Country,* all four titles deriving from a single passage in William Bradford's *History of Plymouth Plantation.* John Sanford has been married to the writer Marguerite Roberts since 1938; they are long-time residents of Santa Barbara, California.